ST. MARY'S COLLEGE OF MARYLAND
ST. MARY'S CITY, MARYLAND

DAVID CURTIS DeFOREST
From a Portrait by Samuel F. B. Morse.
Courtesy of Yale University Art Gallery.

42006

DAVID CURTIS DeFOREST AND THE REVOLUTION OF BUENOS AIRES

BY

BENJAMIN KEEN

ASSOCIATE PROFESSOR OF HISTORY
WEST VIRGINIA UNIVERSITY

GREENWOOD PRESS, PUBLISHERS
WESTPORT, CONNECTICUT

Copyright 1947 by Yale University Press

Reprinted with the permission
of Yale University Press

First Greenwood Reprinting 1970

Library of Congress Catalogue Card Number 75-104249

SBN 8371-3970-8

Printed in the United States of America

To

MY MOTHER

PREFACE

THE life of David Curtis DeForest richly documents the contribution of the United States to the movement of Spanish-American emancipation. His colorful career, spanning a quarter-century of revolutionary upheavals along the shores of the Río de la Plata, shows how North American ideological influence and illegal military assistance, and the astute diplomacy of the United States government, helped to inspire, sustain, and bring to a successful conclusion the Argentine struggle for independence. It demonstrates how numerous and varied were the contacts between the United States and Buenos Aires in this formative period of inter-American relations. These historical lessons emerge from a study of the life of one of the greatest of Yankee adventurers, recorded in his own vigorously written journals and letters.

In quoting from the DeForest papers, the principal source for this study, I have modernized the punctuation for the sake of greater clarity, but have retained the original capitalization and spelling. Books and articles have been cited in full at the first reference, but thereafter in abbreviated form.

To all who have helped me in the completion of this work I express my appreciation. In particular, I am deeply indebted to Samuel Flagg Bemis, Sterling Professor of Diplomatic History and Inter-American Relations at Yale University, for his constant advice and encouragement. Professor Leonard Woods Labaree, Editor of the Yale Historical Publications, has offered valuable suggestions and criticisms. I also wish to thank Richard Blanc and Byron Fairchild, who have read and commented on particular chapters. The custodians and staffs of the Yale University Library, the Library of Congress, the National Archives, the Columbus Library of the Pan-American Union in Washington, and the Connecticut State Library at Hartford, have shown me many friendly courtesies. The assistance and inspiration of my wife were invaluable.

B. K.

Amherst, Mass.
February 2, 1946.

CONTENTS

ILLUSTRATIONS

I

"FORTUNE IS A SLIPPERY JADE"

DAVID CURTIS DeFOREST occupies a leading place among the adventurous Yankee traders who in the epoch of Spanish-American emancipation established the first commercial and political relations between the United States and the new states of Spanish America. Merchant, prince of privateers, and diplomat, he took an active part in the revolutionary struggles of the people of Buenos Aires, capital of the provinces known today as the Argentine Republic. His career is a veritable embodiment of the contribution of the United States to the winning of Argentine independence.

The beginnings of DeForest's career are closely linked to the great outward thrust of American commerce after the Revolutionary War. Spurred by their loss of markets in the British Empire, New England's mariners then pushed across the seas in search of trade. Their quest led to the Northwest Coast for otter skins, to Hawaii for sandalwood, to the coasts of Spanish America for the profits of a contraband traffic, and to the seal fisheries of the Antarctic. At the great Chinese port of Canton they exchanged pelts, sandalwood, and specie for silks and teas. From Canton they began the long voyage home, half way around the world.

On such a "circumnavigating voyage" the young DeForest embarked from Boston port on the last day of the year 1800. But he was not to see the wonders of old Canton. Parting company with his domineering captain on the bleak coast of Patagonia, he traveled by devious routes to the town of Buenos Aires, capital of the Spanish province of the Río de la Plata. There he learned to trade "in the smuggling way." As a resident merchant in Buenos Aires he observed the preliminaries of the Argentine *Revolución de Mayo*, and himself stimulated the spirit of creole discontent by his preachment of republican doctrine. On the eve of the revolution, Viceroy Cisneros expelled him from the province. Returning after the events of May 25, 1810, DeForest became an outfitter of patriot privateers that made heavy inroads on Spanish commerce. Later, as diplomatic representative of his adopted country in the United States, he matched wits with Secretary of State John Quincy Adams in an effort to gain recognition of the independence of Buenos Aires. Defeated by the redoubtable secretary, he retired to the town of New Haven in his native Connecticut, where he devoted his last years to philanthropy, to the promotion of cultural relations between the United States and Buenos Aires, and to the annual celebration of the birthday of Argentine independence, the *veinte-cinco de mayo*.

DeForest's European forebears were wool merchants of the little walled town of Avesnes, in the Belgian province of Hainaut. The Religious Wars of the sixteenth century laid waste this once flourishing region, and by the thousands Walloon Huguenots emigrated to neighboring Holland. Among them was one Jesse de Forest, who in 1615 lived in the "goodly and pleasant citie" of Leyden.

Discontent with economic conditions in Leyden evidently inspired Jesse de Forest and a number of his countrymen to try their fortunes in the New World. With the backing of the Dutch West India Company, then engaged in an ambitious program of overseas expansion, the exile from Avesnes in 1623 led a band of Walloon pilgrims on a voyage to the mouth of the Amazon River. On the Oyapok, a stream that separates present-day French Guiana from Northeastern Brazil, they made a settlement. Jesse was exploring the surrounding country when a fever struck him down. "On the 22nd of October 1624," reads an entry in the journal of the expedition, "our said captain died, much regretted by the Indians who had taken a great liking to him. This day we caused him to be buried as honorably as was possible for us, accompanying his body with arms, which we each discharged three times over his grave and our cannon as well." [1] Disheartened by this heavy loss, the survivors soon returned to their families in Holland.

Twelve years later two sons of Jesse de Forest, Henry and Isaac, left their Leyden home to settle in New Netherland. Henry died shortly after his arrival in America, but Isaac lived to become a wealthy merchant and landowner of New Amsterdam. His

---

1. "Journal of the Voyage Made by the Fathers of Families Sent by the Honorable the Directors of the West India Company to the Coast of Guiana," in Mrs. Robert W. de Forest, *A Walloon Family in America* (2 vols., New York, 1914), II, 249.

son, David, founded the Connecticut line of DeForests. About 1694 he left New York and made his way to the growing settlement of Stratford situated a few miles up the Housatonic River. There he met and married Martha Blagge, daughter of a local merchant, and in time acquired a considerable holding of land. He left behind him a large progeny—plain farmer folk, diligent churchgoers, exemplary members of the ecclesiastical societies and military train-bands of Stratford.

His grandson, Benjamin DeForest or Deforest, as he sometimes wrote his name, came to manhood on the eve of the War for Independence. The violence of the great struggle reached perilously close to Stratford; the British burned Fairfield, eight miles to the west, and plundered New Haven twelve miles to the east. Poor health prevented DeForest from bearing arms in the war, as did twenty-five men of his name, but he was active on local relief committees aiding the patriot cause. The care of his land and the rearing of his six children, however, were his chief preoccupations. His eldest child, a son called David Curtis DeForest, was born on January 10, 1774, in the parish of Ripton[2] in Stratford.

David was nearing his tenth year when the Revolutionary War came to an end. The peace that followed was an uneasy one. The long, exhausting conflict had disrupted the colonial economy and had given a severe shock to accepted religious and moral ideas. Even steady-going Connecticut, of which Aaron Burr is reported to have said that one might "as soon attempt to revolutionize the kingdom of heaven," [3] experienced profound change in the post-war years.

There was no Shays' Rebellion in Connecticut to alarm the better sort, but other signs of unrest grieved those who held to the ancient order of things. In the town of Windham, "it was a transition period—a day of upheaval, over-turning, uprootal. Infidelity and Universalism had come in with the Revolution and drawn multitudes from the religious faith of their fathers. Free thinking and free-drinking were alike in vogue; great looseness of manners and morals had replaced the ancient Puritanic strictness." [4] As

2. Incorporated in 1789 as the town of Huntington. In 1919 the name was changed to Shelton.
3. William A. Robinson, *Jeffersonian Democracy in New England* (New Haven, 1916), p. 28.
4. Quoted in Richard J. Purcell, *Connecticut in Transition* (New Haven, 1918), p. 10.

for New London, "all accounts agree in speaking of the *manners* of the inhabitants as belonging to the *free* and *easy* style. Jovial parties of all kinds, hot suppers, tavern dinners, card playing, shooting matches, and dancing assemblies were popular. Merchants and other citizens congregated around the coffee houses, told stories, cracked jokes, and complimented each other with brandy, ginsling and old Jamaica, as matters of course every day of the week, Sundays . . . not wholly excepted." [5]

At Yale College, a stronghold of Congregationalist orthodoxy, students dismayed President Timothy Dwight by taking the names of Voltaire and Rousseau. The Reverend William Bentley, noting the degeneracy of the times, observed that Thomas Paine was universally read in Connecticut. Toward the close of the century, Federalist oligarchs perceived even more ominous portents in the rise of Jeffersonian heresy, recruiting its first disciples among the merchants and workmen of the shore and river towns.

In this era of transition DeForest passed his formative years. The new climate of opinion nourished a lively intellectual curiosity, fostered indifference to religious dogma, engendered a worldly and acquisitive temper. In time of adversity DeForest's forebears had searched their consciences and their Bibles to learn wherein they had offended their stern and jealous God. David, who had read *The Age of Reason*, would instead rail at fortune, that "fickle Damned Bitch of a Goddess," or would compare himself to another roving pagan, the famed Ulysses, and lament his vain search for "darling Penelope: 30 or 40,000 dollars." Disciple of Paine and Jefferson, talk of the rights of man would fall naturally from his lips; and to the rulers of revolutionary Buenos Aires he would teach the maxim of "the patriotic sages of North America . . . *that an uninstructed cannot long be a free people.*"

The economic life of Connecticut was also adjusting itself to new conditions. The return of peace found agriculture in a sorry plight. Loss of the vital West Indies trade, sharply curtailing the market for farming and domestic produce, made the burden of taxation unbearably heavy for the small farmers of the state. Their dissatisfaction was reflected in the steady exodus of emigrants from Connecticut, an occurrence common to all New England. It has been estimated that between 1790 and 1820 approximately 800,000 persons departed from the three states

5. Frances M. Caulkins, *History of New London* (New London, 1895), p. 581.

of Massachusetts, Rhode Island, and Connecticut. Before the
Revolution the population of Connecticut had been growing at
the rate of 28 per cent in every decade; between 1790 and 1800
it increased only 5½ per cent.[6]

Some of DeForest's generation abandoned the exhausted and
tax-burdened acres of their fathers for the more abundant, cheap,
and fertile lands of the frontier. Others, no less enterprising,
entered the counting-room or took service before the mast. The
increased protection given United States commerce by the establishment of the Federal Government, and this country's neutrality
during a cycle of European wars, presently stimulated Connecticut shipping. Despite frequent seizures and adverse admiralty
decisions, profits were large. The towns of the lower Connecticut
Valley and Long Island Sound once again drove a thriving trade
with the West Indies, their vessels taking grain, butter, meat,
tobacco and other products to be exchanged for sugar and molasses which were later turned into rum.

The coastwise, West Indies, and European commerce did not
afford employment for all the available capital, seamen, and
mounting tonnage. Enterprising merchants and mariners traced
out new trade routes. In 1785 the New London Gazette, noting
the return of two Sag Harbor ships from successful whaling
voyages to the Brazil Banks, boisterously exhorted: "Now, my
horse jockeys, beat your horses and cattle into spears, lances,
harpoons and whaling gear, and let us all strike out: many spouts
ahead! Whales plenty, you have them for catching."[7] Before
1800 New Haven had a South Sea Fleet of about twenty ships
engaged in seal fishing in the Antarctic. The skins were sold at
Canton, and the vessels returned home laden with silks and teas.
On the barren coast of Patagonia was a tract of land two miles
long, known to mariners as "New Haven Green," a rendezvous
where sealers from that city dried the skins of slaughtered animals.[8] Connecticut sealers and whalers, like their comrades of
Massachusetts, smuggled goods into lonely coves on the east and
west coasts of South America, gaining valuable specie for the
Canton trade as well as the disfavor of Spanish officials. Occasionally they introduced the no less contraband commodity of repub-

6. The above figures are taken from James T. Adams, *New England in the
Republic, 1776–1850* (Boston, 1926), pp. 191–192.
7. F. M. Caulkins, *History of New London,* p. 640.
8. Edward E. Atwater, *History of the City of New Haven* (New York, 1887),
pp. 497–498.

lican ideas. These activities tended to undermine the Spanish colonial system and furthered the rise of the spirit of independence in South America.

The town of Stratford, DeForest's birthplace, and neighboring Newfield (modern Bridgeport), where he first engaged in business, shared in this general expansion of commerce. When David and his brother John came to Newfield in 1796, Water Street was lined with stores and wharves, and local merchants were carrying on a brisk trade with Boston, New York, and the West Indies.[9] Newfield's skippers occasionally ventured far from the beaten sea paths. The redoubtable Captain Ezekiel Hubbell sailed his ship *Enterprise* to Chile, and narrowly escaped imprisonment in a Spanish dungeon after a daring effort to smuggle his cargo ashore. Then he made for Canton, calling and trading at Nootka Sound, the Sandwich Islands, and the Russian settlements near Kamchatka on the way. Clearing from Canton in January, 1802, the *Enterprise* came to anchor in the Sound off Newfield on June 27, with a valuable freight of Bohea tea and silks, after an absence of nearly three years.[10]

Similar odysseys of the sea, with their exciting themes of high adventure, travel to distant lands, and fabulous profits, were told and retold on the wharves and in the counting-rooms and inns of maritime Connecticut. "Such a romance was there regarding those South Sea ships," remarks the historian of New Haven's commerce, "that very many of the young men of the town were lured to enrol themselves among the companies which manned the sealing fleet, not only to add to their worldly store, but to be able to say to their friends at home that they had been 'round the Horn,' and to 'the place where Captain Cook was murdered'; and such a voyage was . . . something to boast of in New Haven, and none of the ships which left our port for the Pacific but carried representatives of the most respected families of the town." [11]

Merchant princes and sea captains now rivaled Connecticut's ancient ruling class of country squires and parsons in prestige and influence. An expanding money economy, creating new wants and

9. Samuel Orcutt, *A History of . . . Stratford and Bridgeport* (New Haven, 1886), p. 493.

10. *Ibid.*, pp. 612–615.

11. Thomas R. Trowbridge, Jr., "History of the Ancient Maritime Interests of New Haven," in *Papers* of the New Haven Colony Historical Society (New Haven, 1882), III, 148.

aspirations, caused discontent with the rural folkways of the past. Widening horizons of commercial opportunity beckoned young men of parts and ambition. The economic drift of the times and the social values which it generated alike impelled DeForest to turn to a life of trade and to the sea. Thus, all unknowingly, he would revert to an earlier family pattern, to the ways of his long dead and forgotten ancestor Jesse de Forest, wool merchant of Avesnes, who also roved, traded, and sought his fortune in distant lands beyond the seas.

Benjamin DeForest died in 1784, aged only thirty-five, leaving to his wife Mehitable Curtis eighty-five acres of land, a large well-built house, two barns, and a home lot, the estate of a farmer of fair means of that period. With the proceeds of this property the widow could maintain herself and her brood of six young children in what appears to have been modest comfort.

Little information has come down to us concerning the childhood of David C. DeForest. His bold and adventurous temper manifested itself at an early age. A few months after his father's death, according to family tradition, David ran off to become a sailor, was brought back, but some years later ran off again to sea.[12] Complete obscurity surrounds these youthful escapades.

We do not know the extent of DeForest's formal education. He very likely attended the district school at Ripton, a one-story cellarless structure where the children sat on long benches in the middle of the room and the teacher before them, his back to the blazing, crackling fire. Here Dilworth's ancient *Spelling Book* and *Arithmetic* were the standards of instruction. It appears doubtful that David's formal schooling ever advanced beyond this point, for the pretentious Academy at Stratford was not erected until 1804. There is good reason to believe that as a lad DeForest served an apprenticeship in a mercantile establishment; in a letter to his brother John he speaks of himself as having been bred to common commercial pursuits.[13]

A list of books in the possession of David and John DeForest in 1798 points to the early formation of intellectual and literary tastes along well defined lines. Here is found no ponderous work

12. John W. De Forest, *The de Forests of Avesnes, and of New Netherland* (New Haven, 1900), p. 112.

13. DeForest to John H. DeForest, Boston, Dec. 29, 1800, DeForest Journal, Vol. 1, Yale University Library.

of divinity, such as might have graced the small library of their parents, but rather such flowers of eighteenth century skepticism and social criticism as Paine's *Age of Reason* and Volney's *Ruins of Empire*. On the lighter side, the collection included Sterne's *Sentimental Journey* and Goethe's *Sorrows of Young Werther*. A *History of South America* (perhaps William Robertson's *History of America*), may have stimulated a youthful desire to see the lands conquered by Spanish valor and treachery. There were works too of a practical nature, the *Seaman's Assistant* and the *Lex Mercatoria*, useful possessions for the prospective merchant and mariner.

Upon reaching his majority, David received his share of the paternal estate and promptly decided on a commercial career. His brother John, then nineteen, had similar notions, and the result was that they merged their slender resources and efforts. In August, 1796, the brothers established a business in Newfield. The only available information concerning the nature of the enterprise is that it was a "dry goods and grocery store." [14]

Hardly had a month gone by, when disaster struck the nascent firm. Robbers entered the store, murdered the clerk, a country lad named Shelton Edwards, and set the building on fire. A New Haven paper gave the following account of the incident under a Newfield date line:

"About ten o'clock on the evening of Thursday last, the store of Messrs. David and John DeForest of this place was discovered to be on fire. The neighborhood was immediately aroused, the store opened, and after considerable exertions of the inhabitants, the fire was extinguished; tho' not until the greater part of the goods in the Store were destroyed. The lad who slept in the Store was then searched for, and was discovered to be murdered, and mangled in a most shocking manner; and cash to the amount of almost nine hundred dollars was missed from the desk." [15]

Recovering from the shock of this catastrophe, the brothers somehow managed to raise the means for a new venture. The first months of 1798 found them at Sullivan, a pioneer settlement on Penobscot Bay, Maine, then a district of Massachusetts. There they kept a store, and shipped lumber and other products to the West Indies.

14. S. Orcutt, *A History of Stratford . . . and Bridgeport*, p. 594.
15. *Connecticut Journal* (New Haven), Sept. 21, 1796.

Misfortune dogged the young partners. Their vessel was condemned at Cap Français in Haiti as unfit for sea, and was sold for the benefit of the underwriters. An auction of their property failed to cover the firm's debts. Among the first entries in DeForest's letterbooks are pleading, cajoling letters to importunate creditors. To one the brothers wrote, "We beg of you not to urge the taking of our bodies, for we are in a distant country from home, and must go to Gaol of necessity." [16] To another they complained whimsically, "Fortune is a damned Slippery Jade, and we hardly know how to manage her; however, honesty shall be our guide under any circumstances, whatever may be said to our disadvantage in your part of the world." [17] In order to fend off sheriff's deputies the brothers barricaded themselves in their house, and kept spies on the lookout for unwelcome visitors. On one occasion a deputy ran three miles to catch his quarry unawares, "but a friend who discovered him and guessed his business was more nimble of foot and arrived at our house about 5 minutes first." [18]

While David stayed in Maine to salvage what he could from his shattered fortunes, he packed his young brother off to Salem to study French and prepare himself otherwise for a mercantile career. To a Connecticut friend he wrote dejectedly, "I shall probably have my Business in this country closed by the 1st of October, which will complete four years' race after wealth, honor and happiness, and so disagreeable is my Situation that I cannot promise myself better." [19]

To his brother John the twenty-four year old DeForest addressed grave homilies, urging the student to make the most of his opportunities. "Time is Cash," he wrote sententiously, "Credit is Cash, Knowledge of Business is Cash. Who would be destitute of Cash, if in their power to obtain it, but such as have no pride, no ambition, no thought for the morrow. From daylight to 9 o'clock at night, an ambitious Young Man will never spend an Idle moment, when all that he can value himself upon is a three months'

16. David and John DeForest to Job Nelson, Sullivan, March 31, 1798, DeForest Letterbooks, Vol. 1, Yale University Library.
17. David and John DeForest to Messrs. Hull and Mansfield, Sullivan, March 31, 1798, *ibid.*
18. David and John DeForest to General R. Hunnewell, Sullivan, March 31, 1798, *ibid.*
19. DeForest to Daniel Allen, Sullivan, May 21, 1798, *ibid.*

Opportunity of gaining that Knowledge by which he is to be supported through life." [20]

DeForest now looked about for new roads to "wealth, honor and happiness." The gathering conflict between the United States and France caused him to speculate concerning the merits of a military career. Publication of the "X Y Z dispatches" in the spring of 1798 fanned the flames of Federalist war agitation. Congress hastily prepared for war, levying taxes, creating an army and a navy. Early in August, DeForest called on General Henry Knox of Boston, a stout, rubicund veteran of the Revolution, to apply for a commission in the new army. The general was friendly, and complimented the young man on his excellent appearance.[21] DeForest's application met with moderate success. He did not obtain the captaincy to which he ambitiously aspired, but the records of the War Office show that on March 3, 1799, he was appointed first lieutenant in the 15th Regiment, United States Infantry.[22] In May of that year he received equally cheering news from Connecticut. The general assembly of that state, acting upon a prayer for an act of insolvency for the DeForest brothers, had resolved that after delivering to their creditors all their estate both real and personal, "except such Wages and Emoluments as the said David may be entitled to providing he shall join the Army of the United States . . . the Persons of the said David and John, and all the property which they shall in future acquire be, and the same are hereby discharged and exonerated from all liability for said Debts contracted as aforesaid." [23]

DeForest's hopes for a career of military glory were of course doomed to failure. He spent the greater part of his year of bloodless service in an encampment at Oxford, Massachusetts. Meantime "honest little John Adams," increasingly suspicious of Hamilton's desire for war and of his influence in the presidential cabinet, kept the door open for a peaceful settlement of the imbroglio with France. The tide of public opinion rose rapidly against the war; recruiting lagged; and in later years Adams recalled that the army was as unpopular "as if it had been a

20. Charles D. Gray to George D. Gray, Sullivan, (?) 1798, *ibid*. These names were doubtless assumed by the brothers in order to mislead their creditors.

21. DeForest to Isaac Mills, Boston, Aug. 7, 1798, *ibid*.

22. F. B. Heitman, *Historical Register and Dictionary of the United States Army* (2 vols., Washington, 1903), I, 364.

23. Records of the State of Connecticut, Vol. 6, 1797–1801, Connecticut State Library, Hartford.

ferocious beast let loose upon the nation to devour it." [24] In the fall of 1799, after receiving assurances from Talleyrand that good treatment and respect would be accorded to American plenipotentiaries, the President resumed negotiations with France, a treaty settled the quarrel, and the new army was soon disbanded. On June 11, 1800, the encampment at Oxford broke up, and one week later Lieutenant DeForest was honorably discharged from the service.

David set out for Boston, where in the company of some brother officers he celebrated his release from the tedious routine of camp life. High spirits soon gave way to depression, however, as he reflected on his dubious prospects in "this World of dangers and difficulties." Walking the streets of Boston, he ruminated on his hard lot.

"I thought, I pondered, I knew not which way to turn. Already past the time of life when the young men of our country usually begin business, I considered time as precious indeed. A year, a month, or even a day, was worthy of my particular notice and should be used with the greatest prudence and economy. To have thought or done otherwise would have been a crime."

At last he came to a decision that was to shape his career in an unpredictable way.

"I concluded to go to Sea, to engage as a common Sailor, and depend only on my own exertions, for future promotions. It was a singular conclusion for one who had never labored, and perhaps will cause some of my friends many mortifications when thinking on the subject. I can easily anticipate their thoughts and the remarks many of them will make respecting my conduct, but I hope there are some who are not altogether so unsensible, and whose friendship for me is never the less, than when the Sphere in which I move[d] was far more exalted than at present." [25]

He had no difficulty in securing a place before the mast in that heyday of American commerce. On August 28, 1800, he sailed from Boston in the merchant ship *Orislow* bound for Liverpool, England. They anchored in the Mersey River on the last day of September. DeForest was amazed at the multitude of vessels that thronged the great port. "Here," he wrote, "you may see ships belonging to any commercial Nation in the World, ex-

24. Claude G. Bowers, *Jefferson and Hamilton* (New York, 1925), p. 421.
25. DeForest to John H. DeForest, Boston, Dec. 29, 1800, DeForest Journal, Vol. 1.

cepting of such as are at war with England." Great Britain was then at war with Napoleonic France and her satellites. Eager to gain knowledge of the "Manners, customs, and particularly of the Manufactures of this Country, which to any American, is a subject of very great curiosity," DeForest took advantage of his ship's stay in port to make a tour of the counties of Lancashire and Cheshire.

The intensive cultivation of the English countryside won his admiring comments. He plied farmers along the road with questions concerning "the manner in which they cultivated their Lands, the quantity of produce raised, their grazing fields, their Herd of Cows, on what kind of grass fed, their manner of manufacturing Cheese, how it is colored and with what, etc. etc." He had words of praise for English agricultural technique, but the parochial spirit and ignorance of the English countryman elicited his censure. "The people of England," he observed, "do not possess the hospitality of Americans, nor do the peasantry of that Country possess knowledge of Men and things in any proportion to that which American Farmers and tradesmen possess." The reason for this state of affairs, he thought, was the heavy duty laid on newspapers. "Poor people, of course, cannot be at the expense of reading the News of the Day. They have it (if they know it at all) from the Noble and the rich, who put such a coloring on it as they wish it to have, consequently it is not to be wondered at that the peasantry of the Country are so little informed." [26]

Manchester, center of English cotton manufacture, seemed to DeForest an "immense workshop." He marveled at the great height of the five-, six-, and seven-story structures in which carding, spinning, and reeling operations were carried on. From the cellar dwellings of the wretched weavers rose the hum of looms. Questioning of these workers revealed bitter discontent with their conditions. "They will readily tell you," DeForest wrote his brother, "that 'tis with difficulty they support themselves and families, that they have no other mode of obtaining a livelihood, that they would willingly embark on any enterprise, however desperate, to rid themselves of hard hearted poverty. Should they wish to leave the country, Government would say, No. Should they ask redress of grievances, Government turns a deaf Ear.

26. DeForest to John H. DeForest, Cape Verde Islands, Feb. 6, 1801, DeForest Letterbooks, Vol. 1.

They impute their wants to the War, they groan for peace. Unhappy people, how unpleasant does [their] condition appear when compared with that of the mechanics or peasantry of America." [27]

The approaching departure of the *Orislow* made DeForest end his tour and return to Liverpool. At the close of December, 1800, he was back in Boston, and well content with his decision to follow the sea. He wrote brother John that Captain Owen F. Smith of the *Diana* had invited him to come as second mate on a voyage to Canton, that he had considered the matter, decided to accept, and would sail the next day. From Israel Munson and Company of Boston, he secured on credit a stock of watches, knives, and other notions with which to trade on the way.

On the afternoon of December 31, 1800, a large number of persons gathered on Boston's Long Wharf to see the *Diana* set sail for China. The start of a "voyage of circumnavigation" was no ordinary event, and must be attended by some ceremony. At two of the afternoon the *Diana* weighed anchor; the crew gave three cheers, returned by the crowd on the end of Long Wharf; the ship stood down the harbor, was abreast of the lighthouse at six in the evening, discharged her pilot, and proceeded to sea "with a fine breeze from the northwest."

27. *Ibid.*

II

"DOING BUSINESS IN THE SMUGGLING WAY"

THE *Diana* had a complement of twenty-four men, most of them Massachusetts lads in their 'teens or early twenties. Oldest of the crew was Captain Owen F. Smith, thirty years of age, followed by First Mate Reuben Glover, twenty-seven, and Second Mate DeForest, twenty-five years old. Jeremiah C. Barker, a youth of twenty-two, filled the post of ship's doctor.

Their first destination was the Cape Verde islands, where sealers customarily broke voyage to obtain salt for the treatment of sealskins, and fresh provisions as a precaution against the dreaded scurvy. The lookout sighted land on January 31, 1801. Two days later the ship dropped anchor in English Road, under the lee of the island of Mayo. There they stayed six days, taking on provisions and overhauling the vessel. From the Cape Verdes the *Diana* squared off in a southerly direction, making for the sealing grounds off the coast of Patagonia. Favorable trade winds sent the ship scudding along her course. Soon all hands were industriously whittling great numbers of wooden pegs to be used in the drying of sealskins.

Toward the end of February, while still on the high seas, a violent dispute arose between Captain Smith and his second mate. To his journal DeForest confided that the master of the *Diana* was a drunkard and a tyrant. Wearying of alleged persecution, on February 21 he proposed to quit his post and pay for a passage to Rio de Janeiro. Captain Smith would not hear of it. He swore savagely at DeForest, charged him with mutiny, and threatened to confine him to his stateroom should he renew his request.

Remonstrance was useless; DeForest maintained a prudent silence. But bad feeling between the two men persisted. Efforts at mediation by First Mate Glover and Dr. Barker only achieved a brief, uneasy truce. Nursing his grievances, DeForest set down in his journal an ancient maxim of the sea: "So considerable is the power and influence of a Ship's Commander that persons while under them and at Sea, ought to be cautious how they quarrel with them, for very few who are present will remember anything wrong on the Capt's side and everything on the side of his opponent." [1]

The *Diana* was drawing near the coast of Patagonia. Early in March the ship was on soundings, and DeForest had his first glimpse of hair-seals, sporting in the water. Moving leisurely down the coast, they sent out parties to search the shore line for the little rock islands that were the favorite resorts of these animals. In the Bay of Camarónes they found their first prey. DeForest and a party of four men landed on a rock island and killed about 100 hair-seals in forty minutes. A single blow on the head with a stout club crushed the frail skulls of the animals. Later came the arduous task of skinning the seals and cleaning off the blubber, a grueling chore performed with a "beaming knife," after which the skins were pegged out to dry.[2]

Moving southward, the *Diana* came to anchor off Puerto Deseado, an isolated Spanish frontier post with a garrison of thirty-two men. There DeForest saw Patagonian Indians, large and well made men, but not the giants of whom he had read in the works of early travelers. The Americans received a cordial welcome from the local *comandante*, who came to dine on board their vessel and closed his eyes to a brisk contraband trade between the intruders and the inhabitants of the place. The ancient Laws of the Indies were little regarded in this remote borderland of the viceroyalty of La Plata. Zorilla, guanaco, and lion skins were bartered for Yankee rum and dry goods. Such was DeForest's introduction to "doing Business in the Smuggling Way."

Casual and illicit contacts of this kind established the first commercial relations between the United States and the viceroyalty of La Plata. Contraband traffic carried on by English and American sealers and whalers on the east and west coasts of South America was a perennial source of annoyance to higher Spanish

1. DeForest Journal, Vol. 1.
2. For the early days of the sealing industry, see A. Howard Clark, "The Antarctic Fur-Seal and Sea-Elephant Industry," in G. B. Goode and others, *The Fisheries and Fishing Industries of the United States* (Washington, 1887), Section 5, Vol. 2, 400–467.

authorities during the last decades of the colonial era. The mode of its operation is suggested by a royal order of January 20, 1784, which complained of "the clandestine commerce plied by foreigners in our American ports, which they enter on the pretext of stress of weather and the necessity of repairing their ships; and flouting the laws of hospitality and the Law of Nations they introduce their goods despite all the precautions that prudence dictates." This order enjoined that foreign vessels be forbidden entrance on any pretext whatever.[3]

In the closing years of the eighteenth century Spain's distresses in Europe compelled a temporary liberalization of her colonial trade policies, making possible the establishment of United States commerce with La Plata on a more regular and extensive basis. In 1796 Spain became an ally of France; British naval power promptly drove her shipping from the seas; and her communications with the American colonies were almost completely disrupted. Hard necessity drove the Spanish court to promulgate the royal order of November 18, 1797, permitting peninsular merchants to trade with the overseas provinces in neutral ships from national or foreign ports, provided that the goods carried were non-contraband in character (only slaves, specie, and produce were allowed), and that the ships made a return voyage to Spain.[4]

These restrictions, absurd in the face of the British blockade of the peninsula and the unlimited demand of the colonies for all manner of goods, were ultimately disregarded. Even the conservative *consulado* or tribunal of commerce of Buenos Aires concluded that the return voyage to Spain should not be insisted upon, because the requirement could not be adequately enforced; and declared that compliance with the spirit of the royal order demanded the free export of the produce of the country and the import of needed commodities.[5]

By reason of "the location of its ports, the abundance of its merchant marine, and its neutrality toward the two most formi-

3. Facultad de Filosofía y Letras, *Documentos para la historia argentina, comercio de Indias, 1713–1809* (Vols. V, VI, and VII, Buenos Aires, 1915–1916), VI, 269.

4. Ricardo Levene, *A History of Argentina,* translated and edited by William S. Robertson (Chapel Hill, N. C., 1937), pp. 110–111. For the text of the order, see *Documentos para la historia argentina,* VII, 134.

5. Archivo General de la Nación, *Documentos referentes a la guerra de la independencia y emancipación de la República Argentina* (2 vols., Buenos Aires, 1914–1917), I, 293.

dable powers, France and England," in the words of a contemporary colonial observer, the United States was particularly favored by the new dispensation.[6] Yankee merchants were quick to take advantage. The Spanish minister to the United States wrote in 1799 that about five American vessels had already made trading voyages to La Plata. The lucrative nature of this traffic can be gauged from his statement that these ships purchased jerked beef in La Plata at a dollar and a half per quintal, and sold it in Cuba for ten.[7]

At the same time that American trade with La Plata increased, numerous English vessels, flying the American flag and pretending United States registry, came to share in the profitable neutral commerce.[8] These developments aroused Spanish mercantile jealousy, and governmental fears that the supposedly neutral trade was actually strengthening Spain's powerful enemy. Consequently, on April 20, 1799, a new order went forth, revoking that of November 18, 1797, because, "far from experiencing the favorable effects toward which this sovereign dispensation was directed, . . . it has redounded entirely to the private injury of our vassals of America and Spain, and to the increase of the industry and commerce of the enemy." [9]

American vessels nevertheless continued to arrive in the Plate estuary, bringing cargoes that had been ordered before revocation of the permissive edict, and pleading ignorance of the new state of affairs. So lax was the enforcement of the new decree that on July 18, 1800, the Spanish king addressed a vigorous reprimand to the viceroy of La Plata, asserting that the introduction of foreign goods into the colony continued with complete freedom, and insisting on more effective compliance with the law.[10]

This admonition was evidently heeded. At the time of DeForest's first visit to La Plata in 1801 the ban on neutral trade was being enforced with considerable vigor. The net result was to turn this commerce back into illicit channels, in which it henceforth moved, with few exceptions, until the decree of November 6, 1809,

6. *Documentos para la historia argentina,* VII, 175.

7. [Carlos Martínez de Irujo], *Observations on the Commerce of Spain with Her Colonies, in Time of War* (Philadelphia, 1800).

8. Emilio Ravignani, "El virreinato del Río de la Plata, 1776–1810," in Academia Nacional de la Historia, *Historia de la nación argentina* (Buenos Aires, 1936–   ), IV, Section 1, pp. 172–173.

9. *Documentos para la historia argentina,* VII, 158.

10. *Ibid.,* pp. 181–182.

issued by Viceroy Cisneros on the eve of the Argentine Revolution, opened the ports of La Plata to allied and neutral vessels bringing cargoes of any kind.[11]

Leaving Puerto Deseado, the *Diana* moved slowly down the coast in search of seal rookeries. Presently there arose a new controversy between Captain Smith and his second mate. The captain determined to land a sealing party on an island that appeared to DeForest to be privately owned. His objections to the undertaking provoked an explosion of wrath. "Captain Smith was in a passion with me and agreed to set me and my effects on Shore, but at about 10 at night he weighed Anchor and put to Sea, altering his plan of Sealing and forfeiting his word with me. On my remonstrating against it he said he should keep me, but that I might do duty or not as I chose. I made my election and determined to do no more duty on board the Ship, but consider myself detained here as a prisoner." [12]

Arrival on the scene of the sloop *Prudence* of Nantucket, Captain John Paddock, broke this awkward deadlock. The newcomers had been sealing at South Georgia, a mountainous, perpetually snow-covered island several hundred miles east of Cape Horn, and were bound for La Plata for repairs and provisions. Captain Smith grudgingly agreed that DeForest might transfer to the sloop and take passage for the Plate estuary. He was not yet to quit the coast of Patagonia, however, for the two commanders decided to pool their crews and take the *Diana* southward in search of better sealing, leaving the smaller vessel in James Harbor. There DeForest and two others remained, keeping guard over the sloop until the return of the sealers from the south.

Early in June the *Diana* returned, with a catch of 500 hair- and fur-seal skins, and a story of narrow escape from foundering on rocks. It was July 2, 1801, before the *Prudence* set sail for La Plata, DeForest on board. They anchored off Montevideo on the nineteenth of the month. In his journal DeForest recorded his

11. There is much useful information on early American commerce with La Plata in Harry Bernstein, *Origins of Inter-American Interest, 1700–1812* (Philadelphia, 1945), pp. 33–51. See also Arthur P. Whitaker, *The United States and the Independence of Latin America, 1800–1830* (Baltimore, 1941), pp. 14–16, and Charles L. Chandler, "United States Merchant Ships in the Rio de la Plata (1801–1809) as Shown by Early Newspapers," *Hispanic-American Historical Review*, II (1919), 26–54.

12. DeForest Journal, Vol. 1.

first impressions of the Platine landscape. "What little of the country I saw appeared to be as delightful as I have ever seen. There are no fences. The Ground is almost perfectly level and productive of almost every luxury of life. It is covered with innumerable Herds of Cattle, Sheep and Horses, and fruit trees in abundance. The Town consists of Houses uniformly one story high, and appears like a very neat little place." [13] Less inviting was the reception accorded by the Spanish authorities to the American visitors. When Captain Paddock and DeForest attempted to go on shore, they were stopped at the head of the pier and ordered out of port.[14]

Through the intercession of a more fortunate countryman, Captain Ray of the *Hope*, they were permitted to take on some sorely needed provisions before leaving. From him they learned that the reason for the official hostility was the large-scale smuggling which American vessels had lately engaged in at Montevideo and Buenos Aires. Such were the proportions of this traffic, he declared, that an order had been received to admit no more United States ships unless actually in such distress that they could not proceed without repairs.

Quitting inhospitable Montevideo, Captain Paddock lifted anchor and set sail for Rio de Janeiro. On July 31 the *Prudence* was hailed and stopped by a Buenos Aires brigantine, the *Volcán*, cruising in search of Portuguese enemy vessels.[15] During the search the captain of the boarding party, a hectoring, swaggering brute, according to DeForest, stole a watch from Captain Paddock's trunk and compelled him to sell a hand organ for half its price.

A few days later, the *Prudence* rode at anchor in the blue and sparkling waters of the bay of Rio de Janeiro. Over these waters, circling the bay, towered lofty and strangely shaped mountains.

13. *Ibid.*
14. The *Telégrafo Mercantil* (facsimile edition, Buenos Aires, 1914) of Buenos Aires, July 22, 1801, carried the following news item, apparently referring to the *Prudence:* "Montevideo, July 22. On the 19th instant an American sloop entered this port, coming from Puerto Deseado, whose garrison she had aided with provisions which were immediately replaced, and yesterday afternoon she sailed for her destination."
15. The farcical "War of the Oranges" between Spain and Portugal was ended in Europe by the Treaty of Badajoz, June 8, 1801, but news of the treaty did not reach La Plata until December of that year. Diego Luis Molinari, "La política lusitana y el Río de la Plata," in *Historia de la nación argentina*, V, Section 1, p. 439.

On the narrow strip of land between the shore and the mountains stood the capital of the Portuguese viceroyalty of Brazil. "The most squalid and filthy abode of humans under the sun," according to an English traveler of the period, the shabby, ugly houses and dirty, narrow streets formed a striking contrast to the magnificent natural surroundings.

DeForest went ashore intent on gaining as much information of the country and its trade as he could. He took lodgings in the city with another newly arrived American, Thomas Halsey of Providence, Rhode Island, with whom many years later he was to have far from friendly dealings. Early in September arrived the ship *Monticello* of Philadelphia, one of whose crew conveyed to DeForest the pleasing news that his brother John had lately been seen at Santiago de Cuba, in good health and making a profitable voyage.[16]

The foreign trade of Brazil, a monopoly of the mother country, was largely in the hands of English merchants whose ships, laden with European manufactures, came to Rio after supposedly touching at Portuguese ports.[17] Despite all precautions to prevent smuggling, DeForest observed, "a person who speaks the language and understands the business may effect it." He could not dispose of his own little adventure, however, for the city was glutted with European goods, chiefly because the war in progress between the Spanish and Portuguese colonies hindered the customary contraband trade with La Plata.

DeForest resolved to seek a more promising field for his enter-

16. In the Dyer White Papers, Yale University Library, there is a letter from John H. DeForest to Dyer White at New Haven, dated Santiago de Cuba, September 25, 1800, that graphically depicts the woes of a neutral trader in the era of the Napoleonic Wars. "In our passage from St. Croix to this port, we were gratified with being taken under the parental care of one of his 'Sovereign Majesty's' servants; who, from his tender affection for us, came near granting us a safe conduct to Jamaica: indeed, nothing but our being destitute of a *valuable* cargo, prevented him from doing that generous office. After *protecting* our vessel for 18 or 20 hours with an officer and arm'd soldiers, and finding we had nothing on board, but a little *salt*, he inhumanly withdrew his paternal care, and oblig'd us to shift for ourselves. 'Twould be ingratitude in me, however, not to acknowledge that this generous minded *Chevalier* assured me, on his taking leave, 'that, should providence permit us to fall in his way on our return home (at which time we should undoubtedly be more worthy his notice) he would certainly renew his fraternal embrace; and, enfolding us in his arms, would not let go his grasp until we were safely lodg'd in the *pure* and uncorrupted bosom of some vice Admiralty Judge.' "

17. For the commerce of colonial Brazil, see Roberto C. Simonsen, *Historia economica do Brasil* (2 vols., Rio de Janeiro, 1937), II, Ch. 4.

prise. He thought of going to Buenos Aires in the *Prudence,* chartered by a Spanish merchant to take a cargo to La Plata. But the merchant, learning that the American planned to bring his wares, would not admit him on board. Next he planned to try the market at Rio Grande, a port near the disputed Spanish border. Formidable obstacles barred this project. Foreigners might not travel in Brazil without passports, very infrequently granted, and no Portuguese would risk imprisonment and confiscation of property to give DeForest passage to Rio Grande. "While at Rio de Janeiro I learned thoroughly the mode of doing business there in the Smuggling way, but I found great difficulty in getting away from there in a Portuguese vessel."

At last he came upon a skipper who would brave the dangers of carrying DeForest to Rio Grande. He was one André da Cunha Rego, the young owner of a *zumaca* or smack about to sail for Rio São Francisco. "I felt very much relieved indeed for I had worried myself exceedingly for a passage away to sell my goods and learn the business of the country."

They took furtive leave of Rio de Janeiro on September 24, 1801. To avoid suspicion DeForest stayed on board an English vessel putting out to sea until they were six or eight leagues from port; then he transferred to Cunha Rego's tiny bark. After fourteen days at sea and three "Gales of Wind," which the superstitious crew sought to conjure by attaching a sacred image to the quarter rail, to DeForest's great amusement, they dropped anchor at Rio São Francisco. Presently André returned from a visit ashore with a disturbing report. The *comandante* of the place was a gloomy fellow who showed no mercy to foreigners found in his domain. Recently he had imprisoned two such intruders and the captain of the ship that brought them.

It was decided to keep DeForest hidden in the boat while Cunha Rego transacted his business in town. Three weeks the smuggler remained pent up in the ship's tiny cabin, much of the time rolled up in a blanket to prevent recognition, and subsisting on an unpalatable diet of jerked beef and the Brazilian preparation of ground cereal known as *farinha.* Meanwhile André attempted to sell some of his friend's wares. The results were not gratifying. "Not only the Rulers of the place," complained DeForest, "but some of the Merchants at this infernal Hole appeared disposed to strip me of everything I had." [18]

18. DeForest to Israel Munson and Co., Rio Grande, Dec. 25, 1801, DeForest Journal, Vol. 2.

Cunha Rego finally wound up his affairs at Rio São Francisco, and they bore away south for Santa Catharina, the next port of any size on the coast. DeForest was in a mood to throw discretion to the winds. On arrival at Santa Catharina he resolved "to make a bold push for a passport, and either get in Prison or my Liberty." Cautious inquiry by the helpful André yielded the information that the governor of the place, Curado by name, was a man of liberal principles, possessed of an excellent knowledge of English and French. DeForest promptly dispatched Cunha Rego with the message that an "English Gentleman of distinction" was in the harbor without a passport, and desired to speak with his Excellency.

Governor Curado sent back a favorable reply. That evening, no doubt wearing his finest garments: coat of broadcloth, swansdown vest, cashmere breeches, and silk hose, DeForest called at the governor's residence. Assuming the consequence of a gentleman of fortune on his travels, a pretension which he supported by display of his old officer's commission, he regaled the Portuguese official with an account of his adventures, with certain judicious omissions and deviations from the facts. In conclusion, he requested the governor to grant him a passport to Rio Grande.

Curado listened, smiled graciously, but probably was not deceived. Fortunately for the impostor, the governor of Santa Catharina was not in sympathy with the exclusive policies of Lisbon. He reminded DeForest that the Portuguese government was very suspicious of foreigners, and its officers generally shared the principles of their government. As for himself, he had been educated in Paris, and was free from those jealous feelings. He invited DeForest to be his guest for the duration of his stay in Santa Catharina. Should he wish to depart, however, his passport to go to Rio Grande by land or sea would be ready on the morrow.

The next morning Governor Curado handed DeForest his passport, and the two men parted with expressions of mutual respect and an exchange of gifts. After settling accounts with the faithful André, the smuggler boarded a vessel bound for Rio Grande, taking leave of Santa Catharina with the comment that the women of the place were "handsomer than I have seen elsewhere in Brasil, but . . . they do not look like the pretty Girls of Connecticut."

He landed at Rio Grande, southernmost port of Brazil, on November 16, 1801. In time of peace, he learned, the port was a

center of contraband trade with La Plata, to the amount of $200,000 a year. War between Spain and Portugal had interrupted this traffic, and markets were extremely dull. Failing to sell his goods, DeForest resolved to cross into Spanish territory. Suspension of hostilities on the frontier at the end of December, upon announcement of the treaty of peace of June 8, 1801, aided his plan. On January 13, 1802, in company with a number of Spanish merchants, lately prisoners of war, he set off across the plains for Buenos Aires, some 500 miles away. A priest of Rio Grande, "my good old friend, Padre José Alves Chaves," had provided him with letters of introduction to influential personages on the Spanish side of the border.

In high spirits, the party moved southward over the grassy plains of Rio Grande do Sul. While the older and more sedate travelers rode in carts, DeForest and a young merchant, Don Francisco Galup, generally rode on horseback, desiring "to visit every house we saw within two miles of our road, to converse with the inhabitants, to get every information relative to the country in our power, to eat bread and milk, and make love to the buxom wenches, who uniformly gave preference to the Inglez, as they are pleased to call me, all having a high regard for the English nation." [19]

On January 22 they came to the Spanish frontier post of Santa Teresa, where DeForest presented letters of introduction to the *comandante* and to a local merchant, both of whom treated him with much politeness and attention. A few days later he arrived in Montevideo, where another letter of introduction secured him an invitation to stay at the home of an unidentified merchant.

From Montevideo he sent home a boastful account of his prodigious wanderings, "never before made by a stranger, and an infidel."

"Picture to yourself," he wrote, "a young man deserting his ship, on board of which he was but a petty officer, on the uninhabited coast of Patagonia; arriving in Brasil, where he could neither speak nor understand a word that was spoken by the inhabitants, and where he had not a friend to look to for advice or assistance; flying from Rio de Janeiro without a passport, and contrary to the laws of the country; traversing all the Southern

19. DeForest to Isaac Mills, Montevideo, March 10, 1802, in Louis E. de Forest, ed., "A Trip through Brazil in 1802," *Brazil* (New York), Year IX, no. 101, March, 1937.

part of Brasil; introducing himself to the Governador of St. Catherine who speaks English and French, as a young Gentleman of fortune on his travels, and by him invited to live at the Palace all the time he should be there; arriving in this province, introduced to people of the first respectability, received by the Comandant of S. Teresa, and Governor of Maldonado, as a companion, and as such introduced to their families and friends, and in two days going to Buenos Aires, the capital of the viceroyalty, with some excellent letters, and an increased share of assurance." [20]

As he reflected on these experiences, it became clear to DeForest that society bestowed its favors on those who professed to be least in need of them.

"I suppose you will conclude that I possess as much impudence as vanity and that a man of twenty-eight years of age, without property or very particular friends, ought to reduce his feelings, and his actions, to a level with that of his circumstances. I think differently. He who has a good opinion of himself is sure to have the good opinion of others. If a man is poor, he may travel through all parts of the world, at less expense, by assuming the character of a Gentleman, than that of a blackguard. 'Tis ingrafted in our nature to do, unasked, a thousand favors to a man who appears not to be in want of them. But the poor devil who comes modestly before us, and tells us by his actions that his property, or family, does not entitle him to the rank of Gentleman, receives no favors." [21]

DeForest wrote that he would come home by way of Spain as second mate of an unidentified ship. By the time of his return he expected to be possessed of a considerable knowledge of trade and navigation. He suggested that his friends have ready for him a vessel of 400 tons, completely equipped and furnished for a two-year voyage—presumably to La Plata. He closed in a vein of whimsical gaiety. "I ought to be making money, but fate has decreed otherwise. Like Ulysses, I expect I must yet be tossed about a considerable time longer before I shall be able to see and possess my darling Penelope: 30 or 40,000 dollars." [22]

The Yankee Ulysses noted the presence of thirty-two American merchant ships detained in the Río de la Plata. Some had been

20. *Ibid.*
21. *Ibid.*
22. *Ibid.*

there as long as eight months, awaiting permission from Spain to load cargo and leave the river. DeForest thought that failure to secure such permission would prove disastrous to the outfitters. "I am confident the merchants on whose account the ships have come will never be able to make good the damage." [23]

On March 16, 1802, the smuggler boarded a Buenos Aires-bound sloop, without a passport or other official sanction. The capital of the viceroyalty lay some 200 miles from the mouth of the river, on its southwest shore. Twenty-four hours after leaving Montevideo, the sloop anchored in the harbor of Buenos Aires. A rude cart drawn by oxen took DeForest and his baggage from the shore to the inn of the Three Kings.

An almost complete gap in his journal and letterbooks obscures DeForest's movements during the next four months. Much of this time he presumably passed in doing business and in gaining a knowledge of the language and trade of the country. He was confined to his lodgings for several weeks with a severe cold. He evidently suffered no molestation from local authorities, despite the time-honored ban against the residence of foreigners in Spain's colonies.

When his diary resumes, on July 13, 1802, DeForest is most startlingly installed as a guest in a monastery of the Franciscan Order, called *el Regulador*.[24] He evidently wished to improve his knowledge of Spanish by avoiding contact with English-speaking friends in the city. Perhaps he also thought to court the favor of the influential Catholic clergy by display of interest in the "*santa fé romana, católica, y apostólica.*" At any rate, the simple regimen of the monastery appears to have been to his liking. "Peace and quietness reign here, Poverty is the order of the day, of course no cause of envy exists to lessen the enjoyment of their humble Meal and still more humble apparel."

The pious brethren regarded DeForest in the light of a prospective convert and spent much time with him in religious discussion. When in early August he announced his intention of leaving the monastery, without having embraced the faith, they sorrowed for him as for a lost soul. "Poor Don David," he quotes

23. DeForest to Isaac Mills, Montevideo, March 12, 1802, in L. E. de Forest, ed., "A Trip through Brazil in 1802." For a list of these ships, see C. L. Chandler, "United States Merchant Ships in the Rio de la Plata (1801–1809)," pp. 26–28.

24. According to DeForest, this name was applied to monasteries of the Franciscan Order whose regimen followed the precepts and example of St. Peter of Alcantara.

them as saying, "he for whom we have such a great respect, and whom it was our expectation to have seen made a Christian before his departure, is now going out into the World, to mix with his Countrymen who have no regard for Religion, and who will undoubtedly turn to ridicule everything they may discover in him appertaining to Religion. He is lost forever, we very much fear, but our Prayers shall daily be offered up for him, that he may be convinced of the necessity of embracing our Holy Religion; that he may embrace it, and finally, that he may be received into heaven, and with all other Good Catholics enjoy happiness for ever and ever." [25]

DeForest took cheerful leave of his kind hosts on August 11, 1802. From the Father Superior, Padre Montero, he carried letters of introduction to a wealthy merchant of Buenos Aires, Francisco Ignacio de Ugarte, and to a "very respectable clergyman of Montevideo." Preparing to depart from La Plata, he invested the proceeds of the sale of his goods in a stock of nutria skins and ostrich feathers. He did not sail for Spain, as he had planned, but instead took ship for England. On December 6, 1802, he embarked from Montevideo in the *Three Sisters* of Philadelphia, Captain John Ansley, "laden with hides and bound to Falmouth and a market."

25. DeForest Journal, Vol. 2.

III

"A HIGHLY DANGEROUS TRADE"

THE *Three Sisters* anchored in Falmouth port on March 6, 1803. While the ship discharged cargo, DeForest went ashore to view the countryside of Cornwall and inspect the famous tin and copper mines of this region. He visited the rotten borough of St. Mawes, boasting some 600 inhabitants, and was amazed to learn that this little town sent two members to parliament. "And what is still more extraordinary, there are but Five Votes given in. Very unequal representation." [1]

At Redruth, he descended into one of the mines. "We were underground about three Hours, in which time we went under houses and Streets. Saw a great Number of People at Work, sometimes going on perpendicular Ladders, then crawling down the rocks, then on slanting Ladders, then on Planks laid across deep caverns, then walking a subterraneous road horizontally, then wading in Channels of Water, then over shoes in Mud and Gravel, till we arrived at the, or nearly, to the lower end of the Water Engine, about 500 feet, perpendicular height. Here we saw two poor, though apparently happy, Devils, who were driven from some 50 feet below by the Water and were waiting for the Engine to clear it. On our return we took various other roads and directions till we arrived by another outlet at the surface where we once more had Daylight. Mudded from head to foot, and most intolerably fatigued, I ran to the Office, stripped, washed and redressed myself. The Miners gave me what they called Cornish wine, made of Rum and molasses." [2]

Some days later the *Three Sisters* sailed for London, DeForest on board. They came into the Thames River on March 19, and that evening the trader dismounted from a "caravan coach" in the English capital. He found lodging at the Virginia and Maryland Coffee House in Cornhill. The next day he consigned his stock of nutria skins and ostrich feathers for sale to Thomas Wilson, merchant of the City.

1. DeForest Journal, Vol. 2.
2. *Ibid.*

Portents of war clouded the English spring of 1803. Formal hostilities with France had ceased in 1801, but bitter commercial warfare between the two countries and British alarm over the advancing tide of Napoleonic power on the continent threatened a rupture of the Peace of Amiens. In Plymouth harbor DeForest had seen a great array of the "wooden walls of old England," guns on board and drawing one tier of water, "a thing uncommon in time of Peace, which plainly shows that the Government are jealous of the French." He found the business world of London sensitive to every turn in the developing crisis. On March 29 it was reported that Pitt and Dundas were coming back into power, "which plainly shows that war is inevitable." Stocks immediately fell 5 and 6 per cent.

In Paris the British ambassador, Lord Whitworth, was engaged in weighty negotiations with the government of the first consul. Stubbornly he resisted the French demand that Britain evacuate the strategic island of Malta. Rumors concerning the progress of these discussions ran in the English capital, exciting alternate fears and hopes. On the morning of May 5, DeForest noted in his diary, "Notice was up at the Mansion House that Lord Hawksbury [British foreign minister] had written to the Lord Mayor that the dispute with France was amicably adjusted. Before 12 o'clock, however, the Letter was found to be a Forgery. All London was in an uproar. Stocks had risen all at once to 7¾–8% higher than yesterday." In a thronged House of Commons he heard Fox, Canning, Addington, and other political leaders discuss the great question of the day until debate waxed so warm that visitors were ordered to withdraw. On May 14 came word that Lord Whitworth had left Paris. "THE DIE APPEARS TO BE CAST," was DeForest's comment. Two days later the British king announced the rupture of negotiations, proclaimed an embargo and the issue of letters-of-marque against French commerce.

Meanwhile Napoleon's embarrassments in Europe had brought a gigantic windfall to the Young Republic across the seas. Fearing that his recently acquired province of Louisiana would fall into British hands at the outbreak of hostilities, Napoleon decided to sell it to the United States and use the proceeds for his military campaigns. Our plenipotentiaries in France, James Monroe and Robert Livingston, hastened to seal the magnificent bargain. They purchased the vast and ill-defined territory for 60,000,000 francs plus the assumption by the United States of claims of its citizens not to exceed 20,000,000 francs. DeForest gave scant attention to this epochal event. "A second report," he noted briefly in his diary on May 17, "that Louisiana has been ceded to the United States by the French Government, in consideration of a certain sum of Money, said to be $6,000,000, payable in Debts due from the French Government, and money."

Time passed swiftly for DeForest as he roamed through London, center of world commerce and industry, repository of innumerable historic monuments and landmarks. He made the customary visits to St. Paul's, Westminster Abbey, and the Tower of London. He browsed in Lackington's book store, reputed the largest collection of books in the world, and jotted in his diary the edifying fact that Lackington was once a very poor man and began by peddling songs and pamphlets. He strolled into "Pidcock's Collection of Wild Beasts," and regarded with curiosity "a very singular animal, Elephant." From the din and bustle of the roaring city he found relief by excursions to the neighboring countryside. At Twickenham he came to the house built by the "so justly celebrated Alexander Pope." Strangers were forbidden entrance, but "the Watch Words, Potosi, or Mexico, overcome in this Country, all such Mandates." DeForest left the hallowed spot with a tribute to the philosopher-poet. "Farewell Pope, I revere and respect your Memory."

Early in August, his nutria skins and ostrich feathers sold, DeForest sailed for America in the ship *Gosport*. He landed at Norfolk, Virginia, on September 24, and from there proceeded by water to New York. Yellow fever raged in the city when he arrived, and many inhabitants had fled. "Gloomy looks the Morn," the traveler wrote in his journal. "No one moving, this beautiful City deserted, silent as the Grave, not a Boy hallooing, or a Sailor quarreling, nor a single ring of a Bell." Some days later he disembarked at New Haven from a New York packet boat, to be warmly greeted by his brother John, now a rising country merchant of Watertown, Connecticut.

The brothers set out by stagecoach for this inland town, the home of their mother and step-father, Edward Lockwood, Sr. As they rode over the rolling Connecticut countryside, David's mind turned back to the flat, treeless, and sky-filled plains of La Plata and Rio Grande do Sul. "I was much surprised that the Country should appear so beautifully, when considering its roughness.

The Craggy Hills, the Groves of Timber, the Rivers and the Brooks—all appeared to possess charms innumerable." They arrived at Watertown on the afternoon of October 14, and the returned wanderer was soon regaling his parents and brothers with accounts of his South American exploits.

DeForest's experiences and observations in La Plata had convinced him that this region offered a rich field for American commercial enterprise. Lacking the means for an independent venture, he broached the subject of a trading voyage to the Plate estuary to several merchants. His overtures met with a cool reception. Established firms, basking in the sun of a lucrative neutral trade with Europe and the West Indies (undiminished until the *Essex* decision of 1805 inaugurated a new restrictive policy on the part of the European belligerents), were not disposed to embark on hazardous expeditions to the forbidden Plate ports. Reports of the prolonged detention of American vessels in the river in 1801–1802 heightened skepticism about the prospects of the Plata trade. Unable to gain support for his cherished scheme, DeForest cast about for other ways to fill a depleted purse.

Organization of the Louisiana territory, then under discussion in Washington, suggested the possibility of an interesting employment. DeForest wrote to Secretary of the Treasury Gallatin, expressing gratification with an administration "so well in accord with my own sentiments of propriety," and conceiving "the acquisition of Louisiana, and consequently the entire command of the Mississippi and all its branches" to be almost invaluable to the United States. He closed by requesting the office of surveyor in the new possession.[3] Despite the support of Pierpont Edwards and Abraham Bishop, Republican party leaders in Connecticut, his application seems to have been denied.

DeForest went to New York in May, 1804, in search of commercial employment. He had not abandoned hope of revisiting La Plata. An entry in his diary notes that on May 5 he wrote to the American consul at Santiago de Cuba, requesting that he "inform me by Letter to Buenos Ayres (directed to care of Don Francisco Ignacio de Ugarte) what are the prices of Slaves, Beef, Tallow, Flour and the probable Markets for Months." In New York he discussed a trading voyage to La Plata for nutria skins with several firms, including the prominent New Haven merchant, Ebenezer Townsend. Nothing came of these negotia-

3. DeForest to Albert Gallatin, New Haven, Jan. 10, 1804, *ibid.*, Vol. 3.

tions. At the end of June, DeForest was dispirited and morose. In his diary he inveighed against rich merchants who calculated that "others must dance attendance at their will." Everything relating to him, he complained, went wrong-end first.

A sudden stroke of fortune revived his spirits. On July 2 he received an offer to take command of the schooner *Daphne* on a trading voyage to the Guianas and West Indies. In his capacity of captain and supercargo he would receive wages of twenty-two dollars a month, 5 per cent commission on all property sold, 21½ per cent on all bought for the owners' account. DeForest accepted the offer with alacrity. "Pleasant times in a gloomy season," he wrote in his diary, "I have been so accustomed to disappointments that I fear all will miscarry."

Laden with beef, pickle, and codfish, the *Daphne* sailed out of New York harbor on July 5, her destination the French colony of Cayenne. East of the Bermudas they caught the regular trade winds and ran them down to Cayenne, casting anchor in port after a passage of thirty-three days. DeForest found little demand for his articles, and decided to try the markets of neighboring Dutch Surinam and British Guiana. He touched in turn at Paramaribo and Demerara, but came away almost empty handed. Bewailing his luck, he continued northward, entered the Caribbean, and ran for Tobago in the Windward Islands. He found three American vessels in the harbor of Scarsborough, all complaining of poor sales. Nothing remained, he decided, but to make a dash for Martinique, braving the numerous British cruisers that roamed these waters.

In the early dark hours of September 7, the shadowy bulk of Martinique came in sight. At sunrise they slipped into the great bay of Fort Royal without incident and came to anchor off the town. DeForest went ashore resolved to sell his cargo at whatever price it would bring. In the course of the day he bargained it away for "somewhere about New York prices," investing the proceeds in molasses. He consoled himself with the thought that he had done as well as he could, for indisputably markets in the West Indies were all very bad.

Damning all Fort Royal, DeForest stood out to sea in the middle of the hurricane season. Two days out, a British privateer stopped the *Daphne* and sent her into Tortola for examination. No cause for detention was found, and they were permitted to go on. Cape Hatteras was astern on September 24; the next day

they ran into a heavy gale. The heavily loaded craft rolled pre-
cariously in the troughs of great seas; their foresail was soon
blown to pieces. On the twenty-sixth the gale abated, but it was a
momentary respite.

"We poor Devils who cannot see the length of a Man's Nose
consoled ourselves by saying, 'to be sure we have lost our Foresail,
our most valuable sail, yet we have a fine S. W. breeze, we know
exactly our Longitude and will be in New York in Three days.'
Little did we know what was then brewing—that all the Infernal Spirits were laying their heads together and plotting a Jig for
us to dance—and a hell of a Jig it proved indeed.

"For at 2 P. M. a Black Cloud appeared at the S. W. It flew
like lightning from the Place of its Birth to where we were, and
much ado. We got in our sail, except our Jibs Bonnet, under
which we scudded all the afternoon, the wind whistled, the Seas
were mountain high. At Dark, not daring to scud any longer,
because we could not see to avoid the Seas that every moment
threatened us with destruction, we hove to again under our little
Bonnet. She lay to but poorly, her head constantly knocking
off, and we rolling in the Troughs of the Seas. 'Twas a situation,
in my opinion, very dangerous. We feared to set our reefed
Mainsail for 'twas worn so thin that I was confident 'twould immediately blow to pieces, but something must be done. We of
course set Just the Peak of the Balanced reefed Mainsail (about
one third). She came to better but still it would not do so that
we could feel safe and free from the dangers of the immensely
heavy Seas by which we were surrounded." [4]

Hurried consultation with the mate and crew revealed general
agreement that the ship must be lightened if she were to outlive
the gale. With a heavy heart, DeForest gave orders to pump the
contents of ten hogsheads of molasses overboard. The *Daphne* immediately came to the wind much better, became more lively in
the water. All evening and until late the next morning it blew
tremendously from various points, then gradually abated until
they could make some small sail. The following day (October 28)
the sea was smooth, the weather pleasant. In his cabin, dining
on beef and spiced meats, washed down with excellent brandy
and port wine, DeForest mourned the eternal loss of ten hogsheads of molasses.

"Don't trouble me no more," he wrote in his diary, "ye spirits

4. *Ibid.,* Vol. 4.

of Bad Sales, Molasses and Foresail. If I have not done as I ought, 'tis the best I could, and if I am to be censured, let those who do it, consider every circumstance relating to the business of this very unpleasant Voyage, and I am sure I cannot suffer much in their opinions."

They came safely into New York port, November 3, 1804. For all DeForest's misgivings, his employers professed to be satisfied with his management of the voyage. Settlement of accounts found him richer by several hundred dollars. Fortified with this inconsiderable capital, supplemented by a loan from the firm of Dunham and Lord of Boston, he immediately set about preparing for a smuggling voyage to Brazil and La Plata. He chartered a small schooner, the *Jefferson* of Vinalhaven, Captain Nathaniel Mitchell, and loaded her down with naval stores, in great demand at Buenos Aires.[5]

On the eve of his departure, DeForest wrote to President Jefferson a letter of application for the post of United States consul to the "Vice Kingdom of Buenos Ayres." [6]

"Having passed some time in South America near the close of the French Revolutionary War," he set forth, "more particularly in Brasil and La Plata, and having witnessed many of the difficulties into which our Countrymen plunged themselves from their ignorance of the customs and trade of La Plata, and being satisfied that the carrying trade of the Country must devolve on neutrals should Spain be again engaged in war with England as appears highly probable,[7] I have thought of Establishing myself in mercantile business at Buenos Ayres immediately after the expected war shall have been declared." He closed by assuring the President that his appointment as consul would enable him to render important services to American commerce with La Plata.[8]

DeForest took the *Jefferson* out of New York port on February 2, 1805, his destination the Cape Verdes. After a brief stop there

5. In 1799, pitch cost $2 or $3 a barrel in the United States, but sold in Buenos Aires at $40 a barrel. [C. M. Irujo], *Observations on the Commerce of Spain with Her Colonies.*

6. The names *virreinato de Buenos-Ayres* and *virreinato del Río de la Plata* were used without distinction in reference to the colony.

7. Hostilities between Great Britain and Spain, halted by the Treaty of Amiens of March 27, 1802, were renewed in December, 1804.

8. DeForest to President Thomas Jefferson, New Haven, Jan. 25, 1805, DeForest Journal, Vol. 4.

for provisions, they set course for Brazil. On April 22 the schooner dropped anchor in the harbor of Rio de Janeiro, described by DeForest as "the most grand and romantic in nature." Employing the traditional formula of Yankee smugglers in South American waters, he pleaded the need of repairs to his ship in order to secure permission to remain in port. Judicious management of the officials who came on the customary visit of inspection ensured approval of his request. Before long he had smuggled forty barrels of tar aboard a Portuguese vessel, "and could have smuggled another thousand with equal security." He discovered that with proper measures any kind of contraband trade could be plied at Rio. "Everything is bought and sold for Money—Men, Merchandise, and some Women." With an eye to future trading ventures to Brazil, DeForest noted in his diary that cotton cambrics were gaining popularity in the country, and promised to become an article of great consumption.

The *Jefferson* slipped out of Rio harbor on May 30, bound for a rendezvous in the bay of Ilha Grande, a day's sail to the south, where DeForest was to secure an unidentified freight from one Manos da Costa Guimaraes. This obscure transaction miscarried, but a visit ashore netted the smuggler 150 pieces of valuable brazilwood. He hastened to put to sea, "apprehending difficulty and danger on account of my being near the bottom of a deep bay engaged in a highly contraband trade." As they neared the entrance to the bay a Portuguese government brig stood for them, causing DeForest extreme disquiet. Fortunately a fine breeze sprang up and permitted them to evade the inquisitive vessel and get into the open sea.

Moving south, the *Jefferson* reached Montevideo on June 27, 1805. Again DeForest pleaded distress, and, strange to say, inspection by Spanish officials found the schooner in a pitiful condition, with water in the hold and sails and riggings torn. Her master was sent to the governor of Montevideo, Pascual Ruíz Huidobro, who treated DeForest with politeness, but asked that he make all possible haste in getting ready for sea. "Thus ended this very important day," the smuggler wrote in his diary, "and I returned on board much fatigued, went to Sleep, and was as quiet as a Lamb."

The next day he offered his cargo of pitch and boards for sale to the government. He proposed to use the money thus obtained to pay for his ship's repairs, and requested permission to expend any surplus for the purchase of jerked beef. After interminable parleys and inspections his offer was accepted. But first the viceroy must approve the transaction. By dint of great exertions and some bribing DeForest had his petition forwarded to Viceroy Rafaél de Sobremonte at Buenos Aires. Meantime the cargo of the *Jefferson* had been unloaded and stored in the warehouse of one Villardebo, a *regidor* or councilman of Montevideo.

Six weeks went by without any word from Buenos Aires. DeForest grew impatient, and called on Governor Ruíz Huidobro to plead for greater dispatch in the matter. "You have nothing to complain of," brusquely replied the Spaniard. "In my opinion you left Brasil to come here on commercial reviews, your pretended distress is all a hoax." No amount of disavowals could shake the governor's well founded suspicions.[9]

DeForest wrote an English correspondent that the Buenos Aires government had lately grown very severe in its treatment of foreigners. There was a widespread suspicion that British ships were intervening in the neutral trade to La Plata under cover of the United States flag. Americans in the Plate ports resented this trickery and did all in their power to expose the impostors. United States trading voyages to the river had of late been attended by a singular fatality. A notable exception was the voyage of the *Rufus* of Boston, just arrived with a cargo of 396 slaves, with only ten deaths on the passage. "The profits on

9. The technique of illicit trade to the Spanish-American colonies had not changed radically in more than half a century, as shown by the following description of smuggling procedure, written in 1741: "Ships frequently approach the *Spanish* coasts under pretense of wanting water, wood, provisions, or more commonly to stop a Leak. The first Thing that is done in such a Case, is to give Notice to the Governor of their great Distress, and as a full Proof thereof, to send a very considerable Present. By this Means Leave is obtained to come on Shore, to erect a Warehouse, and to unlade the Ship; but then all this is performed under the Eye of the King's Officers, and the Goods are regularly enter'd in a Register as they are brought into the Warehouse, which when full is shut up, and the Doors sealed. All these Precautions taken, the Business is effectually carried on in the Night by a Back-door, and the *European* Goods being taken out, Indigo, Cochineal, Vinellos, Tobacco, and above all Bars of Silver and Pieces of Eight are very exactly packed in the same Cases, and placed as they stood before. But then, that such as have bought may be able to sell publickly. . . . A Petition is presented to the Governor, setting forth the Stranger's Want of Money to pay for Provisions, building the Warehouse, Timber for repairing the Ship . . . ; in Consideration of all which, Leave is desired to dispose of some small Part of their Cargo, in order to discharge these Debts." John Campbell, *A Concise History of the Spanish America* (London, 1741), quoted in Madaline W. Nichols, *The Gaucho* (Durham, N. C., 1942), pp. 29–30.

them and her return Cargo will undoubtedly be great, and I heartily congratulate the fortunate Owners." [10]

At last came the long awaited permission for DeForest to load a cargo of jerked beef. On September 14, 1805, he sailed the *Jefferson* out of Montevideo, happy at the prospect of "making so much by my little Voyage as to be able . . . to Kick Poverty out of doors. Should such an event happen, I swear I will conduct with prudence and make myself and friends as happy as possible." Off the Brazil Banks they ran into shallow, rock-strewn waters, and narrowly escaped destruction when a squall came up. They made the ship fast, and prepared to take to their single boat if the cables should part and the *Jefferson* go on the rocks. The next morning the tide came to their assistance, and by dodging some rocks and running over others they got into a clear open channel which led to the sea. They cast anchor near some small islands (the Abrolhos group), and from the master of a Portuguese sailing boat they had information how to escape from this perilous coast. "God is good," exclaimed their informant, "or you never would have got clear."

Steering to the north, they rounded the bulge of Brazil and made for the Caribbean. At Trinidad, DeForest learned that the ports of Cuba had been thrown open to neutral trade because of the renewal of hostilities between Spain and Great Britain.[11] He had planned to take his cargo to New Orleans, but now decided to go to Habana instead. Off Santo Domingo they witnessed a running fight between an English packetboat and a French privateer. At dawn a party from the corsair boarded the *Jefferson*. They reported that they had attempted to board the British craft, but found her too heavy, losing five men killed and six

10. DeForest to Thomas Wilson, Montevideo, August 25, 1805, DeForest Journal, Vol. 4. A Spanish royal order of November 24, 1791, permitted foreigners to engage in the slave trade to the Indies on an equal footing with Spaniards. This permission was prolonged down to 1810 by the royal orders of September 4, 1800, and April 22, 1804. For the slave trade to La Plata, see the erudite introduction of Diego Luis Molinari to Vol. 7 of *Documentos para la historia argentina*. A. P. Whitaker, *The United States and the Independence of Latin America*, pp. 15–16, discusses the importance of the slave trade as a factor in the development of United States commerce with La Plata. Georges Scelle, *Histoire politique de la traite négrière aux Indes de Castille* (2 vols., Paris, 1906), is indispensable for the first two centuries of the slave traffic in Spanish America.

11. For a careful study of United States commerce with Cuba in the period 1779–1809, see Roy F. Nichols, "Trade Relations and the Establishment of United States Consulates in Spanish America," *Hisp. Am. Hist. Rev.*, XIII (1933), 289–313.

wounded in the action. The boarding officers conducted themselves with much civility, DeForest noted in his diary, but their men stole a few things. Two days later a privateer of unknown nationality stood for the *Jefferson*, but drew off when the American ship maneuvered in the manner of an armed vessel. "Oh how I hate these Plundering Rascals," DeForest fretted, "of whatever nation they may be." He did not foresee his own future as a promoter of privateering enterprise.

They came to the Cuban port of Batabano, some fourteen leagues distant from Habana, on December 8, 1805. The *comandante* of the place, a "crabbed, drunken Rascal," would not permit DeForest to go overland to the capital until appeased with a bribe. Leaving Captain Mitchell in charge of the vessel, the trader set out for the "famous City of Havanna," two days' journey. On arrival he consigned his cargo of beef for sale to José Matías de Acebal, merchant of the capital. A purchaser was soon found, and on December 16 DeForest began to discharge cargo, "a very pleasant thing, as I had long wished to do it." His voyage gave him, after paying every charge, a profit of more than 1,000 per cent on his investment of less than $1,000.[12]

DeForest sailed from Habana for the United States on January 20, 1806, in the brigantine *Actress*. He landed at Baltimore on February 11, and there discussed the prospects of a trading voyage to La Plata with Captain Thomas Tenant, a prominent merchant. He went on to Washington, and like other travelers of the time was struck by the forlorn and formless appearance of the capital. "Washington," he noted in his journal, "is by nature as well situated as a City could possibly be, but it is nothing but Country as yet, made up of two or three little Clusters of Houses in different parts of the City Plot. Lots and buildings are very low indeed, and no Purchasers. Not a single Vessel of any description is owned here, every necessary of life is said to be very high. Each settlement in the City is contending with the others. On the whole, it is at present a place of no business of any kind except Quarrels and Law Suits."

Congress was in session, with much debate over President Jefferson's foreign policies. "Attending Congress almost every day," DeForest jotted in his diary, "but have a most contemptible opinion of their abilities, as a body."

12. DeForest to John R. Wheaton, Baltimore, Feb. 17, 1806, DeForest Letterbooks, Vol. 2.

He had a conference with the President, and was much cha-grined to learn that Jefferson had not received any letters in support of his application for a commission as consul to Buenos Aires. The President asked his caller many questions about South America. Lately he had received and dined a more celebrated adventurer, the swarthy Venezuelan Francisco de Miranda, who doubtless unfolded to Jefferson his plans for the liberation of his homeland from Spanish rule. Now Miranda's New York-based expedition was on the high seas, headed toward the coasts of Venezuela and disaster, while the Spanish minister to the United States, the Marqués de Casa Irujo, was proclaiming to all the world the perfidy of the American government in conniving with desperate adventurers at subversion of the provinces of a friendly power.[13]

DeForest's attitude toward the Miranda affair is not without interest. In February, 1806, he received a number of letters from a New York friend, Dr. John H. Douglass, who appears to have been an enthusiast for the cause of Spanish-American liberation, and to have acted as a kind of recruiting agent for Miranda's expedition.[14] These messages evidently invited DeForest's partic-ipation in the filibustering venture. His reply was guarded and cool. "I hardly know how to address you on the subject of *that* Expedition, not being sufficiently informed, but can assure you that I should not like to engage in any warlike enterprise, how-ever plausible it might appear, except under the banners of some Established Government, and I certainly have no disposition to change my character as a Neutral American. However, being totally ignorant of your plan, I cannot judge of its Quality, of course, shall not hazard a doubt of its propriety." [15] About the

13. For Miranda, see the classic biography by William S. Robertson, *The Life of Miranda* (2 vols., Chapel Hill, N. C., 1929), and an earlier but still useful work by the same author, *Francisco de Miranda and the Revolutionizing of Spanish America* (American Historical Association *Annual Report, 1907,* Washington, 1909, I, 189–540). For the diplomatic aspects of the Miranda affair, see Henry Adams, *History of the United States of America* . . . (9 vols., New York, 1891–1898), III, 189–196.

14. A "John H. Douglass, physician," is listed in *Jones's New-York Mercantile and General Directory for . . . 1805–6.* For his testimony in the trial of Colonel William S. Smith, Miranda's chief American aide, see *The Trials of William S. Smith and Samuel G. Ogden* . . . (New York, 1807), pp. 126–128.

15. DeForest to Dr. John H. Douglass, Washington, Feb. (?), 1806, DeForest Letterbooks, Vol. 2.

same time he wrote friends in Baltimore of a "secret expedition supposed to be bound for La Guaira," and expressed strong disapproval of the project.[16]

Why did the adventurous DeForest frown upon a plan to bring the blessings of independence and free trade to the Spanish-American colonies? The reasons are not far to seek. First, the participation of United States citizens in Miranda's expedition was bound to impair the standing of all American traders in Spain's colonial ports, rendering more hazardous and difficult DeForest's future ventures to La Plata.[17] Second, should the filibusters succeed and one or more of the colonies achieve their independence, an unlikely event, the special conditions favoring United States commerce with Spanish America at this period would disappear. The new states would at once make peace with Britain and open their ports to the world, and England, by virtue of her immensely superior trading position, would soon replace the United States as the chief carrier to their markets.

DeForest voiced fears of this kind in two letters written in the spring of 1806. "The Opposition in this Country," he informed an American firm in Habana, "have taken much pains to make it appear that our Government ought to be implicated in the Expedition of Miranda. They have failed, in my opinion, and I cannot suppose that Spain will consider it aggression on our part, whatever may be the depredations of Miranda. I am very sorry, however, that the expedition was ever undertaken, for I think it will be injurious to the Interests of this Country to have another Independent Nation on the American Continent." [18] To an English correspondent he expressed the view that Miranda's enterprise would not affect adversely United States commerce with Spanish America, "unless Miranda should succeed and establish

16. DeForest to Robert and John Oliver, Feb. 21, 1806, *ibid.*

17. Spanish anger at alleged United States complicity in the Miranda affair is reflected in the royal order of July 29, 1806, advising the viceroy of Buenos Aires "concerning the conduct that should be observed with the American ships that attempt to carry on contraband trade." The order called for an end to toleration of "the insults of these strangers on our American coasts, for heartened by impunity they do not cease to repeat them, as we have seen recently in the case of the expedition projected by the traitor Miranda, prepared in one of the ports of the United States with the design of attacking one of the provinces of Costa Firme." *Documentos para la historia argentina,* VII, 334–335.

18. DeForest to Gray and Bowen, Boston, May 16, 1806, DeForest Letterbooks, Vol. 2.

another Independent Nation on this Continent, which might possibly injure us in our carrying trade, but what we should lose Great Britain would probably gain." [19]

With the fate of the filibusters still uncertain, DeForest prepared for a second trading voyage to La Plata. He planned to employ a strategy long familiar to foreign intruders in Spain's American possessions: the introduction of contraband wares under cover of the legal slave traffic. In May, 1806, he purchased the brigantine *Jane*, and assembled a cargo of dry goods suitable for the Plate market. The *Jane* cleared from Boston on the twenty-ninth of May, her destination the island of Goree, a notable center of the slave trade on the Gold Coast of Africa. On the eve of his departure, DeForest resolved to remain for several years at Buenos Aires as a commission merchant. This decision, he noted in his diary, was "altogether accidental, and if anything clever grows out of it I shall feel very happy indeed."

19. DeForest to Thomas Wilson, Boston, May 28, 1806, *ibid.*, Vol. 3.

IV

"REIGN OF TERROR AND CONFUSION"

THE passage of the *Jane* to the shores of Africa seems to have been bare of incident. DeForest does not disclose how his polyglot crew of two Swedes, two Scotchmen, a Frenchman, an English boy, and an American cook fared together under the command of Captain John Hooper of Manchester, New Hampshire. His journal notes only that in the vicinity of the Canary Islands the weather grew thick and foggy, the winds baffling, but before they got to the latitude of 18° it hauled westwardly, and so continued until they cast anchor at Goree on July 7, 1806.

A barren rock in the sea, only 900 yards long and 330 yards wide, Goree lies about a mile from the peninsula of Cape Verde, westernmost salient of the Old World. The Dutch purchased the island from its native ruler in 1617 and made it a base for their slave trade with the American colonies. Late in the seventeenth century the French Compagnie du Sénégal acquired this emporium, but during the French Revolution and the Napoleonic Wars it fell into British hands. At the time of DeForest's arrival, an English garrison under the command of a Major Lloyd was stationed on the island.

A population estimated by DeForest to number some 1,500, consisting chiefly of French mulattoes and their numerous slaves, lived on Goree. The former class, he noted, appeared to be the lords of the little island. The slave trade was in their hands; in boats of five, eight, and fifteen tons they ranged along the coast and ventured up into the dim recesses of the great river Gambia to procure their human commodities. Negro chieftains, collecting their commissions in gold and trinkets, often assisted in these manhunts. The shackled captives were brought to Goree, and there, in the *maison des esclaves*, were exhibited to prospective buyers. Numerous ships of United States registry called at Goree for cargoes. The standard price of a human chattel was $120 to

$130, barter price in rum or tobacco, but so many American ships had been coming to the island lately that slaves could not be purchased at that price for cash in hand. The *Rufus* of Boston had sailed for La Plata on June 11 with a cargo of many young slaves. DeForest doubted that they would bring much profit at Buenos Aires, "for most of the slaves sent to that market are transferred to that of Lima for sale, and I have been told that grown slaves there are of much greater value than little ones." [1]

"Not being much acquainted with the Trade," relates De-Forest, "nor willing to run about in the Sun, I employed Mr. Ezekiel Madden an American to assist me." This strategic move greatly vexed the mulatto slave traders, who lodged a protest with the governor of the island. Obscurity veils DeForest's further transactions on Goree. Presumably he purchased only a small token number of blacks as a cover for the more profitable contraband trade. His business soon done, he cleared on July 15 for La Plata.

The *Jane* entered the Plate estuary some three weeks later. In the morning of September 14 they made out a number of warships lying off Montevideo. Presently a man-of-war approached the American ship. The English boarders did not allay DeForest's fears. They explained that Sir Home Popham's squadron had the Plate ports under blockade. At the end of June an expeditionary force under Sir William Beresford had captured Buenos Aires. Little more than a month later, in an astounding reversal of fortunes, the Spaniards had rallied under an obscure officer named Santiago Liniers and retaken the town, making prisoners of General Beresford and his men. Having volunteered this information, the boarders ordered DeForest to go down to the commodore's ship, the *Diadem*.

Sir Home, a tall, pleasant-faced man in his middle forties, received DeForest in his cabin. He confirmed that the ports of La Plata were closed to trade; he could not say when the blockade would be lifted. By way of amends he invited DeForest to sit down with him to a dinner of roast lamb and cabbage. The smuggler passed an agreeable hour with his English host, then returned to the *Jane*, much perplexed at this interference with his plans.

1. DeForest to Thomas Wilson, Goree, July 12, 1806, DeForest Letterbooks, Vol. 3.

Unknown to DeForest, the fountainhead of his difficulties was that same Francisco de Miranda of whose ill-starred expedition against Venezuela he had so vigorously disapproved. Miranda had inspired the British effort to wrest La Plata from the supposedly inept hands of Spain. In 1803 the revolutionist was in London, working to secure British support of his plans for the emancipation of Spanish America. There he struck up a friendship with Popham, a naval captain whose conduct was being investigated for alleged financial misdemeanors.[2] Popham soon became a convert to Miranda's cause. In a lengthy memoir (dated October 14, 1804), the promoters outlined to the British ministers their project for the liberation of Spain's American empire. Miranda was to lead English land forces against northern South America; Popham was to command an expedition of three thousand soldiers against the viceroyalty of La Plata. The planners argued that this stroke at Spain would greatly reduce the revenues of her French ally and increase Great Britain's trade and importance.[3] Execution of this program, accepted in principle by the British ministers, was so long delayed that Miranda, losing patience, departed for the United States where he prepared his ill-fated *Leander* expedition against Venezuela.

In the meantime Sir Home had gone to sea in command of naval forces sent against the Dutch colony at the Cape of Good Hope. Soon after the fall of the Cape, Popham determined on his own responsibility to make an attack on Buenos Aires. He was strengthened in his decision by advices from an American sea captain lately come from La Plata who assured him that Montevideo and Buenos Aires were in a defenseless state, and that the natives would welcome their British liberators.[4] Popham evidently believed that success in the enterprise would vindicate his unauthorized conduct. On April 14, 1806, Popham's squadron set sail for La Plata with a regiment of soldiers under the command of Sir William Beresford on board. In the wake of the expedition followed a great number of merchantmen eager to pour a mass of English goods through the prospective breach in the Spanish colonial system.

2. W. S. Robertson, *Life of Miranda*, I, 257.
3. *Ibid.*, pp. 275–276.
4. Carlos Roberts, *Las invasiones inglesas del Río de la Plata* (Buenos Aires, 1938), p. 72.

Victory had come with astonishing ease. The viceroy of La
Plata, Rafaél de Sobremonte, fled with great celerity to the provincial town of Córdoba upon the approach of the enemy. On
June 27, 1806, Beresford's veterans entered the capital and ran
up the British colors over the fort. To revive the feelings of the
stunned *porteños*, Beresford immediately issued a proclamation
in Spanish and English guaranteeing to the inhabitants the rights
of private property, administration of justice, worship of the
Roman Catholic Church, and freedom of trade. A great store of
public treasure and merchandise fell to the invaders. But Popham
and Beresford had mistaken both the temper and the capacities
of the people of Buenos Aires. United in a sacred fury against
the English *herejes*, creoles and old Spaniards joined in planning
the expulsion of their unwanted liberators. Led by the French-
born captain of the port of Ensenada de Barragán, Santiago
Liniers, a volunteer army fell upon the British occupants on
August 12, 1806, and utterly routed them, capturing General
Beresford and 1,200 of his troops. On his flagship in the river,
Popham, helpless to aid his outnumbered comrades, could do no
more than proclaim a strict blockade of the Plate ports and await
the coming of reinforcements from England and Cape Colony.

This was the state of affairs when DeForest arrived in the
middle of September. After drifting about for three weeks, with
the situation unchanged, he resolved to go south to the Patagonian port of Río Negro and dispose of part of his cargo there.
He evidently expected Montevideo to be in British hands by the
time of his return to the river, and may have anticipated difficulty
in marketing his goods in competition with the swarm of English
merchantmen awaiting the fall of the key to the viceroyalty. The
half-formed idea of running the blockade to Buenos Aires may
have also entered into his calculations. In the current state of feeling against English-speaking foreigners, the excitable *populacho*
of the capital was likely to treat roughly an *anglo-americano* who
possibly came as a spy and almost certainly as a smuggler.
Against such a contingency, it would be helpful to bring from
Río Negro some proofs of DeForest's friendly disposition to the
Spanish cause.

The *Jane* sped southward to the lonely frontier post on the
coast of Patagonia, and cast anchor at Río Negro on October 15.
"There are here," DeForest noted in his diary, "one friar and two

curates and a great plenty of Superstition." There were also Indians, eager to barter guanaco skins, sea elephant oil, and salt for vests and laces. These purchases and his slaves the smuggler left at Río Negro under the watchful eye of Captain Hooper. The brigantine was made fit and trim in preparation for her return voyage. On November 12, 1806, the *Jane* put to sea, bearing on board the secretary of the *comandante* with dispatches for the viceroy of La Plata.

They made the mouth of the river one week later and stood for Montevideo. DeForest soon discovered that the town was still in Spanish hands. The gunboat *Protector* intercepted the *Jane* on November 19, put a youthful midshipman and three sailors on board, and sent her for Maldonado, the recently captured rendezvous of the squadron. The English captain told DeForest that "they were all in the dark respecting Sir Home's instructions, intimating the improbability of ever conquering the Country, which appeared very probable to me." [5]

With Montevideo out of reach, and the prospect of a ruinous detention at Maldonado before him, DeForest saw only one way out of his difficulties. He must run the British blockade into Buenos Aires. A smart easterly gale had blown up, giving good hope of success in the enterprise. DeForest had taken the measure of the youthful midshipman assigned to the *Jane* and anticipated no difficulty in deceiving him concerning the course of the ship. The three English sailors would probably rejoice at being set free from the man-of-war. Feeling some compunction over the fate that awaited the midshipman, "a well educated and apparently amiable Young Man," the blockade-runner privately informed his crew to make sail for Buenos Aires while he kept the guardian of the ship "in play."

Scudding along before the gale, the *Jane* drove up the river and toward safety. On the morning of November 21 they were over the Ortiz Bank and within short distance of their port. Then DeForest summoned the midshipman to his cabin and gave account of his stratagem. The youth vainly pleaded with his captor to return to Maldonado. Seeking to quiet his fears, DeForest assured him that if they arrived safely, "I would render him every possible assistance, that I would furnish him with money to buy

5. DeForest to Alpheus Dunham, Montevideo, Sept. 3, 1807, DeForest Letter-books, Vol. 3.

the necessary clothing he most stood in need of, and that I would exert myself to have him not considered as a Prisoner of War." As for the three sailors, they displayed great satisfaction "at getting away from the Man of War, and rendered all the assistance they could." That afternoon they anchored outside the bar in the port of Buenos Aires.

In response to the *Jane's* signals for a pilot, a launch in the harbor got under way and came alongside the brigantine. A motley crew of privateersmen and soldiery clambered on board. Some held cocked pistols, others brandished swords. Making great noise and perilous display of their arms, they swaggered fiercely fore and aft in evident enjoyment of their easy prize. At nightfall some withdrew, and the rest undertook to get the vessel into port. Since all were commanders, the *Jane* spent most of the night beating at the bar. DeForest, after two sleepless and anxiety-ridden nights, was past all caring; retiring to his cabin he fell into a sound slumber. He awoke in the morning to find the brigantine anchored in port in three fathoms of water. In the afternoon came the customs officers to make their "great visit." To the vexation of the privateersmen they found all in order. "Hurrah for the Prize, was the topic among these poor Devils."

Buenos Aires, a city of some 40,000 inhabitants, had the appearance of an armed camp. In September Liniers had issued a dramatic call for the formation of a people's militia. Now the narrow, dusty streets were alive with volunteer soldiers. Even the Negro slaves had formed their *cuerpo de esclavos*, and proudly sported knife and lance. Brilliantly uniformed officers dashed by on horseback. Daily the raw levies drilled in the public squares. The nights of Buenos Aires, as of old, were filled with music; strains of gay song issued from the white-washed, flat-roofed houses of adobe. But new martial words had been set to the familiar airs.

DeForest lost no time in calling on Santiago Liniers, hero of the *reconquista*, now military governor of Buenos Aires. Of stately bearing, affable and generous, Liniers was the idol of the populace, whose clamor had compelled the municipal authorities to summon a general congress which invested him with the military functions of the discredited viceroy. The shadows of rivalry had already begun to fall between Liniers and the supremely ambitious Martín Alzaga, influential senior *alcalde*. For all save a small minority, however, he was still the most excellent, the incomparable Liniers; time had not yet brought to light the weakness of character that the brave exterior concealed.[6]

Liniers received DeForest with characteristic warmth, commended him on his blockade-running exploit, and offered to exert his influence in the trader's behalf. Through his intercession, DeForest was able to unload cargo two days later. He was anxious to put his commercial affairs in order before the anticipated second British invasion got under way. The British government had dispatched strong forces to La Plata to consolidate its hold on the Spanish colony. The successive arrival of these reinforcements, numbering some 11,000 men by the beginning of 1807, suggested the seriousness of the approaching effort to recapture Buenos Aires.

Expectantly the city awaited the day of the assault, speculated where the first blow would fall. The answer was given in January when the British laid siege to Montevideo, key to the viceroyalty. Liniers with two thousand men sallied to the relief of the town. The sight of the gallant and tranquil bearing of their *jefe* filled the *porteños* with confidence; they "were making calculations to accommodate such of them [the British] as escaped their swords." [7] The expedition soon returned, their march interrupted by the news that Montevideo had surrendered on February 3. For this disaster Viceroy Sobremonte was again held responsible.

The twice-proved incompetence of the viceroy now led to his complete undoing. Turbulent crowds gathered on the afternoon of February 6 before the doors of the *cabildo*, the municipal council, with cries of "No Vice King, no Royal Audience, down with them, hang them." "God only knows how the business will end here," the alarmed DeForest jotted in his diary, "the Government is extremely weak." [8] Bowing to the popular will, the royal *audiencia*, the high tribunal of the province, decreed the suspension and arrest of the viceroy, itself assumed supreme political and military authority, and confirmed Liniers, the beloved of the people, as commander of all the armed forces. The action against Sobremonte had an unmistakable revolutionary significance: "for

6. Paul Groussac, *Santiago Liniers, Conde de Buenos Aires* (Buenos Aires, 1907), is a masterful evocation of Liniers and his times; C. Roberts, *Las invasiones inglesas*, pp. 376–380, brings together numerous characterizations of Liniers by contemporaries and historians.

7. DeForest Journal, Vol. 6, Jan. 29, 1807.

8. *Ibid.*

the first time the American colonies witnessed the deposition and imprisonment of the legal representative of the king." [9]

Hard on the heels of this event came the spectacular escape of the British General Beresford from his captivity in Luján. "The Town in uproar and confusion. No one has full confidence in his Neighbour. Many are suspected who are of high rank." The account in DeForest's journal, otherwise accurate, mentions the rumor that "the Spanish General *Liniers*, Secretary of the War Department," had made his escape together with Beresford—suggesting the suspicions held in some circles of Liniers' loyalty to Spain.[10]

The flight of Beresford heightened the mood of panic created by the fall of Montevideo. Many English-speaking foreigners in the city were arrested and imprisoned. In the evening of March 3, soldiers routed DeForest from bed and escorted him to a militia barracks. Other Americans seized about this time were Captain Tibbet of the *Diana* of Wiscasset, the captain of the *George and Mary* of Newport, and Jeremiah Donovan, supercargo of the *Mary* of Philadelphia.[11] After languishing for five days in the cold and drafty barracks, DeForest was released on the application of Benito Rivadavia, a prominent Spanish merchant and father of Bernardino Rivadavia, future president of the United Provinces of La Plata.[12] DeForest learned that he had been accused of being an Englishman, consorting with Englishmen, and of preparing a quantity of "segars" with the evil intent of sending them to Montevideo.[13]

For his greater safety, DeForest decided to take lodgings in the home of Rivadavia, with whom he had an obscure commercial connection. He also obtained a written protection from the powerful Liniers. "What an infernal rascally Government it must be," he fumed, "that can cooly and deliberately take a Gentleman out of his Bed and order him to Prison without any cause but their having the power to do it." Brooding over his

9. Bartolomé Mitre, *Historia de Belgrano y de la independencia argentina* (3 vols., Buenos Aires, 1887, 4th ed.), I, 152.

10. C. Roberts, *Las invasiones inglesas,* p. 221, affirms that Liniers indubitably connived in the escape of Beresford, but at the same time holds that Liniers was completely loyal to the Spanish king.

11. DeForest Journal, Vol. 6, April 23, 1807.

12. Alberto Palcos, *La visión de Rivadavia* (Buenos Aires, 1938), a study of the early years of the Argentine statesman, includes much biographical material concerning his father.

13. DeForest Journal, Vol. 6, March 3, 1807.

wrongs, and those of his imprisoned countrymen, he finally composed and sent a bristling memorial on the subject to the royal *audiencia*.

"We are not beasts my Lords," he wrote, "we are Men (or rather we were Men when we first arrived here), we have come to your Country for the Purpose of Friendly Commerce, if you receive us at all, you are bound to give us every protection and every aid in the prosecution of our business." Did their Lordships conceive the United States to be in a state of infancy and therefore incapable of defending the rights of its citizens? "No one doubts its infancy, but pardon me my Lords when I tell you that 'it is an infant lion' which if roused, has already strength enough to make the Spanish Empire tremble to its foundations." He closed with the demand that the marine court decide immediately the case of his impounded vessel and cargo; that the individuals responsible for his arrest and imprisonment be punished in the most severe and public manner; and that he be accorded protection from further insult or injury until his departure from Buenos Aires.[14] What effect this invocation of the infant North American lion had on the deliberations of the august *audiencia*, we cannot tell. In July, however, DeForest had returned to him the *Jane* and her cargo.

The *cabildo*, for reasons of public safety, ordered in April, 1807, that all foreigners should appear and give account of their identity and occupation. DeForest complied, as evidenced by the following curious notation in the census records: "David Forest, of American nationality, musician in the Squadron of Hussars of Pueyrredón, lives in the house of Don Benito Rivadavia." [15] Fortunately the registering officials did not put DeForest's musical prowess to the test. The shrewd Rivadavia may have devised this unique camouflage for his Yankee guest.

An electrifying report ran through Buenos Aires on June 25: a squadron of British transports had been sighted at anchor off Ensenada de Barragán, twelve leagues from the capital. The next day the invaders were off Quilmes, only four leagues distant from the city. In the afternoon, reads the entry in DeForest's journal, "the General was beat. The Troops were collected and reviewed. The General Santiago Liniers told them the Enemy was

---

14. DeForest to "the Royal Audience of the Vice Kingdom of Buenos Ayres," Buenos Aires, April 15, 1807, *ibid.*
15. *Documentos para la historia argentina*, XII, 218.

in offing and that they would soon have an opportunity to meet them. They were unanimous in their declarations of attachment to their General, and willingness to loose the last drop of their blood in defense of their Country. The night was passed by great numbers of Citizens in Serenading the City with various kinds of music, and in rejoicing that the English had at last appeared. For my own part I kept close to my room preferring the charms of security to music." [16]

Eight thousand red-coats landed at Ensenada de Barragán on June 28 and advanced on the city. The crisis was at hand. Liniers with a force of seven thousand troops sallied to meet the enemy at the little stream of Riachuelo de Barracas. "All Buenos Aires," DeForest jotted in his diary," is sure of beating the English, and if they do to give no quarter. Such is the savage spirit many of them possess." [17] At four o'clock in the afternoon of July 2, an aide of Liniers strode into the hall of the *cabildo* with grave news; a part of the British army had eluded the Spanish defenders and made a crossing of the Riachuelo at the ford of Burgos. At five (relates DeForest) the distant firing of musketry could be heard in the city; by six the British were in the suburbs; by seven they had fought their way to the Corrales de Miserere and there put Liniers' men to rout. "All the town in an uproar, Spanish troops returned to the Great Square in front of the Fort, no boasts of having beaten the English, of course very well know their defeat must have been total." [18]

The rashness of Liniers had left the capital dangerously exposed to attack. The energetic senior *alcalde*, Martín Alzaga, rose to the occasion. He caused fortifications to be thrown up on all sides; soldiers and militiamen took positions at the windows and housetops of the streets through which the invaders must pass. Some of the defenders broke open DeForest's dwelling and swarmed on the roof. "Damn the luck," swore DeForest, "I intended to have been clear of soldiers but have got into the midst of them."

In the morning of July 5, after a demand for surrender had been peremptorily refused, the British troops closed in upon the city. As they advanced through the narrow streets they were met by a murderous hail of fire from every window and roof. The end

16. DeForest Journal, Vol. 6, June 26, 1807.
17. *Ibid.*, July 2, 1807.
18. *Ibid.*

of the day found them short of most of their strategic objectives. "The fortunes of this day appear much in favor of the Spaniards," opined DeForest. "Great numbers of English were killed and wounded from tops of the Houses while passing in the Streets beneath, without the power of killing scarce a single man who fired at them." [19]

The British commander, General John Whitelocke, impressed by the tenacity of the defense and his heavy losses, hesitated to continue the struggle. On July 6, he accepted the Spanish terms for his capitulation. The British agreed to evacuate Buenos Aires within ten days and to relinquish the town and fortress of Montevideo. All prisoners were to be returned. The formal treaty ratifying these terms was signed on July 7.

The battle for Buenos Aires had ended. DeForest cautiously ventured into the streets; recoiled at the sight of naked English dead, their clothing stripped by pillagers; noted the extensive damage to the city's buildings. "Damn war and him who invented it," he pungently commented in his diary. A few days later he looked on as thousands of British troops assembled in Retiro Square and marched down to the beach to take ship for England. Defeat at the hands of raw colonial levies rankled in the English breasts; DeForest could hear some angry officers and men cursing General John Whitelocke "for a fool and a coward." [20]

For the first time in many months the trader could communicate with the outside world. He wrote his brother John that he had experienced many disagreeable revolutions at Buenos Aires, but had finally come out "bright as the morning Sun—have the unlimited confidence of the Government as well as of the Populace which latter have ruled that place for a long time past." [21] "During this reign of Terror and Confusion," he informed a friend in North America, "the Populace . . . have had nearly all the power in their mobist hands." [22]

The people of Buenos Aires had indeed tasted power, and

19. *Ibid.*

20. *Ibid.,* July 11, 1807. Upon his return to England, General Whitelocke was tried by court-martial on four distinct charges, was found guilty of three, and was in consequence "cashiered and declared totally unfit and unworthy to serve his Majesty in any military capacity whatsoever." Quoted in Bernard Moses, *Spain's Declining Power in South America* (Berkeley, Cal., 1919), p. 369.

21. DeForest to John H. DeForest, Montevideo, July 20, 1807, DeForest Letterbooks, Vol. 3.

22. DeForest to Alpheus Dunham, Montevideo, July 20, 1807, *ibid.*

would not willingly relinquish it again. In the difficult school of war the heroic *porteños* had gained knowledge of their strength and a vigorous sense of nationality. "I presume to felicitate the Americans," proudly declared Cornelio de Saavedra, hailing the achievements of his legion of *patricios*, "for this last proof of their valor and loyalty, which adds luster to the merit of those who were born in the Indies, and testifies that their spirits know not dejection, that they are not inferior to the European Spaniards, that in point of valor and loyalty they are second to none." [23] Spain's distresses in Europe, rapidly moving toward a crisis, were to prove the golden opportunity of ambitious creoles in Buenos Aires, eager to become masters of their political and economic destinies. The British invasions were only the prelude to the greater struggle for the independence of La Plata.

23. B. Mitre, *Belgrano*, I, 201.

V

"ON VERY SAFE GROUND"

THE British invasion fiasco caused DeForest the liveliest satisfaction. Persuaded that the trade of La Plata must soon return to its former neutral channels, he prepared to remain in Buenos Aires as a commission merchant for the duration of the European war; a matter, he calculated, of two or three years. He disposed of his brig *Jane* by charter to a departing English merchant for the "modest price" of $10,000. To Captain John Hooper at Río Negro, fretfully drumming his heels at that lonely Patagonian post, he sent word to sail for the United States with all the property in his charge, save the Negro slaves, in the first Nantucket fishing vessel quitting the coast. He warned Captain Hooper not to sell the slaves at a sacrifice, but to leave them in the hands of some dependable Spaniard, subject to De-Forest's order.[1]

The Laws of the Indies forbade foreigners to trade or reside in the Spanish colonies. But experience had taught DeForest that in time of war these laws were honored as much in the breach as in the observance. Above all he relied on the enlightened views and easy-going ways of the powerful Liniers.[2] His trust was not misplaced. Liniers tolerated the extensive contraband traffic that sprang up as departing English merchants dumped huge stocks of goods on the Plate market, and even gave these enemy traders permission to remain in Buenos Aires in order to dispose of their merchandise after British troops had evacuated the city.[3] He dutifully proclaimed in force in the province Napoleon's Berlin Decree of 1806, making all British property good prize, but gave

1. DeForest to Captain John Hooper, Buenos Aires, Nov. 3, 1807, DeForest Letterbooks, Vol. 3.
2. At this time Liniers was acting as military and civil governor of La Plata in place of the deposed Viceroy Sobremonte. He was appointed *virrey interino* by the Spanish king in December, 1807, and took office in May, 1808. E. Ravignani, "El virreinato del Río de la Plata," p. 312.
3. Dorothy B. Goebel, "British Trade to the Spanish Colonies, 1796–1823," *American Historical Review*, XLIII (1938), 309.

little effect to the edict of Spain's French ally.[4] To the great
scandal of the royal *audiencia*, he released from prison the North
American adventurer William P. White, who had openly collaborated with the British invaders.[5] When the *audiencia* undertook to purge the country of all foreigners, ordering them to leave
the province in the space of eight days on pain of imprisonment
and summary expulsion at the official convenience, DeForest's appeal to the governor resulted in immediate instructions "to the
Judge Velano that he must not consider me as included in the
general order." [6] With good reason, the merchant commended
Liniers as "possessed of that liberality and generosity of Soul,
which the civilised and well bred part of Mankind alone possess,"
and "the Friend and Protector of the Foreigners who are here." [7]

Nevertheless, a cover of legality for DeForest's commission-
house business seemed desirable. By this time he was thoroughly
familiar with the many ruses employed by foreign traders in
Spanish America. For a certain consideration a young Spaniard "of the first mercantile talents and respectability," a particular friend of Liniers, Juan Pedro Varangot by name, agreed to
act as the ostensible receiver of DeForest's consignments.[8] The

4. Napoleon's Berlin Decree was proclaimed in Buenos Aires on September 27,
1807, in compliance with a Spanish royal order of February 21, 1807. One month
later DeForest wrote: "All however is quiet, and it is not probable that it will
ever be enforced, though many of the bigoted vassals here would like to see it
executed with vigour." DeForest to Stephen Twyecross, Buenos Aires, Oct. 28,
1807, DeForest Letterbooks, Vol. 3.

5. For a biographical sketch of White, see Edward S. Wallace, "Forgotten Men
of Dartmouth: Father of the Argentine Navy, William Porter White, 1790,"
Dartmouth Alumni Magazine, March, 1935; see also Enrique Udaondo, *Diccionario biográfico argentino* (Buenos Aires, 1938). The charges against White are
set forth in "Carta de la Real Audiencia de Buenos Aires a S. M. informando
sobre las graves y escandalosas occurencias acaecidas con el extrangero Guillermo
Withe [*sic*]," in Facultad de Filosofía y Letras, *Documentos relativos a los
antecedentes de la independencia de la República Argentina* (Buenos Aires,
1912), pp. 11–14.

6. DeForest to Stephen Twyecross, Buenos Aires, Oct. 28, 1807, DeForest
Letterbooks, Vol. 3.

7. DeForest to the Honorable Charles Stewart, Buenos Aires, April 20, 1808,
ibid. On January 8, 1808, noting the continued presence of many Englishmen and
North Americans in the capital, the *cabildo* rebuked Liniers for a tolerance "so
contrary to the laws and prejudicial to the interests of the nation," and threatened to appeal to the Spanish king against this "pernicious abuse." Archivo General de la Nación, *Acuerdos del extinguido cabildo de Buenos Aires, 1589–1820*
(45 vols., Buenos Aires, 1907–1934), Fourth Series, III, 16–17.

8. François Depons, *Voyage a la partie orientale de la terre-ferme* (2 vols.,
Paris, 1808), II, 362–363, notes that this ruse was commonly employed by foreign
merchants established at Cadiz.

partners took lodgings together in the home of Francisco Ignacio de Ugarte, one of the wealthiest merchants of the city.

In a circular letter to a large number of merchants in the United States, DeForest announced the establishment of his commission-house. The letter took an optimistic view of the prospects of neutral trade to La Plata. Contrary to a widely held opinion, the writer observed, Spanish colonial ports were not completely closed to foreign commerce. The management of this trade offered difficulties, to be sure, but only enough to deter the ignorant. DeForest mentioned first of all the legal traffic in slaves. "I know of no Voyages," he wrote, "which present so fair a prospect of gain to the undertaker, as these."

Spanish law forbade the introduction of any articles save agricultural implements in slave ships, but DeForest dismissed this apparent difficulty. Let the vessel come in ballast with salt, lumber, wine, or rum, represented as ship's stores, and they could be sold without hindrance. Another type of voyage required a license from the governor of Habana authorizing the bearer to purchase beef in La Plata for the Cuban market. A large variety of articles including spirits, rice, iron, hams, cheese, butter, pickles, fish, and lumber could be brought in ballast to pay for the cargo of beef, and other produce could be exported as well.

Hazardous but extremely lucrative was the direct voyage between Spain and La Plata under Spanish colors. The vessel employed for this purpose should be a small fast-sailing craft capable of eluding the chase of British cruisers. Her cargo must appear consigned from a Spanish merchant to one of his countrymen in Buenos Aires. The voyage could be made in the name of Francisco Ignacio de Ugarte, DeForest's very good friend. Spaniards must compose the crew, save for the American captain who might pass for a mate, but not for a master or supercargo. Barcelona wares were much favored in the Plate markets. Catalonian wines, costing $15 or $20 a pipe in Spain, brought from $150 to $200 in Buenos Aires; olive oil in casks or jars yielded a profit of from 200 to 300 per cent. Before entering the river the ship should call at the near-by port of Rio Grande in Brazil. There lived DeForest's old friend, Father José Alves Chaves, who dispensed not only spiritual advice but useful information on the movements of British cruisers in the estuary. Vessels consigned to DeForest must display on arrival his private signal: a blue jack with a white X at the fore-topgallant masthead. No declaration of cargo should be made before receiving his advice.[9]

Two years before DeForest had unsuccessfully applied to President Jefferson for an appointment as United States consul to Buenos Aires. He renewed his solicitations in a letter to Secretary of State Madison that throws a curious light on the beginnings of Anglo-American trade rivalry in La Plata. He explained that he sought the post because of "the unpleasant situation of Americans and their commerce in this Country." Many English ships entered the river under American colors. These impostors produced papers that frequently were forged or plundered from their rightful owners. Spanish ignorance and venality aided the tricksters to escape, while real Americans were sometimes persecuted and cast into prison on suspicion of being British subjects. If appointed consul or commercial agent in Buenos Aires, DeForest could expose these deceptions and protect his injured countrymen. Spanish law would not admit his formal recognition,[10] but the appointment would please the inhabitants and would be sufficiently countenanced by the government to answer all purposes. With adequate protection the Plate trade could provide steady employment for thirty or forty American vessels. "Notwithstanding the rigid Laws against the introduction of Foreigners," affirmed DeForest, "they are constantly admitted, on some pretence or other and derive much profit from their voyages." [11]

DeForest vainly awaited a favorable reply from Secretary Madison. He could not know that the Jefferson administration had just embarked on policies that tended to extinguish United States commercial contacts with the Spanish-American provinces, leaving our agents there but little employment.[12] In re-

9. Copy of Circular Letter, Buenos Aires, Sept. 15, 1807, DeForest Letterbooks, Vol. 3.

10. A royal order of April 24, 1807, prohibited the residence of foreign agents or consuls in the Spanish colonies. For the text of the order, see *Documentos para la historia argentina*, VII, 363–365.

11. DeForest to the Honorable James Madison, Secretary of State, Buenos Aires, Oct. 1, 1808, DeForest Letterbooks, Vol. 3.

12. At this time the United States had a representative in only one Spanish-American colony, that of Cuba. After 1807 his title of consul was replaced by that of "agent for seamen and commerce" because of Spanish refusal to extend official recognition. Before 1808 the United States had appointed consuls to New Orleans (1798–1803), La Guaira (1800–1807), an agent to Cuba during the American Revolution, and a consul stationed there since 1797. On this subject, see R. F. Nichols, "Trade Relations and the Establishment of United States Consulates in Spanish America, 1779–1809."

sponse to the blockade systems of the great European belligerents (Napoleon's Berlin and Milan Decrees and the British orders-in-council), on December 22, 1807, Congress passed a measure designed to bring France and Britain to terms, the famous Embargo act. By the time of its repeal early in 1809, this enactment had practically destroyed the once lucrative American trade with Spain's Caribbean and South American colonies.[13]

The Embargo blighted DeForest's hopes of attracting United States vessels to the Plate estuary. "There are no American ships come to give us opportunity to ship anything," he complained in April, 1808, "and I fear there will not be any for some time." [14] Yet he vigorously defended the men and measures responsible for this state of affairs. "Americans know little of the distresses of War," he informed his brother John, "or they would not clamour as they do against the only measure by which they can avoid it. . . . I love my country as well as any of its inhabitants; and perhaps should be as great a gainer as any one of my standing in life, were the Embargo to be raised, and the Government of our Country disposed to place us in the degrading situation of accepting without a murmur such commercial privileges as others may please to confer on us, but I had rather beg my Bread. I hope to hear ere long, that the most rigid Commercial measures are adopted against all Nations who continue against my Country their insolent pretensions." [15]

Despite the effects of the Embargo, DeForest prospered during these years beyond all expectation.[16] His letterbooks and journals give the impression of a diversified commercial activity, including the clandestine introduction of British goods, speculation in nutria skins, and the defense of United States firms in suits at law before the Buenos Aires marine court. The opening of Brazilian ports to neutral and friendly commerce in January, 1808, imparted new

13. Timothy Pitkin, *A Statistical View of the Commerce of the United States of America* (Hartford, 1816), p. 192, estimates the value of American exports to Spanish America in 1807 at $12,341,225; in 1808, at $4,177,053. A. P. Whitaker, *The United States and the Independence of Latin America*, pp. 47–52, discusses the Embargo as a factor in the non-fulfilment of Jefferson's "large policy of 1808" toward Spanish America.

14. DeForest to Thomas Brewer, Buenos Aires, April 15, 1808, DeForest Letterbooks, Vol. 3.

15. DeForest to John H. DeForest, Buenos Aires, Feb. 10, 1809, *ibid.*

16. In letters to his brothers, DeForest complacently cites his large gains, unfortunately in a cipher to which we do not have the key. Nor do we possess his account books for this period.

vigor to the Plata trade. "Come try this plan," DeForest wrote his brother, "they can live without you in Watertown. By coming to Rio de Janeiro we can play into each other's hands to much advantage. I think if we don't get into this cursed war, we are on very safe ground." [17] His eye ever on the main chance, he described to friends in Rio how Spanish navigation laws might be circumvented. Let a vessel with Portuguese colors and crew come to Buenos Aires laden with slaves, and represented as having been purchased by DeForest's partner, Juan Pedro Varangot. After introducing as many slaves as she had tons, the ship would be considered as fully naturalized and would enjoy all the trading privileges of a Spanish-built ship. Calico, muslins, silk hose, and other dry goods might be smuggled in with the slaves.[18]

In March, 1809, DeForest purchased an estate with a portion of his growing fortune. Since foreigners were not permitted to hold land in Spain's colonies, the name of Francisco Ignacio de Ugarte, DeForest's friend, figured in the deed of sale as purchaser.[19] The *chacra* lay near the present-day Rivadavia Station of the Argentine Central Railroad, eight miles above Buenos Aires. Fronting the Plata for 400 rods, it was a league in length. A force of nine slaves worked on the land, graced by an old brick house and numerous fruit trees. To his Negroes, DeForest gave names drawn from the annals of war.[20] "For the first time in my life," he proudly entered in his diary on March 19, 1809, "I have slept in a House belonging wholly to myself."

At this time DeForest, now aged thirty-four, began to consider seriously the subject of matrimony. The idea of a union with one of the daughters of Buenos Aires, famed for their beauty and amiability, does not seem to have occurred to him. "I am anxious to go home *to get married*," he wrote brother John, "but am unwilling to neglect my establishment here, which I wish you to take care of and be interested in, if you desire it. At any rate

17. DeForest to John H. DeForest, Buenos Aires, June 12, 1808, DeForest Letterbooks, Vol. 3.

18. DeForest to Charles Twyecross, Buenos Aires, June 12, 1808, *ibid.*

19. This paragraph is based on notations in the DeForest Journal, Vol. 6, supplemented by information drawn from Horacio Zorraquín Becú, *De aventurero yanqui a consul porteño en los Estados Unidos: David C. DeForest, 1774–1825* (Buenos Aires, 1943) (reprint from the *Anuario de historia argentina, IV,* 1942), p. 41 n. Señor Zorraquín Becú has traced the history of the estate with the aid of title deeds and other documents down to its final dismemberment.

20. They were Alexander, Caesar, Pompey, Hannibal, Scipio, Romulus, Hector, Paris, Napoleon.

you must come here, and immediately." "We have but a short time to stay here," he closed plaintively, "and ought for our own happiness do to others, particularly our brothers, all the good we can." [21]

Don David Cortes DeForest—so he sometimes subscribed himself in letters—now wrote and presumably spoke Spanish with considerable fluency and correctness. His circle of acquaintances included some of the most prominent names in Buenos Aires society: Ugarte, Rivadavia, Castelli, Azcuénaga. Their mode of life he made his own. The happy *porteños* of that day, observes a nostalgic Argentine historian, had few cares, worked little, ate well, and slept even better.[22] Manners were simple, diversions few. Religion played a major role in the life of the colony; from morning till night church bells tolled for devotion. At noon the women of the better sort were to be seen on their way to Mass, long black cloaks drawn over their faces, beads and crucifixes on their arms, each followed by a slave carrying a prayer book.[23]

DeForest passed the morning hours at work in his countingroom. At midday all offices closed for the long dinner and siesta, reopening a few hours before dusk. Evening might find him strolling on the *alameda*, the tree-shaded walk near the beach, or taking refreshment with a few friends in the French Coffee House near La Merced Church. There, on the evening of July 24, 1808, he sits at a table with the aged Don Ventura Llorente, formerly prior of the *consulado*, and discusses politics very moderately, "without giving offense to each other." Politics was very much in the air that mid-summer of 1808, but DeForest, as befitted a foreigner on a very uncertain footing in the country, professed an outward neutrality.

He was not always thus discreet. With his friend Juan Larrea, a young Catalonian merchant steeped in the doctrines of French and Spanish liberal philosophers and economists, he spoke much of the rights of man, the governments of the world, and the inde-

21. DeForest to John H. DeForest, Buenos Aires, Oct. 28, 1809, DeForest Letterbooks, Vol. 3.
22. P. Groussac, *Santiago de Liniers,* p. 42.
23. For life and manners in colonial Buenos Aires, see the chapters on social history contributed by José Torre Revello to the *Historia de la nación argentina,* IV, Section 1. Alexander Gillespie, *Gleanings and Remarks; Collected during Many Months of Residence at Buenos Aires and within the Upper Country* (Leeds, Eng., 1818), is an engaging account of conditions in La Plata at the time of the British invasions.

pendence of Buenos Aires.[24] Perhaps he knew that some of his friends, such as the fiery young lawyer, Juan José Castelli, were meeting in unobtrusive *tertulias* to concert revolutionary action. For by the late summer of 1808 the affairs of Spain were in crisis, twilight advanced upon the Spanish Empire in America, and in Buenos Aires formidable factions prepared to contend for mastery of this rich heritage of the Spanish crown.

24. Retrospectively affirmed in DeForest to José Antonio Cabrera and Pedro López, New Haven, Nov. 24, 1811, DeForest Letterbooks, Vol. 5.

VI

"THE IDES OF MARCH"

BET with Mr. Blodget," DeForest carefully noted in his diary on February 13, 1808, "three ounces of gold that the Government of the King of Spain would not continue at Buenos Ayres longer than six months."

News of the arrival of the Portuguese royal family in Brazil, brought that day by the post from Montevideo, inspired this seemingly reckless wager. Fleeing the approach of French invaders, Prince John and his court had sailed from Lisbon on November 29, 1807, under British escort. After a stop at Bahia, where he proclaimed the ports of Brazil open to foreign trade, the prince regent cruised on to Rio de Janeiro, the new seat of his government. The men of Buenos Aires had good reason to apprehend danger from the proximity of the Portuguese court. Spain had connived with the French emperor at the destruction of her neighbor, permitting French troops to march through Spanish territory toward Lisbon. The threat of a vengeful Brazilian attack across the border from the province of Rio Grande was now joined to the menace of a third British invasion. "We are in some expectation of an attack from the English," wrote DeForest, "and many think they will be assisted by the Brasilians, in which case it is feared they will succeed." [1]

The aggressive diplomacy of the Prince of Portugal gave substance to these fears. Newly installed at Rio, Prince John dispatched an envoy to La Plata with an offer to take the people of the viceroyalty under his royal protection. He promised to respect their rights and liberties, and to establish complete freedom of trade. Should they reject his friendly proposals, however, he would be under the necessity of making common cause with powerful England against Buenos Aires.[2] Liniers and the *cabildo*

---

1. DeForest to José da Costa e Abreu, Buenos Aires, March 23, 1808, DeForest Letterbooks, Vol. 3.

2. Ricardo Levene, "Intentos de independencia en el virreinato del Plata (1781–1809)," in *Historia de la nación argentina,* V, Section 1, p. 620.

vigorously rebuffed the Portuguese pretensions. In their dealings with Prince John, in their preparations for defense, the colonial authorities acted like the heads of an independent state. Indeed, Spain, the helpless prisoner of her French ally, could neither aid her colonies nor relieve her own wretched plight. By March, 1808, nearly 100,000 French troops were inside the kingdom. In Aranjuez a mob rose against Godoy, Prince of the Peace, regarded as the author of Spain's misfortunes. To save his favorite's life the aged Charles IV abdicated in favor of his son Ferdinand, Prince of Asturias. Napoleon chose this moment to intervene in the quarrels of the House of Bourbon. He summoned father and son to confer with him at Bayonne in France.[3]

Intimations of the somber crisis of the Spanish monarchy reached Buenos Aires in July, 1808. "The first and certain news," DeForest recorded in his diary, "that the French Troops had possession of Madrid and other parts of Spain and that Carlos IV the King and his son Ferdinand who had been crowned King, as well as the rest of the Royal Familia was at Bayonne in France, where was also the French Emperor and Court." [4] At the end of July the provincial authorities received official word that Charles IV had abdicated in favor of his son, who should be proclaimed king as Ferdinand VII. The ceremony was fixed for August 12, but was postponed in the light of a report that Charles had withdrawn his abdication. To add to the confusion of the time, on August 13 an emissary of Napoleon, the Marquis de Sassenay, arrived in Buenos Aires with dispatches for Liniers. "This day closes," reads the entry in DeForest's journal, "with the whole town gaping with anxious expectation of hearing something important very soon."

In the citadel, after inviting the attendance of the *cabildo* and the *audiencia*, Liniers received the imperial envoy. Before the assembled dignitaries the dispatches he brought were opened and read. They related that Charles IV and Ferdinand VII had renounced their rights to the throne in favor of Napoleon, who ceded them to his brother Joseph, now to become King of Spain. The assembly resolved to ignore these communications. Sassenay was ordered to return forthwith to Bayonne, the proclamation of Ferdinand VII as king was set for August 21. But the cautious

---

3. André Fugier, *Napoléon et l'Espagne, 1799–1808* (2 vols., Paris, 1930), is authoritative on Franco-Spanish relations at this period.
4. DeForest Journal, Vol. 6, July 15, 1808.

and ambiguous address issued by Liniers with the advice and consent of the *cabildo* and the *audiencia* failed to answer the questions in the public mind: it spoke respectfully of Napoleon, assured the people of the emperor's good wishes for Buenos Aires, and advised them to imitate their ancestors, who during the War of the Spanish Succession "awaited the destiny of the mother country in order to obey the legitimate authority which occupied the throne." [5]

With traditional pomp and festivity the ceremony of proclaiming the new king was celebrated on August 21. Official efforts to conceal the fate of the Spanish monarchs, prisoners in France, proved vain; the public cry, as recorded by DeForest, was "Hurrah for Fernando 7th! Fernando or no King!" The merchant interpreted popular sentiment to be against the admission of French troops into the province, and for the speediest possible conclusion of peace and establishment of free trade with Great Britain.[6] Two days later a new emissary, the Spanish officer Goyeneche, arrived in Buenos Aires. His dispatches revealed that all Spain was in flames. A supreme *junta* installed at Seville directed the insurrection against the usurper Joseph. Peace was being made with England, which offered all manner of aid to the Spanish patriots. "Every one here," commented DeForest, "appears perfectly happy with this intelligence."

A small coterie of creole leaders headed by Manuel Belgrano, brilliant secretary of the *consulado*, took special interest in the news from Spain. In the disasters of the mother country they perceived an unexampled opportunity to achieve the independence of La Plata. The British invasions had stimulated the growth of a revolutionary climate of opinion among the creole landowners, merchants, and professional men of Buenos Aires. Revelations of creole capacity and Spanish official incompetence and cowardice had sharpened the latent conflict between natives and old Spaniards. English propaganda had extolled the blessings of free government, and the influx of cheap British goods had suggested the benefits of free trade. But the conditions for the achievement of independence were not yet present. The Argentine revolutionaries did not possess the clarity of purpose and energy of their North American counterparts; the *populacho*

5. For this episode, see Mario Belgrano, "El emisario imperial el marqués de Sassenay," in *Historia de la nación argentina,* V, Section 1, pp. 85–104.
6. DeForest Journal, Vol. 6, August 21, 1808.

of Buenos Aires, still fanatically loyal to their king and the established order, were not to be compared with the democratic and responsive yeomanry and artisans of the thirteen North American colonies. That is why the revolution of Buenos Aires had to await a more propitious moment, and even then proceed by indirection and subterfuge.[7]

"A year passed," recalled the patriot leader Belgrano, "and we had not yet labored in the sense of independence. God himself presented us the opportunity with the events of 1808 in Spain and Bayonne. Then it was that the ideas of liberty and independence quickened in America, and the Americans began for the first time to speak of their rights." [8] Ardently professing allegiance to the dethroned and imprisoned Ferdinand VII, in their hearts the patriots believed that the "beloved" monarch would never return to rule in Spain. They counted on the certain victory of French arms in the peninsula. Accordingly they prepared to set up a new government, nominally ruling in the king's name but actually independent and serving the interests of the natives. By donning the "mask of Ferdinand" they hoped to gain the support of the monarchically disposed people of Buenos Aires, avert premature conflict with the Spanish royalists, and secure the sympathy and even assistance of Britain—Spain's powerful ally.

The prevailing temper of the creole party in the mid-summer in 1808 is suggested in a letter from DeForest to his English correspondent, Thomas Wilson. "There is nothing wanting I assure you, Sir" he wrote, "but good management on the part of the English to have a free trade to this country. Force and flattery ought in my opinion be united to bring it about, and after it is accomplished, to leave the people here to govern themselves, and treat them as an independent Nation in order to insure continuance. All is quiet as yet, but I consider it possible, though not probable, that a Revolution may take place without the assistance of the English." [9]

The most influential advocates of independence, such as Bel-

7. For the antecedents of the Argentine Revolution, see the contributions to Vol. 5, Sec. 1 of *Historia de la nación argentina,* particularly R. Levene, "Intentos de independencia en el virreinato del Plata." B. Mitre, *Belgrano,* I, Ch. 6, describes with great power the gathering conflict between creoles and old Spaniards, the impact of the events of Bayonne and Spain, and the constitutional premises of the *Revolución de Mayo.*

8. "Auto-Biografía" of Manuel Belgrano, in *ibid.,* p. 438.

9. Buenos Aires, August 20, 1808, DeForest Letterbooks, Vol. 3.

grano, Nicolás Rodríguez Peña, and Juan José Paso, recoiled from revolution on the French or North American model. They envisaged a peaceful transition to independence under the auspices of a new monarchy limited by constitutional guarantees. A candidate was at hand: she was the Princess Carlota Joaquina of Portugal, wife of the prince regent and sister of Ferdinand VII. After the events of Bayonne, Carlota proclaimed herself Regent of Spain and the Indies, and through emissaries of her husband laid claim to rule in Buenos Aires in the name of her brother. The patriot leaders opened negotiations with the princess, and carried on an active propaganda in her behalf. They could hardly have made a more unfortunate choice. Carlota was not only morally bankrupt, but of decidedly absolutist views.[10] Divining the true designs of the patriots, she denounced her adherents to Viceroy Liniers, charging that their letters were full of revolutionary principles subversive of the monarchial system and tending toward the establishment of a fanciful and visionary republic.[11] With this the Carlota project went into temporary discard.

Meantime the European Spaniards of La Plata, equally convinced of the impending separation of the colony from the mother country, intrigued to depose Liniers and establish a governing *junta* that would confirm and continue their ancient monopoly of political and commercial privilege. Their leader was the stubborn *chapetón*, Martín Alzaga, senior *alcalde* and hero of the *defensa*. Alzaga and his followers had long been critical of Liniers' alien birth, his tolerance of foreigners, and his evident partiality toward the creole element. With the outbreak of hostilities between Spanish patriots and Napoleon's puppet government, the situation of the French-born viceroy grew precarious. His alleged disloyalty to Spain afforded a pretext for the revolutionary plans of Alzaga and his fellow conspirators of the *cabildo*.

In Montevideo the ultra-royalist Governor Javier de Elío, his

10. P. Groussac, *Liniers*, p. 253, gives a pungent portrayal of the princess. "The elder sister of Ferdinand VII was only thirty-three years old at this time. But she was embittered, prematurely aged, sickly, half-consumptive, consumed with ambition and lust, offering the thrice-repugnant spectacle of feminine vice united with perfidy and ugliness." For a more sympathetic view of Carlota and her pretensions to rule in La Plata, see Julián María Rubio, *La infanta Carlota Joaquina y la política de España en América, 1808–1812* (Madrid, 1920). Enrique Ruiz Guiñazú, *Lord Strangford y la revolución de mayo* (Buenos Aires, 1937), discusses the negative attitude of the British minister at Rio de Janeiro toward Carlota's projects and his relations with the patriots of Buenos Aires.

11. R. Levene, "Intentos de independencia," pp. 638–639.

suspicions aroused by certain equivocal utterances and actions of Liniers, defied the viceroy's authority, charged him with treason, and knocked down an officer sent from Buenos Aires to supersede the governor. A tumultuous *cabildo abierto* supported Elío's actions and chose a governing *junta* (September 21, 1808), composed entirely of European Spaniards. In the capital, meanwhile, Alzaga and his partisans prepared to imitate the example of Montevideo. They fixed the date of their uprising for January 1, 1809, when the *cabildo* should choose its membership for the coming year.

The ceremonies of election began tranquilly on that day. But at a prearranged signal the city bell sounded the alarm, and a turbulent crowd composed mainly of armed European troops poured into the great square. As in Montevideo, their cry was, Down with the Frenchman Liniers! A *junta* as in Spain! A *cabildo abierto*, carefully packed, met and chose a governing *junta* comprising European Spaniards with the exception of two creole secretaries. Successive delegations headed by Bishop Lue informed Liniers of these transactions and urged him to resign. The viceroy, shaken by the sweep of events, offered to comply. But he had barely signed the required document when the commanders of the creole regiments, secretly summoned by Liniers, strode into the hall, Cornelio Saavedra at their head. Informed of the voluntary resignation of the viceroy, Saavedra brusquely addressed the gathering:

"Señores, who empowered his Excellency to yield an office that he legally holds, when the reasons urged upon him for this decision are false and groundless?"

"Señor commander," spoke up arrogant Bishop Lue, "in God's name, the people do not wish his Excellency to remain their ruler."

"That," replied Saavedra, "is one of the many falsehoods brought to play in this comedy. As proof, let Señor Liniers come with us and show himself to the people. If they reject him or declare that they do not want him to continue in command, I and my comrades will endorse his deposition."

Saavedra advanced toward the viceroy and took him by the arm. "Come, Señor," said he, "show yourself to the people and hear their wishes." Liniers and the creole officers went out to the square. Meantime native troops had appeared in force, and the Spanish regiments had melted away. Cheering crowds greeted the popular viceroy with loud *vivas!* and assurances of loyalty.

Punishment for the ringleaders of the conspiracy followed promptly. Alzaga and four other *cabildantes* were arrested and exiled to Patagonia, only to be rescued by a warship dispatched from rebellious Montevideo. Liniers acted to consolidate his power by ordering the dissolution of the Spanish regiments that had turned against him.[12]

"What is extraordinary in this affair," DeForest shrewdly commented in a letter to the American consul at Rio de Janeiro, "is that the old Spaniards were on the side of the cabildo, and the Creoles for the Vice Roy."[13] This assertion is not altogether accurate: on the side of the viceroy were ranged the conservative *audiencia*, numerous other Spanish officials, and some of the European military leaders, while the creole lawyer Mariano Moreno, future tribune of the *Revolución de Mayo*, collaborated with the *cabildo*. But differences of motive separated the Spanish and creole adherents of Liniers. Spanish officialdom supported the viceroy as the legal representative of the crown, as a symbol of the established order threatened by the revolutionary formula of governing *juntas* invoked by Alzaga and the *cabildo*. The creoles, the true party of revolution, rallied to the defense of Liniers because for them he was a symbol of popular sovereignty first asserted in the stormy days of the British invasions; be-

12. The above account is based on R. Levene, "La asonada del 1º de enero de 1809," in *Historia de la nación argentina*, V, Section 1. In his journal DeForest gives the following version of the *asonada*, under date of January 1, 1809:

"The day for choosing and qualifying a New Cabildo. The old Cabildo determined to ruin the Vice Roy and establish a junta of Government, and supposing they had secured sufficient strength among the military, began to sound the tocsin of discord and confusion about one o'clock when the Catalan Corps took possession of all the Grand Square and intercepted all communications with the Fort or Montevideo, stopping all People they thought proper and firing on some. Their power continued united with many Biscayans and Galicians for about two hours, during which time they were negotiating with Liniers, and the different Corps took some Prisoners, insulted many and fired on others. But on the arrival of the Patrician Corps in the Grand Square it became known that the Creoles of the Country were determined to support the authority of the Vice King. The Polizones began to fly in every direction. Negotiations still going on and the Cabildo and many of the Authorities endeavouring to persuade Genl Liniers to resign his authority to appear and gratify the populace, which he consented to do believing the Town really in danger of cutting the throats of each other if he did [not]. His friends remonstrated strongly against such a measure and with the Comandant of Patricios at their head took him to the Grand Square, where he was recd with the strongest demonstrations of joy as the friend of the People and the head of the Government.

"All Malcontents were immediately arrested, and some hove into irons. On this occasion some few were wounded."

13. DeForest to Henry Hill, Buenos Aires, Jan. 4, 1809, DeForest Letterbooks, Vol. 3.

cause under his regime they enjoyed unwonted influence and opportunity to work for free trade and independence; and, finally, because Alzaga's conspiracy threatened to restore *chapetón* supremacy in all its former vigor.[14] From this conflict the natives emerged with a practical monopoly of military power and greatly increased prestige. By invoking the formula of governing *juntas*, moreover, the Europeans themselves had established a revolutionary precedent that the patriots would one day use with notable effect.

Liniers, comprehending the true source and bulwark of his authority, now showed himself more than ever well disposed toward the creole party. The patriot leader Belgrano, long an earnest advocate of commercial reform, utilized the complacent mood of the viceroy to urge the opening of La Plata's ports to British trade as a means of diminishing the importance of rebellious Montevideo and relieving the financial distress of the government. Admiral Sidney Smith, commanding British naval forces in the river, seconded these efforts with the suggestion to Liniers that he follow the example of the governor of Habana and open the ports "for mutual convenience and regional benefits, raising revenue from a tolerated commerce." [15]

A potent argument for legalizing trade with England was the swelling volume of contraband traffic, which afforded no revenue to the provincial treasury, and which Liniers appeared unwilling or unable to halt. Indeed, it was charged that the viceroy connived at smuggling operations for personal profit.[16] About this time DeForest observed that with proper management almost anything could be done in the way of contraband.[17] Smuggling, he wrote to one correspondent, had reached the proportions of a regular system, "paying so much p% to one, and so

14. This interpretation of the *asonada* of January 1, 1809, as essentially a conflict between creoles and European Spaniards is accepted by most Argentine historians of past and recent times (Mitre, Lopez, Groussac, Ingenieros, etc.). Cf., however, the somewhat revisionist view of Levene ("La asonada del 1º del enero de 1809," pp. 694–699), who tends to reduce the episode to a factional struggle against the overweening pretensions of the *cabildo*, in which Spaniards were enrolled without distinction on both sides.

15. Smith to Liniers, March 18, 1809, quoted in D. Goebel, "British Trade to the Spanish Colonies," p. 311.

16. William Dunn to Alexander Cunninghame, July 26, quoted in *ibid.*, p. 309. On Liniers' commercial interests, see also C. Roberts, *Las invasiones inglesas*, p. 299.

17. DeForest to Stephen Twycecross, Buenos Aires, Dec. 18, 1809, DeForest Letterbooks, Vol. 3.

much to another."[18] So open was this traffic become that several English shops, familiarly known as *baratillas*, did business in the capital.[19]

Liniers, perceiving no other solution for the grave financial problems of his government, signified his approval of Belgrano's plan for trade reform in June, 1809.[20] Just then word came to Buenos Aires that the newly installed *junta central* of Seville had deposed the viceroy, and that his successor, Baltasar Hidalgo de Cisneros, was at Montevideo. Action on the proposed measure was therefore suspended.

The removal of Liniers, fruit of Spanish intrigue, angered and dismayed the creole party. They apprehended new efforts to restore European predominance and commercial monopoly. "The musty old Laws of the Indies," observed DeForest, "may be hunted up to incommode us, and foreign commerce may be entirely prohibited. It is generally believed that the Govt of Bs As had completed their commercial system on the very day in which the news respecting the Vice Roy arrived, and that commerce was to be perfectly free and taxed only with a moderate duty."[21] An English merchant noted general resentment at the ill treatment of Liniers by his government, and fear that the ports would be closed to British trade.[22]

Belgrano, Saavedra, and other patriot leaders, meeting secretly in the home of Juan Martín Pueyrredón, discussed a project for offering resistance to Cisneros. But they could reach no agreement as to ends: one was for a *junta*, another for bringing Princess Carlota to rule in Buenos Aires.[23] "The figs are not yet

18. DeForest to Nathaniel Lucas, Buenos Aires, Feb. 4, 1809, *ibid.*

19. Same to same, Buenos Aires, March 25, 1809, *ibid.*

20. R. Levene, "Significacción historica de la obra económica de Manuel Belgrano y Mariano Moreno," in *Historia de la nación argentina*, V, Section 1, p. 709.

21. DeForest to Lewis Goddefroy, Buenos Aires, July 8, 1809, DeForest Letterbooks, Vol. 3.

22. William Dunn to Alexander Cunninghame, Buenos Aires, July 15, 1809; same to same, Buenos Aires, July 26, 1809, Public Record Office, Foreign Office, Spain, 90, Hiram Bingham Transcripts, Yale University Library.

23. R. Levene, "Intentos de independencia," pp. 654–655. The renewed vitality of the Carlota project at this time is suggested by a memorial on the subject in the archives of the British foreign office. Written in Spanish and English, and dated August, 1809, it purports to be an "Address by Inhabitants of Buenos Ayres to their Magistrates proposing the election of Princess Charlotte Joaquina of Brazil, Regent of Buenos Ayres." A second memorial, addressed to the British foreign minister (August 22, 1809), solicits Britain's support "in upholding the House of Bourbon." P. R. O., F. O., Spain, 90, Hiram Bingham Transcripts.

ripe," remarked the judicious Saavedra. Cisneros, doubtful of
the reception that awaited him, remained at Colonia until Liniers
himself came to escort the new viceroy to the capital, where he
took quiet possession of his office on July 29, 1809.

Cisneros, a veteran of Trafalgar, soon found himself adrift
upon a sea of troubles. He discovered, read his official report,
"two formidable parties in the capital; the entire extent of the
viceroyalty in convulsion; diversity of opinions; presentiments of
independence, and other evils to which the state of Spain had
given rise." [24] The revolutionary upheavals of Montevideo and
Buenos Aires reverberated in the distant northern reaches of the
province. In the town of Chuquisaca differences between Spanish
authorities culminated in a struggle for control from which the
audiencia, supported by the creoles, emerged victorious (May,
1809). The spirit of unrest soon spread to the important provincial center of La Paz. There the natives rose under the banner
of independence, with the cry: Death to the *chapetónes!* Under
the leadership of a *junta tuitiva* they organized a government
composed exclusively of creoles, framed a constitution, and in-
stituted extensive reforms. "It is time," boldly proclaimed the
patriots, "to raise the standard of liberty in these unfortunate
colonies, acquired without the least title and ruled with the
greatest injustice and tyranny." [25]

Against these insurgents Cisneros acted with speed and
energy. To the seats of disaffection he dispatched Brigadier
Goyeneche, who crushed the uprising of La Paz with great
cruelty. But in Buenos Aires the new viceroy walked softly,
for he recognized the superior military power of the creoles. He
restored Alzaga and other ringleaders in the tumult of January 1
to their former places of honor, but he dissolved the *junta* of
Montevideo and stripped the Spanish regiments which had taken
part in the *asonada* of their separate identity. Alarmed by the in-
filtration of suspicious strangers from abroad—notably from
Philadelphia and Rio de Janeiro—Cisneros had a census of
foreigners made preliminary to their expulsion.[26] In the list of
names submitted to the viceroy by *alcalde* José Serra y Valle of
the Third Quarter figures that of "D^n David Cortez Laforest

24. B. Mitre, *Belgrano*, I, 279.

25. *Ibid.*, p. 285. For the uprisings of Chuquisaca and La Paz, see R. Levene,
"Intentos de independencia," pp. 602–669.

26. *Ibid.*, p. 665.

[*sic*], captain of an American ship that went to Patagonia, with which he later came hither, and which he dispatched I know not where, remaining in the land to trade. And the same has purchased a *chacra* on the coast of San Isidro. He is an American." [27]

Cisneros, like his predecessor, pondered the means of solving the grave financial crisis of the colony. The need for additional revenue was great, the viceroy's desire to conciliate the creole party was strong; reluctantly he turned to consider the unorthodox expedient of free trade. Two English merchants applied to him in August, 1809, for permission to sell their cargoes. Cisneros passed this petition to the *cabildo* and the *consulado*, with a favorable recommendation. "The general opinion," commented DeForest, "is that the Ports of the River will soon be opened to general Commerce, and on a fair and liberal plane, for, the Treasury is empty, the Government deeply in debt, the interior in commotion, the Govt both unwilling and unable to use effectual force for driving out the English Vessels, of course unable to prevent the Contraband trade and for a variety of other reasons is this opinion formed." [28]

The *cabildo*, representing the monopolists on both sides of the Atlantic, indicated the grave evils that must flow from trade with foreigners, but grudgingly conceded the necessity of the measure. In the *consulado* the proposal of the viceroy won by a vote of seven to five. With breathless interest DeForest followed the fortunes of trade reform. "A majority of the Cabildo and Consulado," he wrote, "approve of the measure. All the Patrician and landed interest make every exertion to support this liberal and patriotic plan. Its opponents are such as have large quantities of Goods on hand, and some rich and infamous old Spaniards, who wish to continue a Connection with Spain whatever may be its situation and Government." [29]

Now Fernández de Agüero, attorney for the *consulado* of Cadiz, submitted to the viceroy an able brief against free trade. This innovation, he asserted, was contrary to the Laws of the Indies and must prove fatal to the merchant marine of Spain, to the agriculture and industry of the province. "The land holders and respectable Creoles then came forward by their Agent in

---

27. *Documentos para la historia argentina*, XII, 288.
28. DeForest to Henry Hill, Buenos Aires, Aug. 14, 1809, DeForest Letterbooks, Vol. 4.
29. DeForest to Oliver Jump, Buenos Aires, Sept. 12, 1809, *ibid*.

support of the proposed measure of the Vice Roy, and in an ex-
position of 24 sheets have lashed the supporters of the Old System of things in a masterly manner." [30]

This was the celebrated *Representación de los hacendados* of
the thirty-one-year-old creole lawyer, Mariano Moreno. More
than a defense of the viceroy's proposal as a temporary financial
expedient, it was an ardent and vigorous argument for the adoption of free trade as necessary to the welfare of the people of La
Plata and in conformity with the laws of political economy as expounded by Adam Smith. Free trade would provide an outlet for
the productions of the country and relieve the distress of the landowners and laborers, it would stimulate commerce, replenish the
provincial treasury, and make possible a greater measure of
assistance to the patriots of Spain. Indignantly Moreno spurned
Agüero's suggestion that this reform might weaken the bonds
between La Plata and the mother country. He cited the observation of the philosopher Filangieri concerning prosperous colonies
to prove the contrary. "Happy under their metropolis they
would not dream of shaking off so light and mild a yoke in favor
of an independence that would deprive them of the protection
of their mother, leaving them with no sure defense against the
ambition of a conqueror, the intrigues of a powerful citizen, or
the perils of anarchy. It was not an excess of riches and prosperity that induced the English colonies to rebel; it was an excess
of oppression that caused them to turn against their mother the
same arms that they had so often employed in her defense." [31]

Argentine historians are not in accord as to the influence of
Moreno's memorial on the course of events leading to the *Revolución de Mayo*. Señor Molinari has sought to demolish the claims
made for the *Representación;*[32] Professor Levene, on the other
hand, ascribes to this writing a far-reaching significance.[33] De-
Forest's comments suggest that it was warmly received and widely
read in cultured creole circles, although Spanish censorship prevented publication at that time. Manuscript copies of the original

30. DeForest to Henry Hill, Buenos Aires, Oct. 5, 1809, *ibid.*
31. For the text of this document, see Norberto Pinero, ed., *Escritos de
Mariano Moreno* (Buenos Aires, 1896), pp. 89–224.
32. Diego Luis Molinari, *La representación de los hacendados de Mariano
Moreno, su ninguna importancia en la vida económica del país y en los sucesos de
mayo de 1810* (Buenos Aires, 1939, 2d edit.).
33. R. Levene, *Ensayo histórico sobre la revolución de mayo y Mariano Moreno*
(2 vols., Buenos Aires, 1920–21), I, 282 ff.; see also by the same author, "Significacción histórica de la obra económica de Manuel Belgrano y Mariano Moreno,"
in *Historia de la nación argentina*, V, Section 1, pp. 732 ff.

circulated in the capital; DeForest notes that he paid eighteen dollars for one. An interested English merchant forwarded a copy of Moreno's memorial to the British foreign minister with an account of the events which led to its composition.[34]

Delighted by the vigorous style and liberal sentiments of this Argentine *Common Sense*, DeForest resolved to bring Moreno's statement before a wider reading public. Accordingly he sent his manuscript copy to English acquaintances at Rio de Janeiro, requesting them to arrange for its publication in an edition of two or three thousand copies. He assured his correspondents that the pamphlet would have a large sale in Buenos Aires. "Profit however would not be the object of you or myself in putting it forward, but the interest and improvement of the Spanish Americans in which most certainly your Country is very deeply and directly interested." He would assume one-fourth of the costs of publication, and expected British merchants at Rio to advance the remainder. Suggesting that Moreno had been consulted on the project, he promised shortly to send a title and introduction, "with a variety of notes which ought to accompany it." [35]

Unfortunately DeForest soon lapsed into silence concerning the progress of his publishing plans. Presumably he failed to secure the support at Rio which he had anticipated. The first publication of the *Representación* did take place at Rio de Janeiro in the early part of 1810, in a Portuguese translation by the economist José da Silva Lisboa.[36] But there is no evidence that DeForest was linked with this project, which differed substantially from his own.

Meantime the three-months-old debate on the viceroy's proposal for trade reform drew to a close. A *junta* of commerce convoked by Cisneros sanctioned a decree establishing a limited free trade with allied and neutral nations (November 6, 1809). DeForest proudly noted in his diary that the first ship to enter the port of Buenos Aires under the new dispensation was the Portuguese brig *Roquete do Sul*, consigned to him by Henry Glover of Rio de Janeiro. "This brig began to discharge on the 14th November, and had the Goods discharged in the Custom

34. Alexander Mackinnon to George Canning, Buenos Aires, Nov. 2, 1809, P. R. O., F. O., Spain, 90, Hiram Bingham Transcripts.

35. DeForest to Nathaniel Lucas, Buenos Aires, Oct. 20, 1809, DeForest Letterbooks, Vol. 4.

36. R. Levene, "Significaccion histórica de la obra económica de Manuel Belgrano y Mariano Moreno," p. 738, ascribes this publication to the efforts of interested British subjects.

House on the 16th and 17th before any other vessel had begun to discharge."

The decree of November 6 soon justified itself as contraband trade gave way to open commerce, with increased receipts from customs accruing to the treasury. Withal vexatious restrictions upon trade remained. Foreigners could consign only to Spanish merchants, duties were unduly high, and one totally impracticable provision declared that payment for imports must be made one-third in money, two-thirds in produce. About this time Juan Pedro Varangot departed for Spain on a government mission, and DeForest secured a new partner to act as the nominal receiver of his consignments. His choice fell on Juan Larrea, syndic of the *consulado*, a young Spaniard of liberal proclivities.[37] A gentleman of handsome fortune, a well bred merchant, in every particular well qualified for a consignee—so DeForest described his new business associate.[38]

In the winter of 1809 gloomy tidings came to Buenos Aires from mother Spain. Inexorably the armies of Napoleon drove toward total conquest of the peninsula. The colonials anxiously discussed what they must do when Spain fell to the invader. Three courses, observed DeForest, were open to the people of Buenos Aires: independence, union with Brazil under Princess Carlota, or submission to the new rulers of Spain. The old Spaniards, intolerant of all foreigners and warmly attached to the mother country, preferred to maintain the peninsular connection under all circumstances. They filled the principal offices of government and therefore possessed considerable strength. But military power rested in the hands of the creoles, and armed force must ultimately settle the question. Serious differences of opinion and a spirit of vacillation obtained in creole ranks. "The most respectable and best informed Natives tho' they much wish a complete independence, doubt their ability to establish it on a firm basis, and will of course (as I believe) throw their influence into the scale of the Princess of Brasil, whose pretensions I think will prevail." [39]

Cisneros, apprehensive of the furtive intrigues of the patriots, but lacking the material or moral resources to act decisively

---

37. For Larrea, see the sketch in E. Udaondo, *Diccionario biográfico argentino.*
38. DeForest to Balch and Godard, Buenos Aires, Nov. 11, 1809, DeForest Letterbooks, Vol. 4.
39. DeForest to Thomas Wilson, Buenos Aires, Nov. 26, 1809, *ibid.*

against them, pursued a vacillating policy of small concessions to the natives coupled with ineffectual efforts to stamp out sedition. At the end of December, 1809, he moved to purge the province of undesirable foreigners. DeForest was among the first to receive the order of expulsion. He had been singled out for banishment, reflected the merchant, because he had property exposed, had lived in Buenos Aires a long time, received the consignments of others, and possessed "too much liberality of sentiment to live in a Country where individuals have no rights." [40] That the viceroy's motives were primarily political is suggested by the simultaneous expulsion of a number of Portuguese and Frenchmen whose conversation on the relations between Spain and her colonies had made them obnoxious to the government. [41]

"Know ye," DeForest addressed himself to posterity in the pages of his journal, "that the new and brutal Vice Roy Cisneros, influenced by some of my private enemies, ordered me out of the Country within Eight days from the 17th December." Vainly he appeared before the Spanish official to plead for an extension of time; Cisneros drove him forth without deigning to reply. Then the exile retreated to an English ship in the harbor, and from this place of refuge carried on an active correspondence with friends on shore, meanwhile peppering his foes with epistolary abuse. Confident of a speedy return to the capital, DeForest renewed his partnership with Juan Larrea for the year 1810, and by means of a fictitious sale arranged to place his *chacra* in Larrea's safekeeping.

Revolution was in the air. In Buenos Aires the patriots awaited the hour fixed by Saavedra: when Seville should fall to the French. [42] DeForest was evidently in the secret; to an English friend he wrote that he would not seek to have the order of expulsion revoked "till after the Ides of March are over." [43] But life on board ship grew irksome, and he determined to voyage to Rio de Janeiro and there await the great and certain tidings. Armed with letters of introduction from the patriot leader Belgrano, he sailed for Rio on February 13, 1810, in the Portuguese bark *In-*

40. DeForest to Oliver Twyecross, Buenos Aires, Dec. 23, 1809, *ibid.*

41. Alexander Mackinnon to George Canning, Buenos Aires, Dec. 18/23, 1809, P. R. O., F. O., Spain, 90, Hiram Bingham Transcripts.

42. A. Zimmerman Saavedra, *Cornelio de Saavedra* (Buenos Aires, 1909), p. 168.

43. DeForest to Oliver Jump, on board the *Seaton,* Dec. 29, 1809, DeForest Letterbooks, Vol. 4.

dustria. He had a fellow passenger in Juan Larrea's young brother Ramón, bound for Spain by way of England.

They landed at the Brazilian capital on March 5, 1810. Hospitable *cariocas* opened their homes to the travelers from La Plata, until DeForest fell ill from high living, "being invited to parties for 15 and 20 days daily after my arrival." To Belgrano he wrote a long and circumstantial account of the latest news from Spain, relating the fall of Seville, the dissolution of the *junta central,* and the apparently impending fall of Cadiz—last stronghold of the Spanish cause.[44] Two and a half months passed by without a hint of revolution in Buenos Aires. DeForest grew restless, decided to heed the urging of young Ramón Larrea and accompany him on the voyage to England. Perhaps while there he would find "a good daring girl for a wife." They sailed out of Rio harbor on May 20, 1810, in the packet-ship *Dispatch.*

One week earlier, the "Ides of March" had dawned in Buenos Aires. On May 13 an English vessel brought to Montevideo news that French armies had burst across the Sierra Morena and swept over the plains of Andalusia, entered Seville, and were threatening Cadiz. The *junta central,* the provisional government that claimed to rule in the name of the captive Spanish king, had fled and dispersed. This was the event that the secret society of the patriots had fixed upon as the signal for revolutionary action. From the unwilling viceroy and *cabildo* they wrested assent to the calling of a *cabildo abierto* which should decide the future form of government of the colony.

This first Argentine congress, from which many conservative notables were barred by the creole militia, voted overwhelmingly to depose the viceroy and establish a governing *junta.* On the historic twenty-fifth of May the clamor of the people compelled a reluctant *cabildo* to abide by these decisions and confirm a government nominated by the patriots. In the newly erected *junta* of nine sat friends and associates of DeForest: Larrea, Castelli, Azcuénaga, Belgrano. On the same day "the patriot *junta* installed itself in the citadel, residence of the ancient rulers of the colony, and began to act in revolutionary fashion while invoking the name and authority of the King of Spain, Ferdinand VII." [45]

44. DeForest to Manuel Belgrano, Rio de Janeiro, April 27, 1810, *ibid.*

45. B. Mitre, *Belgrano,* I, 346. On the *Revolución de Mayo,* see the chapters by R. Levene on "Los sucesos de mayo" and "El 25 de mayo" in *Historia de la nación argentina,* V, Section 2.

VII

"THE DOWNFALL OF MY ENEMIES"

DeFOREST, his Negro servant Joseph, and young Ramón Larrea landed at Falmouth port on July 19, 1810, after a voyage of sixty days. In his diary the exile expressed delight at the appearance of the English countryside, with its variegated pattern of hedges, fields, hills, and dales. In leisurely fashion, with frequent visits to scenes of interest, they journeyed by stage-coach toward London. At Redruth they inspected mines and machinery, at Plymouth they viewed the great navy yard where the king's ships lay, and at the little village of Ashburton they entered cottages where entire families wove serges that the East India Company would later export to India and China. It was the fourth of August before the travelers set foot in the capital. Two days later, at the counting-house of his old friend and correspondent Thomas Wilson, DeForest received and eagerly perused official accounts of the Revolution of Buenos Aires.

"Never, perhaps," the merchant recorded in his journal, "was there a Person more happily surprised than I to hear of the REVOLUTION OF BUENOS AYRES, of the disgrace and downfall of my enemies, and the complete establishment of the Government of my friends. This is the news, and certain news of the day, and I never felt more overjoyed at any circumstance in my life. Now let the infamous Cisneros grind his Teeth and mourn over his follies. He was a savage Villian while in power, and will be a most contemptible wretch out of it. Let him be so. Huzza! Huzza! Huzza for Buenos Ayres! May it be happy, and may its Enemies be damned. May all those who have had rule there and have conducted themselves in an unjust manner be severely punished. And may the Natives of Old Spain, who have no other crime but being Natives, be treated with a compassionate forgiveness, and become good citizens."

Simultaneously with this welcome intelligence, the first diplomatic representative of the patriot *junta* of Buenos Aires arrived in the English metropolis. He was a young naval officer, Matías

Irigoyen by name, dispatched by the revolutionary régime on a mission to London and Cadiz.[1] His instructions charged him to solicit British protection against the aggressive designs of Portugal and permission to export arms and munitions to Buenos Aires. This accomplished, he should cross over to Spain and present to the Cadiz *junta* a message that affirmed the stainless loyalty of the colonials to their captive king. A British warship brought Irigoyen to Britain's shores. Upon landing he discovered that the Spanish central *junta* had fallen and given way to a council of regency. Digesting this information, he concluded that the new régime did not even remotely "unite the qualities prescribed by law for a legitimately constituted government," and resolved to limit his diplomatic dealings to the British foreign office. The emissary carried letters of introduction to DeForest and Ramón Larrea, and the three *porteños* took lodgings together at No. 7, Southampton Street.

Irigoyen had his first interview with Marquis Wellesley, the British foreign secretary, on August 6, 1810. The English statesman expounded with precision the views of his government on the revolution of Buenos Aires. Britain stood ready to mediate the dispute between Spain and her disaffected subjects of the colonies, and greatly desired a reconciliation in the interests of the common struggle against Napoleon. She offered to the patriot *junta* protection against the aggressions of the Corsican, and her good offices in the quarrel with Portugal. But Britain would not aid or abet any movement tending toward the separation of the colonies from the mother country. Therefore Wellesley declined formally to receive the patriot agent and, tactfully alleging legal impediments and arms shortages, refused permission to export materials of war to Buenos Aires. The foreign secretary had conveyed essentially similar views to a delegation from the supreme *junta* of Caracas, headed by the immortal Simón Bolívar, that arrived in London on July 12 to solicit British aid for revolted Venezuela.[2]

1. Documents bearing on this and other early missions from Buenos Aires to Britain have been published by the Archivo General de la Nación of the Argentine Republic in the first volume of its *Misiones diplomáticas (misiones de Matías Irigoyen, José Agustín de Aguirre y Tomás Crompton)* (Buenos Aires, 1937). On these missions, see Daniel Antokoletz, *Histoire de la diplomatie argentine* (Paris and Buenos Aires, 1914), pp. 117–162.

2. C. K. Webster, *Britain and the Independence of Latin America* (2 vols., London, 1938), contains selected documents bearing on British policy, with an

British official coolness toward the suppliants from Buenos Aires and Caracas represented a significant reversal of attitude toward Spanish America. Cautious interest and encouragement to sundry schemes for Spanish-American emancipation under English auspices had been for two decades a characteristic feature of British policy. That stormy petrel of revolution, Miranda, had enjoyed British financial support while he plotted the subversion of Spain's American dominions, and such responsible statesmen as the great William Pitt had seriously considered his audacious plans. The filibustering expedition of the Venezuelan against his homeland had not been without implied British sanction. But the events of 1808 in Bayonne and Spain sounded the knell of this liberal policy. In January, 1809, Spain became Great Britain's formal ally in the mortal contest with Napoleon, and now it was to English interest that the Spanish Empire remain intact to provide effective aid to the mother country. Moreover, recent developments in the colonies weakened the force of commercial motives for desiring Spanish-American independence. While there is no basis for the commonly accepted view that in 1810 the Spanish government gave Britain permission to trade with the Indies,[3] by that year financial and political exigencies had compelled a number of colonial governments (notably at Habana and Buenos Aires) to open their ports to British ships.[4] Thus even before the first revolutionary outbreaks in Spanish America British merchants effectively enjoyed free trade with some Spanish provinces, while steady diplomatic pressure on the Cadiz régime gave promise of complete relaxation of the Laws of the Indies in return for British succors of all kinds. Under these conditions, there appeared to be "no special reason why British policy should desire the emancipation of the Spanish Colonies."[5]

interpretative introduction by the editor. William S. Robertson has described the first diplomatic reachings of the revolted colonies toward Great Britain and the United States, with special reference to Venezuela, in "The Beginnings of Spanish-American Diplomacy," in *Essays in American History Dedicated to Frederic Jackson Turner* (New York, 1910), pp. 231–267. For a stimulating comparison of British and American policy toward the Spanish-American revolutions, see Samuel Flagg Bemis, *Early Diplomatic Missions from Buenos Aires to the United States, 1811–1824* (Worcester, Mass., 1940, reprinted from the *Proceedings* of the American Antiquarian Society, April, 1939), pp. 89–93.

3. See, for example, C. K. Webster, *Britain*, I, 10. D. Goebel, "British Trade to the Spanish Colonies, 1796–1823," rejects this thesis in her heavily documented study of the status of British trade in the colonies.

4. This question is carefully studied in *ibid.*, p. 298 and *passim*.

5. C. K. Webster, *Britain*, I, 10.

In the light of these facts, British diplomacy in relation to the Spanish-American struggle for independence pursued a consistent yet flexible course. During the first stage of the conflict it diligently strove to reconcile Spain with her revolted dominions on the basis of imperial reforms that would include the admission of British commerce to colonial ports.[6] Later, when Iberian obstinacy and the victories of Bolívar and San Martín had shattered all hopes of reunion, it encouraged as the next best choice the establishment of congenial monarchial régimes under European princes in the new states.[7] At all stages of the struggle, Britain interposed her formidable might to bar armed intervention by a third party in the dispute.

Irigoyen emerged from his parleys with Lord Wellesley convinced that British policy was governed by Machiavellian precepts, and that Britain would not openly favor the South Americans while Spanish resistance to Napoleon continued.[8] He evidently imparted these impressions to his fellow-lodger DeForest. In a letter to Juan Larrea, now an influential figure in Buenos Aires politics, the merchant bitterly assailed the attitude of the British cabinet toward Spanish America. The people of England, he asserted, rejoiced at the liberation of that interesting part of the world. "But of the Government of England I have a very different opinion. It is selfish in the extreme, and while it is possible to keep the people of Old Spain and Portugal in a state of insurrection, I do not believe that they will perform any act of generosity toward the Spanish Americans." On the other hand, "the people of the United States of America and also the Government are enthusiastic in the cause of all oppressed Nations, and unlike the junta of Cadiz are as anxious to see Spanish America liberated from Spain, as to see Spain liberated from the modern Alexander." The patriots of Buenos Aires, however, he advised in closing, must not look for assistance abroad, but should depend solely on themselves and by their sincerity and exertions avoid the necessity of aid from others.[9]

6. On British offers of mediation, see for the first phase of negotiations, John Rydjord, "British Mediation between Spain and Her Colonies, 1811–1813," *Hisp. Am. Hist. Rev.*, XXI (1941), 29–50; for the second phase, C. K. Webster, "Castlereagh and the Spanish Colonies," *English Historical Review*, XXVII (1912), 78–95.

7. C. K. Webster, *Britain*, I, 26–34, discusses British interest in the establishment of monarchical institutions in the New World.

8. D. Antokoletz, *Histoire de la diplomatie argentine*, pp. 123–124.

9. DeForest to Larrea, London, Aug. 15, 1810, DeForest Letterbooks, Vol. 4.

In recognition of "the gallant and consistent conduct" of the people of Buenos Aires "in bringing to a crisis the long wished for change," DeForest sent for presentation to the new government a collection of books that included fittingly enough the works of the Abbé Raynal, Montesquieu, Voltaire, and Rousseau. These offerings were incorporated in the collections of the public library founded in Buenos Aires in 1810 at the initiative of Mariano Moreno, "for the purpose of encouraging reading and to instruct the people." [10]

To an old and honored friend, now a member of the patriot *junta*, the patron of learning wrote in praise of the educational and cultural undertakings of the new régime, particularly the establishment of a school of mathematics and a public library. He urged the further creation of an agricultural institute, furnished a detailed plan of organization, and sent plants and seeds for a projected botanical garden. "It is an undisputed maxim," he observed, "among the patriotic sages of North America (where I had the happiness to be born) *that an uninstructed cannot long be a free people.*" [11]

In Buenos Aires, however, the first preoccupation of the revolutionaries was with arms, sorely needed to repel threatened attacks by the royalists of Montevideo and their Portuguese allies, and to extend patriot authority into the distant northern reaches of the viceroyalty. Irigoyen, we have seen, vainly appealed to the British foreign secretary for permission to export articles of war. In this extremity the distraught agent resolved to seek to "elude the vigilance of a discreet government [*govierno savio*] and its strict laws," [12] secretly purchasing and smuggling arms out of the country. DeForest readily lent himself to these forbidden purposes; in behalf of Irigoyen (who evidently knew little or no English) he corresponded and otherwise negotiated with interested munitions makers.[13] "Your great want of arms is well known," he wrote Larrea, "I assure you that I am making every possible exertion to have your wants supplied." [14] One must con-

10. R. Levene, *History of Argentina*, p. 264.
11. DeForest to Miguel de Azcuénaga, London, Jan. 5, 1811, DeForest Letterbooks, Vol. 4.
12. Irigoyen to the *junta gubernativa*, London, Oct. 13, 1810, *Misiones diplomáticas*, p. 22.
13. DeForest to Graham, Riggs, and Co., London, Aug. 23, 1810; DeForest to Simon Walker, London, Jan. 14, 1811, DeForest Letterbooks, Vol. 4.
14. London, Oct. 27, 1810, *ibid.*

clude that the British government deliberately closed its eyes to these endeavors, for presently, without having experienced other embarrassments than his scanty funds occasioned, Irigoyen sailed for Buenos Aires with a cargo of armaments and a letter from Lord Wellesley recommending him to the protection of the British minister at Rio de Janeiro.[15]

Active interest in the patriot cause did not render DeForest oblivious of his personal concerns. Tartly he reproached Juan Larrea for devoting too much time to affairs of state. "You will certainly excuse me," he wrote that budding legislator, "for my interest and character must stand or fall with you, and I cannot forego this opportunity of saying to you: That you have it in your power to be the first Merchant in Buenos Ayres, if you will be content to be only that; but to be so, it is necessary that your whole *Time*, *Capital* and *Credit* be applied to the object for which your House is established. The moment you divide them you cease to be first." Predicting that the town of Lima in Peru would ere long be opened to foreign trade, the promoter broached a project for establishing Larrea's brother Ramón as their agent in that provincial capital.[16]

Revolutionary upheavals on the shores of La Plata revived DeForest's waning hopes for a consular appointment to Buenos Aires. Spanish authority had departed from the port, and he could see no reason why the United States should not maintain an agent there. Long years of residence in the Plate area, an intimate acquaintance with trade conditions, his friendship with the members of the patriot *junta;* these and other endowments appeared eminently to qualify the merchant for such a post. He resolved to proceed to the United States and make personal application for the office. Confident of success in his mission, DeForest left England on February 22, 1811, in the *George Augustus* of Philadelphia. He had taken the precaution of writing to Abraham Bishop, Republican party leader of New Haven, and to Postmaster General Gideon Granger, soliciting their patronage and influence to delay any appointment to Buenos Aires until his arrival in Washington.

DeForest, it appears, was unaware that in the spring of 1810, following the arrival in the United States of a delegation from the

15. D. Antokoletz, *Histoire de la diplomatie argentine,* p. 131; A. P. Whitaker, *The United States and the Independence of Latin America,* p. 75.
16. DeForest to Larrea, London, Nov. 29, 1810, DeForest Letterbooks, Vol. 4.

supreme *junta* of Caracas in search of succors and a treaty of alliance,[17] Secretary of State Smith had appointed three "agents for seamen and commerce" to as many actual or prospective centers of revolt in Spanish America. To Vera Cruz he dispatched William Shaler (June 16, 1810); to Caracas, Robert K. Lowry (June 26); to Buenos Aires, Joel Roberts Poinsett (June 28).

"You will make it your object," read Poinsett's notable instructions in part, "wherever it may be proper, to diffuse the impression that the United States cherish the sincerest good will toward the people of Spanish America as neighbors, as belonging to the same portion of the globe, and as having a mutual interest in cultivating friendly intercourse: that this disposition will exist, whatever may be their internal system or European relation, with respect to which no interference is pretended: and that, in the event of a political separation from the parent country, and of the establishment of an independent system of National Government, it will coincide with the sentiments and policy of the United States to promote the most friendly relations, and the most liberal intercourse, between the inhabitants of this hemisphere, as having all a common interest, and as lying under a common obligation to maintain that system of peace, justice, and good will, which is the only source of happiness for nations." [18]

Poinsett, a highly conscious protagonist of North American republican ideals, landed in Buenos Aires on February 13, 1811.[19] The initial misgivings of the patriots over the form of his commission, which was not directed to the revolutionary *junta* nor signed by the President, vanished when Poinsett explained that his credentials were identical with those issued to American agents at Habana and La Guaira. From the outset, British political and commercial pretensions on the River Plate gave the United States representative much concern. Soon after his arrival he advised

17. Composed of Juan Vicente Bolívar and Telésforo de Orea. The mission is briefly discussed in Charles C. Griffin, *The United States and the Disruption of the Spanish Empire* (New York, 1937), pp. 50–52.

18. William R. Manning, *Diplomatic Correspondence of the United States Concerning the Independence of the Latin-American Nations* (3 vols., New York, 1925), I, 6–7.

19. On Poinsett, see J. Fred Rippy, *Joel Roberts Poinsett, Versatile American* (Durham, N. C., 1935); Dorothy M. Parton, *The Diplomatic Career of Joel Roberts Poinsett* (Washington, D. C., 1934); and Charles Lyon Chandler and Edwin J. Pratt, "Vida de Joel Roberts Poinsett," in course of publication in the *Revista chilena de historia y geografía* (Santiago), LXVII (mayo-agosto, 1935), 37–52, and LXXXVIII (enero-junio, 1940), 295–309, to date.

the state department to establish a permanent consulate in Buenos
Aires to keep the English from securing exclusive trade privileges.[20] James Monroe was now Madison's secretary of state.
About this time a group of Baltimore merchants addressed to
Monroe a letter of recommendation in behalf of one Louis Goddefroy, a French merchant domiciled for several years at Montevideo, and currently in the United States to apply for the post of
consul to Buenos Aires. The signers deplored the languishing
state of American commerce because of the European war, and
remarked the expediency of maintaining a resident consul on the
River Plate in view of our lucrative and important trade with that
region.[21] These observations bore fruit; on April 30, 1811, President Madison appointed Goddefroy "Consul for Buenos Ayres
and the ports below it on the River Plate," [22] and at the same time
made Poinsett consul general to Buenos Aires, Chile, and Peru.

Two days later DeForest arrived in Washington from Baltimore where, suspecting nothing, he had encountered and spent
some convivial hours with his old friend and agent at Montevideo,
Louis Goddefroy. Without delay he called on Monroe and from
the secretary of state learned that his long quest was in vain. The
embittered applicant then saw President Madison, but his angry
protests only elicited soft words of regret and promises of patronage at a future opportunity. Rancorous at this perverse preference of the Frenchman Goddefroy over his own highly qualified
self, DeForest returned to his lodgings, seized pen and paper,
and wrote a severe letter of censure to Monroe.

Brooding over his humiliation, DeForest resolved at all costs
to defeat the appointment of Goddefroy as consul to Buenos
Aires. He persuaded the United States senators from Connecticut, Samuel W. Dana and Chauncey Goodrich, to lead the fight
against confirmation at the forthcoming session of Congress. His

20. D. M. Parton, *Poinsett,* p. 6.

21. Robert and John Oliver, and others, to James Monroe, Baltimore, April 1,
1811. National Archives (Washington), Department of State, Appointment
Papers.

22. W. S. Robertson has printed Madison's letter to Goddefroy in "Documents
Concerning the Consular Service of the United States in Latin America, with
Introductory Note," *Mississippi Valley Historical Review,* II (1916), 561–568.
On receiving his appointment, Goddefroy immediately departed for Buenos Aires,
but on arrival in the river was refused permission by the blockading royalists
either to land at Montevideo or to proceed to Buenos Aires. D. M. Parton,
Poinsett, p. 19.

exertions were so successful that the Senate by unanimous vote rejected the nomination of Goddefroy.[23] This triumph salved DeForest's injured feelings, but furthered his own consular hopes none at all, for the irate Madison reportedly vowed to appoint any applicant in preference to the schemer from Connecticut.[24] The Buenos Aires post ultimately went to William Gilchrist Miller, a candidate recommended by Joel Poinsett. DeForest viewed the appointment with an understandably jaundiced eye. He described Miller as a very young man lately arrived at Buenos Aires from the East Indies without property or mercantile credit. "However," he grudgingly conceded, "Mr. Miller is a gentlemanly young man, has a good education, and perhaps may perform the duties of such an office satisfactorily." [25]

From Washington, still nursing his grievances, DeForest departed for the north. In July, 1811, he came to Watertown, Connecticut, where his parents and brothers fondly received the returned wanderer after an absence of six years. It was on a visit to his birthplace, the village of Ripton, that he found the "good daring girl" he sought for wife. Julia Wooster was distantly related to General David Wooster of Revolutionary War fame, and to that Charles W. Wooster who won distinction on the sea in the War of 1812, later enlisted in the patriot navy of Chile, and by his gifts of leadership rose to the rank of rear-admiral in that service.[26] Only sixteen years old, she was already a notable beauty, "a golden-haired woman with a skin like roseate snow," in the adulatory words of a family historian.[27] DeForest was thirty-seven, swarthy, dark-haired, and dark-eyed. Ardently he courted

23. The Senate rejected the choice of Goddefroy as "inexpedient." *Journal of the Executive Proceedings of the Senate of the United States of America* (Washington, 1828–   ), Vol. 2, p. 190.

24. DeForest to Samuel W. Dana, New Haven, Dec. 4, 1811, DeForest Letterbooks, Vol. 5.

25. *Ibid.* The *Dictionary of American Biography* contains no account of Miller. Some of his consular reports are printed in W. R. Manning, *Diplomatic Correspondence*, I, 322–331, 333. Miller arrived at Rio de Janeiro in the spring of 1810 as supercargo of the schooner *Juliet*. At Rio he made the acquaintance of DeForest, then an exile from Buenos Aires. It was agreed that Miller should go to Buenos Aires and be associated with Juan Larrea, assisting him in the conduct of his business. In return Larrea was to lend his name to Miller's commercial transactions, receiving half of the North American's commissions. DeForest to Larrea, Rio de Janeiro, March 16, 1810, DeForest Letterbooks, Vol. 4.

26. On Charles Wooster, see the adequate biographical sketch in the *D. A. B.*

27. J. W. De Forest, *The de Forests of Avesnes*, pp. 121–123.

her, quickly won her consent, and presently, feeling some trepidation, set out to obtain the approval of Julia's parents for the match.

"Took a Horse and Gig," reads the entry in DeForest's diary, "and went to Ripton with a view of asking my beloved little Julia of her Parents. The anxiety caused by this novel and to me most important Journey was very great. I sometimes doubted the propriety of my attempt, the Knowledge of my own mind, and, what was greater than everything else, I feared that she might not alter her's. However, on I went, and before twelve o'clock, arrived at Mr. Ephraim Wooster's the Father of my Julia. Told her my errand, with which she seemed highly delighted, and soon after went into conversation with her Mother, who appeared to be much opposed to the proposed connection. The Father was consulted, Julia cried, the Mother cried, all was confusion, and after Dinner I bade them all farewell and left the House with a positive denial from the Mother."

Next day, however, mature reflection had brought Julia's parents to a more favorable view of the matter.

"Towards Evening Julia's brother arrived at Mr. Butler's and informed me that his Father, Mother and Julia were on their way to New Haven with a view of complying with my proposition, to put her to school, Marry her and take her with me to Buenos Ayres.

"Now I felt that it was too late to recede, and that I was about to enter into an engagement which might prove ruinous to my happiness.

"However, the charms of her I loved presented themselves to my Imagination and dispelled my gloomy fears. I waited on Mr. Wooster and Family at the House of Mr. James Prescott, and indirectly gave them assurances of my satisfaction at their arrival with Julia."

Thereupon Julia was sent to an unidentified school in New Haven for instruction in the management of a well-ordered household and the niceties of social routine. Some weeks later DeForest brought her home, "as innocent and virtuous, as I believed, as when she was carried to New Haven to go to school." That learned man of God, Dr. David Ely of Huntington, joined them in wedlock on October 6, 1811.

Disquieting news from La Plata cast a shadow on DeForest's

JULIA WOOSTER DeFOREST
From a Portrait by Samuel F. B. Morse.
Courtesy of Yale University Art Gallery.

new-found felicity. A letter from an old friend told of developments that boded ill for the merchant's prospects at Buenos Aires. Discord had early arisen among the creole revolutionaries, with a cleavage into liberal and conservative factions. Cornelio Saavedra, president of the governing *junta*, headed the moderates in the patriot ranks; about Mariano Moreno, fiery secretary of the new government, gathered the enlightened youth who desired sweeping political and social reforms. Admission of conservative provincial deputies into the governing *junta* represented a serious defeat for the fervent secretary and his followers. Moreno resigned and accepted a diplomatic mission to Great Britain, but died on the voyage, March 9, 1811. His passing did not content the friends of Saavedra. On April 5 and 6, 1811, they instigated a tumult in the capital that resulted in the dismissal and banishment from Buenos Aires of Moreno's supporters in the governing *junta*, among them Juan Larrea.

DeForest bore this last stroke of misfortune with philosophic patience. "I have ever considered such a thing possible," he commented, "and of course have in all my letters warned Larrea to return as soon as he could from Governmental affairs. . . . If the banishment of Larrea was necessary or acted as a safeguard to the Revolution, I am glad of it—and should be, even if I had lost one half of my property by it." [28]

A few days later the friend of liberty learned that two agents of the reconstructed *junta* had unobtrusively arrived in the United States in the guise of commercial travelers. They went by the plebeian names of José Cabrera and Pedro López, but these pseudonyms concealed the identity of Diego de Saavedra, son of the president of the *junta*, and the merchant Pedro de Aguirre. They carried instructions to purchase quantities of arms and munitions, pledging the public funds of the new régime for their purchases, and were particularly enjoined not to compromise the government of the United States or any other government. A letter from the *junta* to President Madison revealed the true names and objects of the emissaries, and besought his aid for their enterprise. [29]

28. DeForest to Thomas W. Stansfeld, New Haven, Oct. 22, 1811, DeForest Letterbooks, Vol. 5.
29. The best account of this mission is in S. F. Bemis, *Early Diplomatic Missions from Buenos Aires*, pp. 9–16.

DeForest promptly wrote to these agents, making generous offer of his services.[30] In their reply the commissioners from Buenos Aires evidently alluded to the fate of Juan Larrea, for in his next letter the merchant descanted on the singular virtues of that unlucky statesman. "I have always considered him," observed DeForest, "a man of honor, and a particular friend of that beautiful country. We have often spoken concerning the liberty of men, the governments of the world, and much more concerning the emancipation of Buenos Ayres, and his opinions were so much akin to mine and those of my countrymen in this hemisphere, that he won my heart completely. Notwithstanding my great interest in the fate of Larrea, my friends, I can say to you in all sincerity that if the security and tranquillity of the country were increased by his exile, I am perfectly content with it." [31]

There is no evidence that the patriot agents required or made use of DeForest's proffered aid. Received in most friendly fashion by Secretary of State Monroe in the name of the President, and given every facility to purchase and export arms to Buenos Aires, the only limits upon their procurements were financial ones. They finally sailed for La Plata with a shipment of munitions which they brought safely to the port of Ensenada de Barragán on May 19, 1812. "The liberality with which we have been considered by the government and inhabitants of the United States," they wrote Monroe on the eve of departure, "and their favorable disposition toward the cause we uphold remain graven in our gratitude and respect." [32]

At the beginning of the year 1812, DeForest prepared to depart with his young wife for Buenos Aires. He employed the closing weeks of his stay in North America to good advantage, soliciting business for his commission house. Conditions were propitious, for European blockade systems and our own non-intercourse measures were proving most injurious to American commerce. About this time Stephen Girard of Philadelphia made his entrance into the South American field, sending the *Montesquieu* to Valparaiso and the *Rousseau* to La Plata. The reason he gave for these voyages was "the unpleasant prospect of our European commerce, together with my anxiety to employ my ships as advan-

30. DeForest to Pedro López and José Antonio Cabrera, N. Y., Nov. 8, 1811 (in Spanish), DeForest Letterbooks, Vol. 5.
31. Same to same, New Haven, Nov. 24, 1811 (in Spanish), *ibid.*
32. S. F. Bemis, *Early Diplomatic Missions from Buenos Aires,* p. 16.

tageously as possible." [33] Another magnate, John Jacob Astor of New York, ventured into the South American market at this time, perhaps in response to DeForest's solicitations. Astor instructed the commission merchant to purchase for his account four or five thousand dollars' worth of nutria skins at Buenos Aires. DeForest accepted this commission with thanks, but warned the capitalist that if his object was a complete monopoly of the article, "your present order is but illy-calculated to accomplish it." [34] Apparently it was also agreed that in the future DeForest should represent Astor's interests at Buenos Aires. [35]

On February 13, 1812, DeForest, his wife, and his black servant Joseph boarded the ship *Mary*, Captain Edward Garland, bound from New York for Rio de Janeiro. Just seventy days later the mountain-girdled Brazilian capital came into view. There they stayed for several weeks, during which time DeForest satisfied himself that a Spanish squadron maintained a blockade of the River Plate beyond Montevideo. Once before the adventurer had successfully run a blockade of the river, in the days of the British invasions; he resolved to thwart the royalists of Montevideo with equal dexterity. In an ugly little brig, the *Southern Packet*, they sailed for La Plata on May 17. Three weeks later their ship had reached the point where the yellow waters of the great stream merged with those of the Atlantic. At midnight of June 6, 1812, the brig stood off Islas on the southern shore of La Plata. At this appointed spot, under cover of darkness, DeForest and his party took the ship's boat and softly made for shore. They landed about four leagues below Islas and encamped for the night under some willow trees near the bank of the river. In the morning they discovered that a cane swamp more than half a mile wide barred their way to dry land. After passing the entire day in fruitless search of a passage through the bog, they decided to camp another night by the side of the river. At dawn the party began to wade through the marsh, Julia wearing the great coat and boots of the black servant. It was the winter season in these southern latitudes; a two-day frost had covered the swamp with a thick crust that broke under their

33. John B. McMaster, *The Life and Times of Stephen Girard, Mariner* (2 vols., Philadelphia, 1918), II, 146.

34. DeForest to Astor, N. Y., Feb. 11, 1812, DeForest Letterbooks, Vol. 5.

35. Kenneth W. Porter, *John Jacob Astor, Business Man* (2 vols., Cambridge, Mass., 1931), II, 650.

tread. The mud and water almost came to Julia's waist. Twice the fatigued and frightened bride, now in the eighth month of her pregnancy, was about to collapse. DeForest and Joseph supported her, and on they went till they finally came to dry ground.

"On our arrival to the hard land," reads the journal, "under the lee of the monte Talas, I stripped my lovely little wife of her wet clothes, wiped her dry, and put her into my Great coat, which I had cautiously preserved dry, wrapped her up and piled on all the things I could find till she began to perspire. I then wiped her dry again, and dressed her from head to foot in flannels which I had purposely brought with me, when she appeared to be as well as ever she was in her life."

Now the weary travelers set out to find a dwelling, and advanced toward the river. Soon they came to a deep, well-nigh impassable marsh, and so had to retrace their steps to the camp hard by the hill of Talas where they had left a great fire.

"I was sick of a fever. Julia began to despair, and the Black Boy looked as though he had lost all his friends. We returned, and much fatigued, sat down in silence near our fire. Julia cried, I doubted of our fate, and all was sadness for 15 or 20 minutes, when the boy astonished us by crying out 'here is a man.' I started up, and beheld a country man on Horseback, surrounded by a Pack of Dogs which had smelt us out, and shewn their Master where we were."

Their deliverer was a *campesino* of the vicinity. Hospitably he offered to assist the bedraggled pilgrims, went home for a cart, and by sundown had brought them to his *rancho*. On the following day they proceeded to the village of Islas, where a friendly curate afforded them lodgings for the night. They reached the port of Ensenada de Barragán on the ninth of June. Loaded into a lumbering cart, the travelers set out on the last lap of their journey to Buenos Aires. Halfway between Ensenada de Barragán and the capital they came to a post house, met a coach "coming on the run," and that evening, safely ensconced in the house of Juan Larrea, rested from the fatigues and perils of their strange homecoming to La Plata.

VIII

"ADOPTED CITIZEN OF BUENOS AYRES"

THE political face of La Plata had greatly altered since DeForest left Buenos Aires for Rio de Janeiro in February, 1810. The ideal of independence which he and Juan Larrea once ardently discussed had become an effective reality. The government of the United Provinces of La Plata yet professed to rule in the name of the captive Ferdinand VII, but this concession was everywhere evaluated at its proper worth. Against the true loyalists of Peru and Montevideo the men of Buenos Aires waged war; against the king's friends in their midst they employed a revolutionary strategy of terror. Already in 1810 the governing *junta*, then dominated by the stern and unbending Mariano Moreno, had sent before a firing squad the former Viceroy Liniers and other Spanish dignitaries implicated in the rising at Córdoba. A few days after DeForest's return, the government discovered and vigorously suppressed the last and most formidable conspiracy against creole rule, planned and directed by the intractable *chapetón* leader, Martín Alzaga. In his journal DeForest noted with satisfaction that "the Robespierre of the America de Sur" was shot in the Great Square "amidst the most unanimous cries of 'Viva la Patria, y muerte a los Traidores.' " Forty others expiated their part in the plot with their lives. Grimly the diarist expressed a hope that this harsh lesson would have a salutary effect on the survivors. "The chastisement they receive will be felt during the lives of those who are on the stage of action." [1]

The wheel of party fortune in Buenos Aires had made a full turn since DeForest learned of the conservative revolution of April 5 and 6, 1811, so ruinous to the interests of his friend Larrea. The military disaster of Huaqui in June of that year, which lost Upper Peru to the revolution, soon provoked widespread discontent with the timid leadership of Cornelio Saavedra and the unwieldy governing *junta*. In September, 1811, popular clamor moved the *junta* to establish a triumvirate of which the

1. DeForest Journal, Vol. 8, 1812.

driving force was the youthful but extremely competent Bernardino Rivadavia, in whose father's home DeForest had taken
shelter during the difficult days of the British invasions. Between
this executive power and the *junta*, now transformed into a legis-
lative chamber (*junta de conservación*), arose a struggle from
which the triumvirate emerged victorious; presently it dissolved
the *junta*, banished the wretched Saavedra, and assumed dic-
tatorial powers. The ascendancy of Rivadavia betokened a return
to the principles of *porteño* centralism and liberalism proclaimed
by the martyred Moreno. From exile in the interior the triumvirate recalled Juan Larrea and other lieutenants of the great
revolutionary.

The government of Rivadavia accorded a friendly welcome to
DeForest. Two months after his arrival, citing the merchant's
"distinguished merits, patriotism, and adherence to the liberal
system adopted by the peoples," it conferred on him the title of
honorary citizen of the United Provinces of the Río de la Plata.[2]
Gratified by this official mark of attention, and by numerous calls
of old acquaintances who came to pay their respects to the returned exile and his young wife, DeForest expressed belief that
it would continue to his "happiness and interest" to stay in
Buenos Aires for a few years.

News of the American declaration of war on Britain of June
18, 1812, however, soon nullified these favorable auguries. Already United States trade to La Plata had suffered from unsettled
political conditions in Buenos Aires and the forbidding presence
of a Spanish squadron in the river.[3] The Anglo-American War of
1812 dealt a mortal blow to this dwindling commerce. British
warships patrolled the mouth of the Plate estuary and even seized
American vessels within the territorial waters of the United
Provinces.[4] English merchants naturally would not consign to an
enemy Yankee. Under these conditions, DeForest's business prospects appeared in a dismal light.

His relations with Juan Larrea at this time bore an equally un-

---

2. *Gaceta de Buenos Aires*, Aug. 22, 1812.
3. Consul Miller described United States commerce to Buenos Aires in the first
half of 1812 as very trifling, only seven vessels having arrived during that period.
He ascribed this condition to the unsettled state of the country, and asserted that
the presence of an American warship in the river would lead to an immediate
increase of trade. W. G. Miller to James Monroe, Buenos Aires, July 16, 1812,
in W. R. Manning, *Diplomatic Correspondence of the United States*, I, 329.
4. J. R. Poinsett to Monroe, Buenos Aires, June 14, 1812, *ibid.*, I, 336.

satisfactory character. To insistent demands for a settlement of accounts covering the period of DeForest's absence from Buenos Aires, the Catalonian merchant, evidently immersed in political concerns, long gave evasive replies. When, late in 1813, an adjustment was made, the silent partner was dismayed to find that instead of having made money he had lost many thousands of dollars.[5]

With British sea power in effective control of the trade routes to America, DeForest resolved to quit Buenos Aires and commerce for the duration of the war. His *chacra*, conveniently situated seven miles above the capital, offered an ideal site for a rural retirement. With his little family, augmented by the birth of Francisca Tomasa Isabel, born on July 24, 1812, and christened in the great cathedral of Buenos Aires with Doña Tomasa de Larrea as godmother,[6] he departed for the country in September of that year. Under DeForest's direction his Negro slaves soon put the sadly neglected estate in order; flowers, shrubs, and fruit trees bloomed forth. "Having a well chosen little library," he wrote one correspondent, "which engages a considerable share of attention, the days pass by swiftly; and I assure you Sir very pleasantly." [7]

While DeForest reposed on his *chacra* overlooking the broad Plata, "very quietly and stupidly, waiting for a peace and better times," in the debatable mountain province of Upper Peru the patriot troops battled to stem the advance of a royalist army moving southward to an ultimate junction with the Spanish defenders of Montevideo. On September 24, 1812, creole soldiers under General Manuel Belgrano routed the invaders on the plain of Tucumán, and decisively dispelled the danger to the heart of the revolution. DeForest shared the universal sentiment of grati-

5. DeForest to James Smith, Buenos Aires, Feb. 8, 1815, DeForest Letterbooks, Vol. 5.

6. It does not appear, however, that any of DeForest's children were reared in the Catholic faith. In a letter written many years later to the director of a Montreal school attended by his son Carlos, DeForest forbade any religious instruction for his son. "You are pleased to intimate," he wrote, "what I feel and have ever professed—viz. to be perfectly liberal on the subject of Religion, and I assure you, my dear Sir, that I would as soon make my Children Catholics, as of any other Christian Persuasion. But I cannot consent, that any one of them should be spoken to respecting Religion till he arrive at years of discretion." DeForest to Monsieur Roque, New Haven, Nov. 13, 1824, DeForest Letterbooks, Vol. 8.

7. DeForest to Gideon Granger, "Plaza de Washington," Jan. 3, 1813, *ibid.*, Vol. 5.

tude and relief. To Belgrano he sent a letter of felicitation and a copy of Washington's Farewell Address. "Although very little," he wrote, "it is worth reading a great many times, and may be a valuable and appropriate model for you, when, after having established the liberties of your Country, you may be disposed to retire from publick affairs and cultivate some beautiful Chacra, in the neighborhood of mine, on the banks of the delightful Plata." [8]

DeForest thus planted a seed of republican propaganda better than he knew. Early in 1813 a Spanish edition of the Farewell Address was published in Buenos Aires. A reverent preface from the pen of Belgrano introduced the North American classic. In this foreword the patriot general related that the Address first came into his hands about 1805; that he had burned it together with all his other papers at the dangerous and hasty battle of Tacuari in Paraguay; and that having received another copy from DeForest, in his eagerness to make known the teachings of Washington among his countrymen he had undertaken to translate it for publication. Belgrano charged the Argentines to read, study, and ponder Washington's words. "Determine to imitate this great man, that we may reach the goal to which we aspire— to constitute ourselves a free and independent nation." [9]

In turbulent Buenos Aires, however, creole politicians were little disposed to heed admonitions against factional strife. Rivadavia's government soon lost support among decisive sections of the people. Clinging jealously to power, it rejected all proposals to broaden the base of the revolution by summoning a representative assembly of the United Provinces. Opposition to the régime centered in the Patriotic Society, a political club on the Gallic model led by the vehement republican Bernardo Monteagudo, inheritor of Moreno's mantle; and in the Lautaro Lodge, a secret revolutionary order founded in Buenos Aires by two newly arrived soldiers come to offer their swords to the cause, Carlos de Alvear and José de San Martín. With the watchwords of independence, constitutional government, and democracy, a revolt spearheaded by the grenadiers of Alvear and San Martín overthrew Rivadavia's tottering régime on October 8, 1812. In its

---

8. DeForest to Manuel Belgrano, "Plaza de Washington," Dec. 15, 1812, *ibid.*

9. Antonio Zinny, *Bibliografía histórica de las Provincias Unidas del Río de la Plata* (Buenos Aires, 1875), pp. 88–89, relates the circumstances of publication and reprints Belgrano's preface to this pamphlet of thirty-nine pages.

place arose a second triumvirate which proclaimed that the last rights of Ferdinand VII had disappeared and summoned the people to elect delegates to a general constituent assembly.

On his *chacra* DeForest regarded with approval the triumph of the radical wing of the revolutionary party, in whose councils Juan Larrea figured prominently. "Larrea's party," he commented, "is again in power, and appears to have great strength. He of himself has probably more influence than any other Man in the Country; altho he has not any office." [10]

The constituent assembly of the United Provinces of La Plata opened its sessions under hopeful auspices on January 31, 1813. "It is supposed," DeForest had written, "that Independence will be declared; and a Constitution of Government formed on a Plan similar to that of the United States of N. A." [11] The assembly chose to evade these crucial issues, but it suppressed the symbols of royal authority and sanctioned a national anthem that proclaimed the birth of "a new and glorious nation." The congress also enacted a series of important social reforms that reflected the liberal proclivities of its guiding spirits, Alvear and Larrea. The Inquisition, judicial torture, Indian forced labor and tribute, entailment of estates, and titles of nobility were swept away. A memorable law decreed the freedom of all children of slaves born after January 1, 1813. The assembly in conclusion abolished the impractical triumvirate and vested executive power in a supreme director who should rule with the advice of a council of state. They chose Gervasio A. Posadas for this high post, through the intrigues of his nephew Alvear; and in the cabinet of Posadas, Larrea occupied the strategic post of secretary of the treasury. "A rather curious arrangement," observes an Argentine historian. "The management of the public funds was intrusted to a great merchant, a Spaniard to boot, and for many years linked all too closely to all the foreign speculators and merchants of the capital." [12]

It was Larrea, in concert with the Americans William P. White and DeForest,[13] who at the beginning of the year 1814 gave effect

10. DeForest to Thomas W. Stansfeld, "Plaza de Washington," Nov. 21, 1812, DeForest Letterbooks, Vol. 5.

11. DeForest to Gideon Granger, "Plaza de Washington," Jan. 3, 1813, *ibid.*

12. H. Zorraquín Becú, *De aventurero yanqui a consul porteño en los Estados Unidos*, p. 20.

13. C. Roberts, *Las invasiones inglesas*, p. 414, links DeForest with Larrea and White in the creation of the patriot navy, but gives no details. DeForest makes

to a daring plan that changed the face of the Argentine war for independence. At this period the military fortunes of the patriots were at a low ebb. In Upper Peru, General Belgrano was in full retreat after suffering severe defeats at Vilcapugio and Ayohuma. In the Banda Oriental the irrepressible gaucho chieftain Artigas was in open revolt against the authority of Buenos Aires. The siege of Montevideo went ill, for the royalists enjoyed naval supremacy in the river and constantly replenished the fortress with men and supplies. A bold and decisive stroke was necessary to break the ring of Spanish encirclement by land and sea. Larrea's grand design, which won the support of the powerful Carlos de Alvear and of Director Posadas, proposed the creation of a patriot navy which should establish a blockade of Montevideo and thereby compel the capitulation of the royalist stronghold. For this all the elements of a fleet—ships, armaments, crews—had to be assembled in the shortest possible time. As his chief agent in this enterprise of fantastic difficulty Larrea designated an old crony, the American adventurer William P. White, also known to DeForest since the period of the British invasions.

White, aided by DeForest, energetically set about the performance of his assigned tasks. Merchant ships lying idle in the harbor were purchased to make up a naval force mounting 264 cannon. Deserters from English vessels composed the majority of the Argentine crews. A spirited Irish sea captain, William Brown, assumed command of the hastily formed armada. In a series of combats he won undisputed command of the river. The situation of blockaded Montevideo now became hopeless; and in June, 1814, General Vigodet surrendered to a besieging patriot army Spain's last foothold in La Plata.

Great stores of supplies fell to the captors of Montevideo. This booty presented opportunities for private gain that Juan Larrea was quick to apprehend. Mindful of old friends, he offered De-Forest a commission for a state auction house in Buenos Aires or, in DeForest's blunt words, "the sales of the possessions plundered at Montevideo by M[r.] L[arrea] who is First Lord of the Treasury and Prime Minister." [14] The merchant quickly ac-

---

no mention of such activity in his letters or journals. The classic history of the Argentine navy is Angel Justiniano Carranza, *Campañas navales de la República Argentina* (4 vols., Buenos Aires, 1914).

14. DeForest to Thomas Wilson, Buenos Aires, Feb. 8, 1815, DeForest Letterbooks, Vol. 5.

cepted this invitation to return to the ways of commerce. In
September, 1814, his store, situated next to the municipality,
opened its doors. A circular letter to British and American merchants explained his commercial advantages. "I am backed by
my intimate friend Larrea, who is secretary of the Treasury, and
has already given me a great deal of business in sales of government property."[15]

DeForest's first account book with the Buenos Aires government opened September 21, 1814, and closed April 8, 1815. During this period of six months and fifteen days his sales of state
property amounted to $191,704, on which he received 2½ per
cent commission. Meantime the Anglo-American War of 1812
had ended, although many months after the Treaty of Ghent,
DeForest, styling himself "an adopted citizen of Buenos Aires,"
complained to the Supreme Director Pueyrredón of British interference with mail coming to American residents of La Plata.[16]
In September, 1815, the commission merchant sent his first shipment to the United States since his return to Buenos Aires, a
cargo of 2,400 nutria skins consigned to Thomas Tenant of Baltimore with orders to sell immediately on his account.[17] About this
time he wrote John Jacob Astor, advising him that nutria skins,
though scarce, could be had for $1.75 a dozen, and counseled the
New York capitalist to open a trade between Buenos Aires and
Calcutta. Three weeks later he offered a $5,000 draft of Astor's
to one Broghan, asking him to make the necessary inquiries
"about the standing of Mr. Astor."[18] Five out of seven American
vessels which had arrived in the river since August, 1815, De-
Forest boasted in another letter, were consigned to him.[19]

15. Letter dated Dec. 22, 1814, quoted in J. W. De Forest, *The de Forests of
Avesnes*, p. 124.

16. "Copy of Memorial presented to his Excellency, the Supreme Director of
Buenos Ayres, on the 20th day of September, 1815," in *Niles' Weekly Register*
(Baltimore), Jan. 20, 1816.

17. DeForest to John and Benjamin DeForest, Buenos Aires, Sept. 16, 1815,
DeForest Letterbooks, Vol. 5.

18. J. W. De Forest, *The de Forests of Avesnes*, p. 129.

19. DeForest to Louis Goddefroy, Buenos Aires, Dec. 28, 1815, abstract of
letter in John W. De Forest Papers, Yale University Library. Included is an
account of these five vessels, as follows:

William and Charles of Salem, Henry King, master and supercargo, arrived
on August 23 with a cargo of quicksilver, gin, codfish, cordage, lumber, etc.,
valued at $18,000, and sailed for Baltimore on November 18 with 5,000 pesos,
8,000 hides, and other freight.

Schooner *Kemp* of Baltimore, John C. Zimmerman, supercargo, arrived on

An ambitious young creole of Irish ancestry, Patricio Lynch by name, at this time appears in DeForest's counting-room. Their agreement stipulated that Lynch should devote all his "time and attention to the business and interests of the House," turning over to DeForest all the commissions his influence could secure. As junior partner he was to receive a third part of the firm's profits. Presently Patricio's brothers joined him in service. Benito came at nine dollars a month, Manuel at eight, Felix at five dollars a month. This growing force of assistants suggests the mounting proportions of the business. From near and distant lands came wine, indigo, balsam, sugar, tobacco, cochineal, copper and many other articles to rest in the vast and redolent store-rooms. Over these rooms lived DeForest in the ample style of a merchant prince. His household expenses, relates a family historian, amounted to the prodigious sum of $7,000 a year; the table was always set for twenty-four persons.[20] Meantime, keeping pace with waxing prosperity, DeForest's progeny likewise increased. In addition to his first-born, Francisca Tomasa Isabel, there were Carlos María, born September 8, 1813, "a day most glorious in the annals of our family"; Juliana Nicanora, born January 10, 1815; and Jacoba Pastora, born December 30, 1815. All were christened in the great cathedral of Buenos Aires.

At this period, also, Juan Larrea and his party fell on evil days. In January, 1815, the Director Posadas, weary of unprofitable dispute with provincial *caudillos* and insubordinate military, resigned his office. Into his place stepped the youthful and supremely ambitious Carlos de Alvear. For four months he maintained a precarious sway in Buenos Aires. But in the Banda Oriental the gaucho chieftain Artigas ruled contemptuous of Alvear's pretensions, and even took under his protection the

August 29 with a cargo of 500 muskets, gunpowder, cordage, and naval stores valued at $19,000, and sailed for Bordeaux on October 27 with 6,000 hides, etc.

Brig *Expedition* of Baltimore, Captain John Chase, arrived on September 2 with a cargo of 3,000 muskets and other warlike stores valued at $70,000, and sailed on November 9 with 37,000 pesos, 672 bars of copper, 3,200 nutria skins, horse hair, etc.

Brig *Nancy Anne* of Salem, J. B. Osgood, master and supercargo, arrived from Hamburg on December 1 with a cargo of linens, gin, and iron, valued at $36,000, and sailed for Marseilles on January 15 with hides and tallow.

Brig *Favorite* of Boston, Ezra Foster, master and supercargo, ran on shoal near Cape San Antonio on December 17. Came with a cargo of 20,000 Spanish dollars and 100,000 feet of pine boards. "In safety and expected to arrive."

20. J. W. De Forest, *The de Forests of Avesnes*, p. 127.

neighboring provinces of Entre Ríos, Corrientes, and Santa Fé; the army of Upper Peru rejected the new director's authority, proclaiming him suspect and incompetent; and in the distant province of Cuyo, where San Martín was building up and training his army for the fateful campaign of the Andes, Alvear's decrees went unheeded. In April, 1815, national troops dispatched against Artigas mutinied and fraternized with the enemy; in the capital the *cabildo*, long resentful of Alvear's arrogant and headstrong ways, led an uprising against the dictator and proclaimed his downfall. Thus abandoned, Alvear sought safety on an English ship, but his secretary of the treasury did not make good his escape. Thrust into prison and loaded with irons, Larrea had opportunity to meditate on the mutability of power and the vicissitudes of a revolutionary career. Presently the new interim régime of Alvarez Thomas organized a civil commission of justice to sit in judgment on Larrea, among others, charged with misuse of his office for private ends, and also on his colleague William P. White.

Manuel Vicente de Maza, judge of the commission, directed the interrogation of Larrea.[21] What, he inquired at one point in the proceedings, was the motive of public interest that induced Larrea to intrust the sale of state property to the foreigner DeForest, in preference to sons of the country? Lamely the accused explained that DeForest was associated with the creole Patricio Lynch; he, Larrea, had also anticipated certain advantages from this "innovation" (*novedad*). But the prosecutor, unconvinced, on August 18, 1815, listed among other charges against Larrea the sale of government effects with payment of commissions to a foreigner, when the state auction board (*junta de almonedas*) could have done as much with a saving of interest to the necessitous public treasury.

DeForest, meantime, followed the course of the trial from a safe distance. "It is nearly four months," he wrote an English correspondent, "since Mr. Larrea's political fall. He is now in prison, loaded with irons; and when he will be set at liberty is very uncertain. He has several thousand pounds of my money in his hands, which probably I shall never recover." [22]

---

21. For the trial of Larrea, I have drawn on the account in H. Zorraquín Becú, *De aventurero yanqui a consul porteño en los Estados Unidos*, pp. 22–23.

22. DeForest to Thomas Wilson, Buenos Aires, Aug. 7, 1815, in J. W. De Forest, *The de Forests of Avesnes*, pp. 128–129.

On October 9, 1815, the court passed sentence of exile and confiscation of goods upon Alvear's chief lieutenant. Soon he took ship for Bordeaux in France, assuring DeForest that he had $80,000 there and would repay his debts in full. "I hope it may be so," Larrea's former partner commented doubtfully, "he has not for twelve months paid me a shilling on account." In this manner the Catalonian merchant, in whom political idealism and shrewd practicality were so ambiguously mingled, passed forever out of DeForest's life.

The fall of Alvear had brought no solution for the acute political problems of the distracted country. The United Provinces of the Río de la Plata appeared to be in full process of dissolution. Weak economic ties between the vast regions composing the former viceroyalty, and rural hostility for rich and cultured Buenos Aires, underlay the trend toward disunity. Artigas in the Banda Oriental, Güemes in Salta, lesser potentates in other provinces, under the slogan of "federalism" expressed the suspicion of the rude democracy of the countryside concerning *porteño* designs. For decades this problem, in its constitutional aspect of a balance between the powers of the central government and the provinces, was to engross Argentine political thought and activity.

In a letter written to a friend in New York, an extract from which was published in a leading American newspaper, DeForest gave a sober estimate of the military and political prospects of his adopted country. The patriots had recently fought and disastrously lost the battle of Sipe Sipe in Upper Peru, November 23, 1815. "Our physical force," he affirmed, "as well as our military means, are fully competent to the task of defeating all the attempts of Spain to subjugate the country; but we are unaccustomed to self government, and possess, but very partially indeed, the stubborn virtue and determined patriotism of the North Americans. However, the country must and will be independent, notwithstanding all the follies of its inhabitants, who are rapidly increasing in numbers, and even by their defeats are learning the art of war." [23]

Independence was a crucial issue at the provincial congress of Tucumán, summoned by the provisional government that the *cabildo* of Buenos Aires had established after the fall of Alvear.

---

23. *National Intelligencer* (Washington), May 14, 1816.

As an earnest of its desire to achieve a truly national union and avoid imputations of *porteño* supremacy, the Buenos Aires *junta* had selected a site distant from the capital, and hallowed by Belgrano's great victory of 1812. From all the provinces save the Banda Oriental and the three littoral provinces deputies slowly arrived. Not until March 24, 1816, did the congress begin its sessions. Action on a definitive constitution was again delayed; many members viewed with favor a constitutional monarchy under a European king, but no eligible candidate was immediately available and the scheme was repugnant to the democratic sentiments of the Argentine people. There was general agreement, however, on the desirability of proclaiming the independence that had long been exercised in practice. On July 9, 1816, the congress solemnly declared the United Provinces of South America[24] "a nation free and independent of King Ferdinand VII, of his successors, of the mother country and of any other foreign domination"; and to this end the signers, in obvious imitation of the North American precedent, pledged "the security and guarantee of their lives, their property and their reputation." [25] Possibly some of the members had drawn inspiration from two books that DeForest opportunely advertised in a Buenos Aires newspaper on March 31, 1816, as "worthy of the notice of the people in the present crisis." [26] One contained translations of extracts from Thomas Paine's political writings, under the title, *La independencia de Costa Firme justificada por Thomas Paine treinta años ha;* included in this volume were translations of the Declaration of Independence of July 4, 1776, the Articles of Confederation, the Constitution of the United States, and the constitutions of Connecticut, Massachusetts, New Jersey, Pennsylvania, and Virginia.[27] The translator, a Venezuelan patriot named García de Sena, had written the second book, entitled *Historia concisa de*

24. Luis P. Varela, *Historia constitucional de la República Argentina* (4 vols., La Plata, 1910), II, 529 n., affirms that this name was chosen in place of the traditional phrase, "United Provinces of the Río de la Plata," in order to establish a likeness of origins (*paridad de origenes*) with the United States of North America. Both names, however, were used with little distinction during the revolutionary period.

25. The text of the Declaration (in English translation) may be consulted in F. A. Kirkpatrick, *A History of the Argentine Republic* (Cambridge, Eng., 1931), p. 241.

26. *Gaceta de Buenos Aires,* March 31, 1816.

27. William S. Robertson, *Hispanic-American Relations with the United States* (N. Y., 1923), pp. 70–71.

los Estados Unidos desde el decubrimiento de América hasta el año 1807.[28]

All diplomatic ambiguities cast aside, the Argentine people at last stood forth as a "free and independent nation." A grave danger, however, menaced the infant state. The Bourbon King of Spain, restored to his throne in 1814, had already sent to northern South America a powerful army that soon ended practically all patriot resistance in the provinces of Venezuela and New Granada. A like fate threatened his rebellious subjects of Buenos Aires. It was to ward off the anticipated invasion, by crippling attacks on Spanish convoys and seaborne commerce, that the United Provinces now launched a great privateering campaign with the aid of North American ships, commanders, and crews.

28. A North American visitor to Buenos Aires in 1818 observed that these two books had been read "by nearly all who can read, and have produced a most extravagant admiration of the United States." Henry M. Brackenridge, *Voyage to South America . . . in the Years 1817 and 1818* (2 vols., Baltimore, 1819), II, 214.

IX

"A DASH AT THE DONS"

THREE passengers landed at Annapolis on January 17, 1816, from the brig *Expedition*, Captain John Chase, thirty-three days out of Buenos Aires. They were bound on separate yet not unrelated missions. One was a young and handsome South American patriot, José Miguel Carrera, the most renowned of three brothers of tragic destiny.[1] He came to the United States in search of aid for a liberating expedition to his native Chile, lately reconquered by Spanish arms. In his possession were letters from David C. DeForest, commending "Don José Miguel Carrera, late President of Chile, and now in exile," to the favorable attention of merchants Samuel Carp and John Jacob Astor of New York, Walter and Nixon of Philadelphia, and Robert Oliver and Thomas Tenant of Baltimore.[2]

Captain Marcena Monson was the name of the second passenger; he was the confidential agent of David C. DeForest. Monson came of an old and worthy Connecticut family, and his father dispensed spiritual advice to a flock in the town of Huntington.[3] A letter from DeForest to a merchant of Baltimore introduced Captain Monson as one who for some years past had been employed by a New York firm on "voyages of peculiar

1. Benjamín Vicuña Mackenna, *El ostracismo de los Carreras* (Santiago de Chile, 1857, and later editions), is the classic account of the misfortunes of the Carrera brothers and their tragic end. Miguel Varas Velásquez, *Don José Miguel Carrera en Estados Unidos* (Santiago, 1912), first published in the *Revista chilena de historia y geografía*, 1912, num. 7 y 8, is based on Carrera's diary of his stay in the United States. S. F. Bemis, *Early Diplomatic Missions from Buenos Aires*, pp. 30–33, utilizes fresh archival sources as well as published materials in his summary of Carrera's mission.

2. These letters were all dated November 7, 1815. DeForest's letterbook for the period of his major privateering activity is now missing, but I have been able to use a set of transcripts and abstracts drawn off from this letterbook by Col. George Butler Griffin (the son of one of DeForest's daughters) for the use of J. W. De Forest when he was preparing a family history. These notes, which form part of the J. W. De Forest Papers in the Yale University Library, will hereafter be cited as the G. B. Griffin Notes.

3. Myron A. Munson, *The Munson Record* (2 vols., New Haven, 1896), I, 170–171.

delicacy and confidence." [4] Now he was bound for Baltimore, there to negotiate most secretly for the outfitting of privateers to cruise against Spanish commerce under the flag of Buenos Aires. Captain Monson himself, it had been agreed, was to assume command of one of these vessels.

The third emissary was also a seafaring man. Captain Thomas Taylor hailed from the town of Wilmington in Delaware, but in recent years he had been active in the naval service of the United Provinces of La Plata. He, too, was bound for Baltimore in order to "initiate and encourage (*entablar y propagar*) privateering enterprise against the vassals of the King of Spain," [5] and to this end he brought six blank patents for disposal among interested merchants. Taylor had sailed in the *Expedition* by a very scanty margin, for the brig was two days out of the port of Buenos Aires and about to leave the river when he clambered aboard after a hot pursuit along the shore. The observant Carrera, noting the discomfiture of Captains Chase and Monson, confided to his diary that they were put out because they had agreed with David C. DeForest to sail for the United States without Taylor. Behind this intrigue, he surmised, was the interesting circumstance that everyone concerned had privateering patents to dispose of in the United States: Taylor had six, DeForest four, Monson one, Chase one. [6]

With unerring judgment, the voyagers from Buenos Aires had selected Baltimore as the base for their warlike operations against Spain. During the late conflict with Britain this town had gained

4. DeForest to Robert Oliver, Buenos Aires, n. d., G. B. Griffin Notes.

5. Thomas Taylor to the Supreme Director Pueyrredón, Buenos Aires, Feb. 19, 1818, Archivo General de la Nación (Buenos Aires), S[ala] 1, A[rmario] 2, A[naquel] 4, núm[ero] 3. Charles C. Griffin, "Privateering from Baltimore during the Spanish-American Wars of Independence," *Maryland Historical Magazine* (March, 1940), XXXV, 1–25, is an intensive study of the Baltimore end of the Buenos Aires-Baltimore privateering axis, based on United States court records. Two valuable works on the corsairs of Buenos Aires are Lewis W. Bealer, *Los corsarios de Buenos Aires* (Buenos Aires, 1937); and Theodore S. Currier, *Los corsarios del Río de la Plata* (Buenos Aires, 1929). T. S. Currier, *Los cruceros del "General San Martín"* (Buenos Aires, 1944), a case study in privateering based on United States court records, appeared after most of the work on this book had been completed.

6. Carrera's Diary, Nov. 11, 1815, quoted in Miguel Varas Velásquez, *Don José Miguel Carrera en Estados Unidos* (Santiago de Chile, 1912), p. 15. Carrera's rather vague wording is that Chase and Monson, "de acuerdo con Deforest [*sic*], habian violentado el viaje por llegar sin Taylor a los Estados Unidos."

fame through the exploits of its many privateers. Here resourceful shipbuilders had developed a type of craft ideally suited for such ventures, the Baltimore clipper, fast and rakish, designed for speed and ability to sail close to the wind. Fortunes had been made in those years of Baltimore's privateering glory. Then came peace, and, after a brief flurry of activity in the carrying trade to Europe, a great quiet and sadness descended upon the once roistering town. The swift ships were laid up; their crews, prize money spent, lounged about the docks; and even well-to-do merchants and shipowners felt the pinch of hard times. Upon this sorry scene now entered the agents from Chile and Buenos Aires, bringing·promise of employment for idle capital, ships, and crews.

Presently Baltimore felt the stimulating touch of their demand. In December, 1816, after a long siege of failure, José Miguel Carrera sailed away with three ships and a motley band of adventurers, guaranteeing payment by the still inexistent government of Chile to the trusting outfitters, Darcy and Didier. Meantime Captains Monson and Taylor had prevailed upon various merchants to arm and send to sea a number of privateers. Among the first to put out were the *Romp* and the *Orb*, both veterans of the Anglo-American War of 1812. Lest federal authorities interfere in these ventures on the ragged edge of legality, the corsairs cleared as merchantmen with crews of normal size and took on the rest of their complements after leaving port. Once at sea they discarded their prosaic names in favor of the more sonorous *Santafecino* and *Congreso*, hoisted the sky-blue-and-white ensign of Buenos Aires to the mizzen top, fired a salute under the flag amid the cheers of the crew, and set off in search of Spanish prey.

These were the beginnings of a spectacular chapter in the history of North American participation in the winning of Argentine independence. For a space of several years thousands of Americans carried on hostilities against Spanish commerce in privateers built in American shipyards and owned by American citizens. Of this unneutral activity Baltimore was the center, and she gloried in her depravity. When a bill designed to strengthen the neutrality law was introduced into Congress, John Randolph, with his usual acrid wit, called it a bill to make peace between the town of Baltimore and Spain. "We have been informed," exulted a Buenos Aires newspaper, "that the people of Baltimore are the greatest enthusiasts in the United States for the cause of our

liberty. Its merchants have reduced Spanish commerce to an unhappy state." [7] Matters came to such a pass that a respectable
merchant could not procure a crew for his ship waiting to proceed on a legal voyage: "The universal reply was, *he must wait
until another Privateer arrived;* for that every one now in port
had shipped on board some one of these cruizers; and the consequence is, our honest merchants are obliged to send to Philadelphia, (where pirates and privateersmen do not meet similar
encouragement and facilities,) in order to procure seamen to enable them to send their vessels abroad." [8]

To the American Government, engaged in difficult negotiations
with Spain over the Florida question; and above all to Secretary
of State John Quincy Adams, who had the onerous task of replying to the well documented charges of the Spanish minister concerning the outfitting of insurgent privateers within the United
States, in violation of the Treaty of 1795 between Spain and the
United States and the neutrality laws of the United States
itself,[9] the privateering issue was a constant source of annoyance
and embarrassment. The small force of revenue cutters available
for police duties was quite inadequate to patrol the extensive
territorial waters of the United States. In the Chesapeake Bay
area, the principal seat of outfitting activity, the interest of some
public officials in the industry, the tolerance of many citizens for a
practice by which numbers of their townsmen gained a living, and
the sympathy of others for the insurgent cause, gave rise to few
arrests and fewer convictions. Indeed, a letter to a Baltimore
newspaper gave notice that "any judge who should presume to
condemn the privateersmen under South American colors could
not expect to live long, either as a judge or as a man." [10]

Since privateering was at best a business in the twilight zone
of legality, extreme precautions were taken to conceal the identity
of the solid citizens of Baltimore and other seaboard cities who
owned shares in the South American corsairs. Nominal ownership of these craft was vested in the outfitters (*armadores*) of

7. *El Censor,* March 20, 1817, quoted in L. W. Bealer, *Los Corsarios de Buenos Aires,* pp. 36–37.

8. Baltimore *Federal Republican,* in Washington *National Intelligencer,* Dec. 18, 1819.

9. For this legislation, see C. G. Fenwick, *The Neutrality Laws of the United States* (Washington, 1913).

10. Quoted in John Quincy Adams, *Memoirs* (12 vols., Philadelphia, 1874-1877), IV, 186.

Buenos Aires, in the case of vessels sailing under that flag. These men, natives or naturalized citizens of Buenos Aires, secured privateering patents from the patriot government; answered for the good conduct of the corsairs named in these licenses; disposed of prizes when brought to the home port; and generally watched over the interests of the true owners. David C. DeForest, we shall show, was the most active and successful of these agents. Other leading *armadores* were the two Aguirres, Manuel Hermenegildo and Juan Pedro; and a number of Americans, among them Thomas Taylor, William G. Ford, and John Higginbotham.[11] A commission of 10 per cent of the net proceeds of prizes appears to have been the customary share of the Buenos Aires outfitter.[12]

Baltimore rather than Buenos Aires was the fountainhead of that "system of pillage and aggression . . . against the vessels and property of the Spanish nation" of which the Spanish minister to the United States, Luis de Onís, ceaselessly complained.[13] Onís justly charged that "formal companies" had been established in Baltimore to finance privateering operations.[14] The principal syndicate in Baltimore was known as the "American Concern." [15] The typical practice seems to have been for a number of merchants to purchase one or more shares in a privateer. In the case of the Buenos Aires corsair *Tucumán*, DeForest speaks of her "numerous owners." [16] It was admitted on all sides that the firm of Darcy and Didier of Baltimore, whose Buenos Aires representative was DeForest, had the largest single interest in the privateering industry.[17] The customary share of owners, to judge

11. For the privateering patents issued by the government of Buenos Aires during the War for Independence, the authoritative source is *Las presas marítimas en la República Argentina, primera parte, 1810–1830*, in *Estudios editados por la facultad de derecho y ciencias de la Universidad de Buenos Aires*, no. XIII, Buenos Aires, 1927.

12. DeForest to Juan Pedro de Aguirre, Georgetown, Md., Dec. 19, 1818, DeForest Letterbooks, Vol. 6.

13. Onís to J. Q. Adams, Washington, Nov. 16, 1818, in W. R. Manning, *Diplomatic Correspondence*, III, 198.

14. Luis de Onís, *Memoria sobre las negociaciones entre España y los Estados Unidos . . .* (Mexico City, 1826), p. 70.

15. C. C. Griffin, "Privateering from Baltimore," p. 5.

16. DeForest to Lynch and Zimmerman, New Haven, Oct. 14, 1819, DeForest Letterbooks, Vol. 6.

17. Manuel Aguirre to the Supreme Director Pueyrredón, Washington, Aug. 30, 1817 (copy), Archivo General de la Nación (Buenos Aires), S.1 A.2–A.4, no. 9; A. J. Carranza, *Campañas navales*, III, 90 n.

from entries in DeForest's ledgers, was one-half of the proceeds from the sale of prizes.

A murky atmosphere of secrecy, suspicion, and thinly disguised anxiety emerges from such of DeForest's privateering correspondence as has come down to us. Principals in Baltimore complain of the excessive charges of the Buenos Aires *armadores;* these agents in turn darkly hint at misuse of patents in the United States; fear is expressed that aggrieved parties will resort to the courts and bring to light matters that were better hidden.[18] The use of fictitious names (DeForest thus becomes Don Carlos Cortez de Güemes in certain privateering connections),[19] the guarded and reticent language, the sudden disappearance of famous corsairs which presently turn up at lonely *rendezvous* to undergo change of name, patent, and captain, for no clearly apparent reason—these and like circumstances contribute to the prevailing mood of mystery and to the difficulties of the student who would unravel the tangled skein of privateering affairs.

Along the trade routes of the Pacific, in West Indian waters, and off the very shores of Spain, the corsairs of Buenos Aires hunted down their Spanish quarry with prodigious success. It has been estimated that "the damage relative to the total tonnage of Spanish merchant ships must have been much greater than that done by the *Alabama* and other Confederate cruisers to United States shipping." [20] The Spanish minister to the United States, suggesting a plan for the annihilation of these scourges of the sea, indicated an involuntary respect for their prowess. He proposed that Spanish armed ships should cruise in squadrons of six or eight, attacking individual corsairs and avoiding all combats in which they did not enjoy a decisive superiority. What a disgrace, fretted the excitable minister, that a band of wretched pirates in a miserable schooner should dare proclaim a blockade of all the ports of Cuba and make a jest of our navy! [21]

The very effectiveness of the patriot privateers contributed largely to their eventual downfall. Once Spanish shipping had been swept from the seas, less scrupulous elements, made desperate by

18. Much illustrative material is contained in letters from DeForest to Darcy and Didier, Juan Pedro de Aguirre, John Higginbotham, and others, in the DeForest Letterbooks, Vol. 6.

19. J. W. De Forest, *The de Forests of Avesnes,* p. 133.

20. C. C. Griffin, "Privateering from Baltimore," p. 10.

21. Luis de Onís to Irujo, Washington, Dec. 24, 1818, Archivo Histórico Nacional (Madrid), Estado, Legajo 5643 (L. C. photocopies).

the dearth of prizes, began to attack flags of all nations. Spreading political disintegration in the United Provinces of the Río de la Plata, moving toward the anarchy of the "Year XX," made difficult any strict control over vessels flying the Buenos Aires ensign. In this last degenerate period of privateering activity, the patents issued by the shadowy government of Artigas in the Banda Oriental, at war with Portugal as well as with Spain, became increasingly popular among prize-starved corsairs. Some of the more predatory brethren of the privateering fraternity turned to slave-dealing. Lying in wait in the waters about the Dutch island of St. Eustatius, Danish St. Thomas, or Swedish St. Bartholomew, they fell upon slavers come from Africa, murdered or otherwise disposed of their crews, and sold their human cargoes in "legal" fashion to planters of nearby islands. The United States consul at St. Bartholomew grew vehement in reporting the outrages perpetrated under patriot colors. "Without exaggerating," he asserted, there were "not less than fifteen hundred men" aboard the privateers cruising in these waters, "chiefly *Citizens* of the *United States* one half of which at least, are concern'd in slave dealing, and I may very justly add, that not one of them but considers a *Guinea Man* a very profitable Prize!" [22]

By the year 1819 the privateering industry had come to display all the characteristics of piracy. Horrifying tales of pillage, murder, and mutiny reached the United States, turning the once favorable opinion of patriot corsairs into hostility. An influential Washington newspaper rejoiced that it was no longer fashionable to confound privateering and patriotism, and that even in Baltimore agents could no longer be found to transact any kind of privateering business.[23] Some months later, the same journal had to deplore that there were still seven or eight privateers in Baltimore harbor, and "*encouragement* enough left for them to be fitted out." [24]

The irresponsible and piratical conduct of many privateers cruising under the flags of Buenos Aires and Venezuela moved the United States to make vigorous representations to these governments. Commodore Oliver H. Perry, dispatched on a mission

22. Robert Monroe Harrison to J. Q. Adams, St. Bartholomew, Dec. 1, 1820, National Archives (Washington), Department of State, Consular Letters, St. Bartholomew.
23. *National Intelligencer,* July 3, 1819.
24. *Ibid.,* Dec. 4, 1819.

to South America, was instructed to inform the Supreme Director Pueyrredón at Buenos Aires that "many of the privateers commissioned by the South American Governments have become common nuisances to the peaceful commerce of all Nations. That we have seen proclamations from Pueyrredon at Buenos Ayres and from General Arismendi at Margarita themselves declaring some of such Vessels Pirates. That of others the Crews have revolted and murdered or turned on shore their Captains; attacked, plundered and ravaged defenceless islands, robbed indiscriminately every vessel that came within their power; seduced the crews of some, to join them in their depredations, suborned others to make false declarations of property; to alter and disguise the marks upon bales or cases of Merchandise—transshipped whole cargoes, and stranded captured Vessels to escape the detection of their guilt, or evade the redeeming process of the law. . . . That ministers of friendly nations have complained and it was impossible to regard this state of things without effort for effectual interposition." [25]

Perry did not live to lay this formidable catalogue of complaints before Pueyrredón, but his instructions accompanied John M. Forbes when that veteran diplomat departed to take up the post of consul in Buenos Aires. Forbes succeeded where others had failed; on October 6, 1821, largely through his influence, the government of Bernardino Rivadavia abolished privateering under the flag of Buenos Aires. For some years longer, however, pirates thinly disguised as patriot privateers continued to roam the Spanish Main, waging impartial war against the commerce of all nations.

We cannot state with certainty when or how DeForest first became interested in privateering enterprise. Perhaps the successful pioneering cruise of Captain Thomas Taylor in the *Zephyr*, made in the summer of 1815,[26] stimulated his imagination, ever susceptible to projects that combined the elements of hazard and a high rate of profit. About this time a group of foreigners resi-

---

25. J. Q. Adams to Smith Thompson, Washington, May 23, 1819, National Archives (Washington), Department of State, Domestic Letters, Vol. 17. Extracts from this letter have been printed in W. R. Manning, *Diplomatic Correspondence*, I, 101–102.

26. L. W. Bealer, *Los corsarios de Buenos Aires*, p. 20.

dent in Buenos Aires petitioned the supreme director for permission to outfit privateers to cruise against Spain,[27] and DeForest may have been of their number. At any rate, it is certain that he was one of the first to conceive and act upon the happy notion of "making a fortune by a dash at the Dons." [28] In this endeavor he was notably successful. No less a figure than John Quincy Adams testified, though in a censorious spirit, that DeForest was "among the persons most deeply and extensively concerned in the privateers commissioned by that [Buenos Aires] Government." [29]

Under date of September 20, 1815, the merchant drafted a letter, copies of which were to go to John Jacob Astor of New York, George Crowninshield of Salem, Thomas Tenant and the firm of Darcy and Didier, both of Baltimore. He proposed to these magnates that they should outfit corsairs to cruise against Spanish commerce under the flag of Buenos Aires. "I lend my name to these privateers," he wrote, "and shall expect my reward in a commission of 10% on sales of prizes, holding myself to remit net proceeds as real owners may direct, and under all circumstances will protect and defend to the utmost the interests of the privateers, officers and men. To cover you from any censure by our govt. or prosecution from any irritated subject of his Catholic Majesty, I enclose to you a formal order to purchase for my account, arm and equip a ship or vessel and in my name to send her to sea with orders to capture such Spanish ships as she may meet and send them here for condemnation. Blanks in the commission you will please fill up according to circumstances." [30]

Under this arrangement, Thomas Tenant was to outfit a privateer to be called the *Potosí;* John Jacob Astor, the *Criollo de Buenos Aires;* Darcy and Didier, the *Congreso;* George Crowninshield, the *Tucumán.* Two days later, however, there was a change of plan; DeForest now wrote Tenant that he had decided to send all four commissions to the Baltimore merchant. Tenant and his friend Didier were to keep the whole secret to themselves if they wished to outfit all four vessels; if not they should take their com-

27. *Ibid.,* p. 15.
28. DeForest to Thomas Reilly, Buenos Aires, Nov. 9, 1815, G. B. Griffin Notes.
29. J. Q. Adams to Smith Thompson, Washington, May 23, 1819, cited above, note 25.
30. G. B. Griffin Notes.

missions first and send the others to Astor and Crowninshield, respectively.[31] These documents DeForest sent to Baltimore by the *Dorothea*, Captain Adams, sailing October 5, 1815. Presumably they were of an unauthorized, makeshift character, for not until October 23 did the promoter secure from the patriot government patents for the four privateers named above and two others: the *Mangoré* and the *Tupac-Amarú*.[32] These six licenses went to the United States on November 9, 1815, in the *Expedition*, owned by Darcy and Didier of Baltimore. Captain Marcena Monson, it will be recalled, also sailed on this ship, intrusted by DeForest with the management of his privateering interests in the United States.

In a letter to the owners of the *Expedition*, DeForest observed that the government of the United Provinces had granted only two other general privateering commissions, one to the *True Blooded Yankee*,[33] the other to Captain Thomas Taylor's ship, the *Zephyr* or *Céfiro*, since lost at sea. He acknowledged that privateering patents had been given to a number of vessels gone to cruise in the Pacific, but they were strictly forbidden to operate elsewhere.[34] He had not been able to prevail on the government to grant him more than six licenses, ruefully admitted the merchant, but these were "sufficient to make business for any one house." [35]

At this time DeForest also made contracts with "the most Excellent the Director of the State," Ignacio Álvarez Thomas, which governed the mode of disposal of prizes and other routine matters. The privateers were to send their captures for Buenos Aires, together with the papers necessary for condemnation proceedings, but in the event of a blockade of the river they could proceed to the Patagonian port of Río Negro, dispatching the required documents overland to the capital. Prize cargoes would be free from custom-house duties, paying the government only 15

31. DeForest to Thomas Tenant, Buenos Aires, Sept. 22, 1815, G. B. Griffin Notes.

32. *Las presas marítimas,* p. 204.

33. Otherwise known as the *Invencible,* Captain David Jewett, which departed on her first cruise in July, 1815, with a patent issued on June 23, 1815. A. J. Carranza, *Campañas navales,* III, 216–221.

34. This presumably refers to the famous expedition of Brown and Bouchard to the Pacific in 1815–1816. Ricardo Caillet-Bois has described this expedition in *Nuestros corsarios,* I, *Brown y Bouchard en el Pacífico, 1815–1816* (Buenos Aires, 1930). There is a convenient account in L. W. Bealer, *Los corsarios de Buenos Aires,* pp. 105–122.

35. DeForest to Darcy and Didier, Buenos Aires, Oct. 30, 1815, G. B. Griffin Notes.

per cent of the auction sales, and the captured vessels, their armament, tackle, and apparel were to pay no duty whatever. The
government, however, claimed a preferential right of purchase
of these articles, "at fair prices." Privateering patents were valid
for one year from the time of leaving port, but could be prolonged if deemed convenient by new and special commissions.[36]
Meantime official instructions were being prepared for the
guidance of DeForest's commanders. Article 1 of the instructions
to the captain of the *Mangoré* permitted him to "commit hostilities against, capture, or burn" every Spanish vessel, unless there
be on board "some person of rank, sent by the Spanish Government in a public character toward that of the United Provinces;
in which case you will allow him to proceed on his voyage unmolested." Article 2 warned the corsair to respect Spanish goods
not contraband of war, found under neutral flags, "as a convincing proof of the desire of the Government, to preserve friendship
and good Harmony with powers in amity and with neutrals."
Article 5 reflected the persistent patriot fears of a Spanish military expedition against Buenos Aires. Should the captain learn
that such a force was *en route* to the shores of La Plata, his chief
care must be to cut off transports, following the route of the
enemy "with a view to capture, burn and destroy as many vessels
of the Spanish convoy as possible—this service to be considered
the most important that can be rendered to the American cause."
Article 7 declared that vessels under the Spanish flag trading between the ports of Brazil and La Plata must not be molested,
"from political considerations which the Government reserves to
itself." Article 9 instructed the commander to obtain, while cruising in the Pacific, "every information you can . . . of the number of regular troops at Lima; those detached throughout the
kingdom of Chile; those sent by the Viceroy Abascal to the
succour of the army oppressing Peru; the general opinion in
Lima concerning the present state of the Peninsula; the opinion
of those people of the cause of the United Provinces; of the persons of respectability and character they consider attached to
the cause of liberty; the parties of Patriots still existing in Chile.
All these declarations you will insert in your journal." Article 10

36. "Contract . . . for the arming in North America of two Privateers under
the flag of the United Provinces to cruise against the Spanish Nation. The said
vessels to be named the Tupac-Amaru and the Mangore." Jonathan Meredith
Papers, Manuscripts Division, Library of Congress.

struck a humanitarian note. "Should you go near the islands of St. Felix and Juan Fernández, you will make signals, so that the colours of the State to which the Privateer belongs may be known: and in case there should be any Patriots exiled there for being such; you will receive them on board if they can effect their escape and forward them to this place by first opportunity." [37]

Instructions of this tenor were issued to the commander of each privateer, together with the vessel's patent, a copy of the privateering ordinance of 1801,[38] a set of officers' commissions, and a covering letter from DeForest. "As a citizen of B[uenos] A[ires]," he wrote Captains Marcena Monson and John Chase of the *Tupac-Amarú* and *Mangoré*, respectively, "I lend my name to the owner of this privateer and take upon myself all responsibility attaching to this situation. You will, therefore, be at all times on your guard as to rendering me liable to vexatious law suits, and have nothing to do with a prize of doubtful character or one that is not of considerable value." [39]

Thus instructed, and fortified with documents that attested the unimpeachable legality of their proceedings, DeForest's captains were ready to take command of the cruisers that one by one cleared from the port of Baltimore, presently to hoist the flag of Buenos Aires, mount the armament that had been stowed in the hold, and make for the Caribbean and other fields of privateering activity. Among the most celebrated of these corsairs were the *Congreso*, the *Potosí*, the *Tucumán*, the *Tupac-Amarú*, and the *Mangoré*.

Captain Joseph Almeida of the *Congreso*, the former *Orb* of Baltimore, was "a rough, open-looking, jovial jack tar," according to John Quincy Adams who met him in 1819, "who can neither write nor read." [40] No mercenary spirit, by his own account, but a sacred thirst for vengeance inspired this native of the Azores and veteran of the Anglo-American War of 1812 to take up arms against Spain. Attempting to run the blockade into patriot Car-

---

37. "Secret Instructions given by the Government of the United Provinces, to the Commander Mr. ———— for the cruize of the ———— named Mangore." Jonathan Meredith Papers, Manuscripts Division, Library of Congress.

38. Until November 16, 1816, when a formal privateering code was promulgated, the United Provinces used the Spanish privateering code of 1801. L. W. Bealer, *Los corsarios de Buenos Aires*, pp. 19–23.

39. DeForest to Marcena Monson and John Chase, Buenos Aires, Oct. 30, 1815, G. B. Griffin Notes.

40. J. Q. Adams, *Memoirs*, IV, 377–378.

tagena in 1815, Almeida had been captured by the Spaniards and thrust into General Morillo's singularly unpleasant dungeons, where he languished until released early in 1816. Swearing to revenge himself upon his jailors, Almeida departed for Baltimore and there assumed command of the *Orb*, outfitted for privateering service under a patent granted to DeForest. The corsair cleared from Baltimore in the guise of a merchantman on May 16, 1816. Thirteen days later she hoisted the flag of Buenos Aires, took the name *Congreso*, and like an avenging fury swept down on the commerce of Spain both in the West Indies and in peninsular waters. No less than six prizes of sufficient value to be sent for condemnation fell to her commander on this first cruise. When the *Congreso* came to anchor at Buenos Aires in October, 1816, her patent was about to expire, whereupon Captain Almeida purchased the vessel at public auction and secured a patent in his own name.[41] One suspects that this change of ownership was fictitious, but the reasons for the manipulation are not apparent. The *Congreso* arrived at Baltimore from a second successful cruise in the West Indies on April 2, 1817. She vanishes from sight after that date; but it appears that under the names of *Tyger* and *Pueyrredón*, with Captain John Daniels in command, this notable corsair continued to sail the seas as late as 1819.[42]

Captain Almeida not only settled some old scores with his first cruise, but enriched himself and the owners of the *Congreso*. He got a 5 per cent commission on the sale of cargoes, twelve shares of prize money as captain at 465 pesos each, and the one and one-half shares of "York Davy his Black Boy," the whole amounting to 19,506 pesos.[43] The true owners in North America received 79,744 pesos. DeForest is credited with thirty and one-half shares of prize money, amounting to 14,184 pesos. Each common sailor got a wage of one peso a day and one share of prize money. Privateersmen, however, sometimes never saw the full amount of their shares; a long time frequently elapsed before captured cargoes were realized and the proceeds distributed, and impatient

41. A. J. Carranza, *Campañas navales,* III, 84–85.
42. See the list of privateers, under *Orb,* in C. C. Griffin, "Privateering from Baltimore," p. 9.
43. All privateering figures are taken (except when other sources are indicated) from the DeForest Ledger, no. 2, where they are embedded in a number of individual accounts. They are given in Spanish pesos or silver dollars. I have omitted fractions of the dollar. Presumably Spanish and American silver dollars were roughly equivalent in value.

or needy sailors occasionally disposed of their prize tickets at a loss. Thus George Cochrane sells his share worth 465 pesos to DeForest for 375 pesos; and prizemaster William Frisby of the *Leona* similarly disposes of his eight shares for 3,200 pesos.

Brief yet spectacular was the career of the *Potosí*, the former *Spartan* of Baltimore. Her commander was Captain John Chase, late of the *Expedition*. The privateer sailed out on her first and only cruise early in 1816. Cruising in front of Cadiz, she fell in with the Spanish armed merchantman *Ciencia*. The Spaniard offered fierce resistance; but was soon humbled and forced to strike his colors. Chase transferred part of the cargo and treasure to the amount of some $20,000 to his ship, sent the prize to Port-au-Prince for condemnation,[44] and incontinently departed for the Chesapeake with his loot. Spain's minions in Baltimore exerted themselves to track down these privateering spoils. The Spanish minister Onís inveighed against the piratical activities of Chase and the complacence of Baltimore customs officers, affirming that in the hands of Henry Didier were more than $20,000 taken from the *Ciencia*.[45] Despite the ministerial fulminations, Chase continued to reside in calm and security at Norfolk, where Spanish agents discovered him enjoying the fruits of his depredations.[46] The great hue and cry raised by Onís, however, was decidedly embarrassing, and the owners of the *Potosí* evidently judged it convenient for the corsair and her captain to drop out of sight, in a manner about to be related.

From a privateering letter of DeForest's, we learn that the value of the captures of the *Potosí* amounted to 81,552 pesos. DeForest acknowledges receipt of 4,077 pesos, perhaps only partial payment of his commission. To General William H. Winder of Baltimore and three other attorneys, he paid 500 pesos for unspecified legal services.[47]

In June, 1817, the *Potosí* sailed out of New Orleans port. In the tranquil waters of the Gulf she came to anchor, and a strange little ceremony was enacted on board. Captain John Chase yielded

44. The stipulation in the privateering code of 1816 that required prizes to be sent to Buenos Aires for condemnation was frequently violated on one pretext or other. L. W. Bealer, *Los corsarios de Buenos Aires*, p. 25.

45. Luis de Onís to James Monroe, Washington, Feb. 12, 1817, W. R. Manning, *Diplomatic Correspondence*, III, 1918–1919.

46. Onís to Monroe, Washington, March 11, 1817, *ibid.*, p. 1921.

47. DeForest to Patricio Lynch, New Haven, May 11, 1819, DeForest Letterbooks, Vol. 6.

up his command to Captain George Wilson; the *Potosí* simultaneously became the *Tucumán*.[48] These formalities completed, the
corsair set off to cruise in the Caribbean, then to the Bay of Cadiz,
laying effective blockade to that Spanish port. An aggressive and
experienced sea fighter, Captain Wilson yet had in his character
a touch of idealism and a flair for dramatic expression. From his
anchorage in front of Tenerife, he reported to the Buenos Aires
ministry of war that he had taken twenty-four Spanish ships, of
which he sent four to Buenos Aires, burned four, and returned
the others to their owners. "The reason for abandoning these
craft was that for the most part they belonged to very poor men:
such men as would doubtless shake off the yoke of the imbecile
government of Spain, if they but could." [49]

The *Tucumán* came to anchor at Buenos Aires on December 3,
1817. There is no record of the value of her captures. At this
time, William P. Ford, an American who was a naturalized citizen
of the United Provinces and had an obscure association with
DeForest, purchased the *Tucumán* at public auction together
with the unexpired term of her commission.[50] Clearly this negotiation was linked with the impending departure of DeForest for
the United States, and the consequent necessity of finding a new
armador to pose as the privateer's owner and receive her captures.

The *Tucumán* sailed from Buenos Aires, bound for a cruise
in the Bay of Cadiz, on March 6, 1818. Her patent running out
on the passage, she took the name *Julia DeForest* on the strength
of a commission that Ford had secured on January 10, 1818.
Under this winsome appellation, the corsair operated with considerable success in Spanish and West Indian waters. In June,
1819, Captain Wilson brought his ship into the island of Margarita, a favorite *rendezvous* of the privateering brotherhood.
Her commission having expired, Captain Joseph Almeida now
came forward to purchase the vessel and outfit her for service
under the flag of Venezuela and the name *Almeida*, Wilson con-

48. For the successive incarnations and movements of the *Potosí*, I have relied
principally on an unsigned and undated relation (perhaps a deposition) in the
Jonathan Meredith Papers, Manuscripts Division, Library of Congress.

49. A. J. Carranza, *Campañas navales*, III, 235.

50. The patent of the *Tucumán* had been issued to DeForest on October 23,
1815, but remained deposited with the Buenos Aires secretary of war until
January 10, 1818, when it was granted to the outfitter for one year, made retro-
active to June 3, 1817, the date of the sailing of the *Tucumán* (late *Potosí*) from
New Orleans. *Ibid.*, III, 234–235.

tinuing as commander. In August, 1819, the privateer cleared
from Margarita on a cruise and in early October fell in with a
Spanish armed packet; in the ensuing action Captain Wilson
suffered wounds and the corsair's sails and rigging were badly
shattered. Shortly after this the *Almeida* limped into the Chesapeake for repairs. Here the manuscript relation on which this
account is mainly based abruptly ends; but from another source
we gather that as late as December, 1820, Captain Wilson, having recovered from his wounds, operated in West Indian waters
in command of the *Bolívar* (presumably the former *Almeida*), a
privateer of ten guns and one hundred men.[51] Whether any genu-
ine transfers of ownership accompanied these changes of identity
of the old *Spartan* or *Potosí*, it is not possible to determine.

One masterful stroke brought Captain Marcena Monson of
the *Tupac-Amarú* such success as this adventurous son of Connecticut had not dreamed of. He took his ship, the former *Regent*
of Baltimore, to sea at the end of December, 1816. Twenty-three
days later, off Cape Verde, a Spanish sail came in sight. She was
the *Triton*, a fine new ship of the Philippine Company, bound
for Spain with a precious freight of silks and other Eastern
merchandise. Monson swooped down on his quarry; but there was
no tame surrender. For two and a half hours the sea resounded
with the roar of their broadsides; the *Triton* fighting with her
twenty-two guns, the *Tupac-Amarú* with her twelve, eighteen-
and six-pounders. The Spaniard fought stubbornly and well:
when the *Triton* struck her colors twenty of her crew of eighty-
five lay dead upon the deck. The corsair had not gone unscathed;
among her fallen was young Lieutenant Francis Bulkley of New
Haven.[52]

Captain Monson was done with cruising; he sent his fabulous
prize for Buenos Aires with all the speed her shattered sails and
rigging could muster. The entire privateering world marveled at
the splendor of his windfall. After deducting 83,790 pesos for
duties and other local charges, there remained a net product of
640,000 pesos. Captain Monson got a 5 per cent commission on
the sales of the *Triton*, twenty shares of prize money, and one-

---

51. Robert M. Harrison to J. Q. Adams, St. Bartholomew, Dec. 1, 1820, National Archives (Washington), Department of State, Consular Letters, St. Bartholomew.
52. The New Haven *Columbian Register*, July 19, 1817, mourned this fatality
in an editorial note.

third of the gains from a joint speculation in prize tickets with DeForest, a total of 54,944 pesos. The heirs of Lieutenant Bulkley received ten shares of prize money, and one extra "allowed by Captain Monson on account of the extraordinary gallantry and good conduct of the unfortunate Capt. Bulkley," making 7,122 pesos in all. Each common sailor rejoiced in a prize ticket worth 647 pesos, in addition to wages of one peso a day. To the anonymous owners went the lion's share, 304,189 pesos. It is not clear what part of the proceeds fell to DeForest, but it must have been at least as large as Monson's.

Captain Monson, having made his fortune, now thought only of how to keep it untroubled by attentions from inquisitive grand juries. He retired from privateering practice, made his way back to the United States, and settled down to a secluded existence at Astoria, Long Island. His exploits, however, lived on in the memory of his Connecticut neighbors and associates. Thus in old New Haven it was told that "one Marcena Monson was captain of a privateer . . . that on a certain occasion they encountered a Spanish galleon loaded with treasure, engaged in a bloody battle and brought the wreck of the vessel safely into Buenos Ayres, that after making a fortune at privateering, Monson returned to his native land, and built himself a large and handsome house at Astoria." [53]

Captain Livingston Shannon, a New Yorker who had served as first lieutenant on the first cruise of the *Tupac-Amarú*, commanded the privateer when she sailed from the Río de la Plata on July 9, 1817, with a new patent obtained by DeForest on May 28, 1817.[54] In one hundred and fifteen days of navigation they sighted only one Spanish sail, the *Santo Cristo de la Salud*, taken September 1 near the Azores. Shannon sent this ship with her rich freight of cacao, coffee, and cotton for Buenos Aires; but $50,000 in coin found aboard were divided among the crew in conformity with privateering practice. The subsequent history of the *Tupac-Amarú* contains little of interest. As for Captain Shannon, finding privateering under the flag of Buenos Aires unprofitable, he looked about for greener pastures, and in December, 1820, cruised in the Caribbean in command of the *Invencible*, ten guns, with a patent issued by Artigas.[55]

53. M. A. Munson, *The Munson Record,* I, 171 n.
54. *Las presas marítimas,* p. 204.
55. Robert M. Harrison to J. Q. Adams, St. Bartholomew, Dec. 1, 1820, cited above, note 51.

Like so many of his comrades, Captain James Barnes of the *Mangoré*, the former *Swift* of Baltimore, had obtained his privateering novitiate in the Anglo-American War of 1812. Sailing from Baltimore in the guise of a merchantman at the beginning of August, 1816, the *Swift* entered the service of the United Provinces at Port-au-Prince toward the end of the month. In December the *Mangoré* returned to port laden with Spanish spoils which Captain Barnes declared to custom-house officials in the most natural and routine manner. After repairing and provisioning his ship, Barnes prepared to go to sea again, but at the demand of the vigilant Spanish minister the *Mangoré* was detained and embargoed in port. Legal trammels, however, could not long embarrass a privateering captain in the genial and sympathetic atmosphere of Baltimore. Soon the corsair was free to sail under bond, but now ice in the river impeded her departure. Meantime the angry Onís complained that Barnes was very tranquilly and publicly taking out of his ship "the effects plundered by him, which it is calculated, exceed eighty thousand dollars in value, without any impediment being put to his proceedings by the authorities at Baltimore." [56]

Despite these strictures, the *Mangoré* sailed from port in March, 1817, bound on a cruise in the waters about Cadiz. In four months Captain Barnes took twenty-one prizes; of these the most valuable was *La Esperanza*, a ship of the Philippine Company, captured in collaboration with the privateer *La Independencia del Sud*, Captain James Chayter. From this cruise Barnes put into Buenos Aires in August, 1817. The commission of the *Mangoré* was now about to expire, and DeForest, her nominal owner, had already resolved to leave shortly for the United States. These circumstances probably prompted the sale of the vessel to the *armador* John Higginbotham, who on November 20, 1817, secured from the government of the United Provinces a patent for a privateer to be known as the *Pueyrredón*, in honor of the new supreme director of the state.[57] Under this name, the old *Mangoré* continued to operate against Spanish commerce until November, 1819, when she entered the service of Artigas as the *Tigre Oriental*.[58] As late as December, 1820, a

56. Luis de Onís to James Monroe, Washington, Feb. 11, 1817, W. R. Manning, *Diplomatic Correspondence*, III, 1917.

57. A. J. Carranza, *Campañas navales*, III, 231.

58. L. W. Bealer, *Los corsarios de Buenos Aires*, p. 219.

corsair of this name, commanded by one Murray, cruised in the Caribbean.[59] There is no record of the value of the captures of the *Mangoré*, but it is known that Darcy and Didier of Baltimore had a heavy interest in this privateer.[60]

The privateering business had many ramifications, and De-Forest utilized all of them to put money in his purse. He had a large interest in the prizes taken; he bought up the shares of officers and men; the "house" bought the cargoes sold by him as auctioneer and speculated in them. In these last years of his stay in Buenos Aires, DeForest's financial affairs assume a rather complicated character. Patricio Lynch, lately head clerk and junior partner, turns into Patricio Lynch and Co.; and still later into Lynch, Zimmerman, and Co.[61] About this time DeForest also aided Lynch's young brother Estanislao to set himself up in business at Santiago de Chile in company with the American Henry Hill, who had come to Buenos Aires as supercargo of the *Salvaje* in José Miguel Carrera's ill-starred expedition.[62] In later years DeForest ever regarded this fomenting of mixed North and South American commercial enterprises as one of his chief claims to honor.[63]

By the close of the year 1817, it would appear, DeForest had attained that goal of "wealth, honor and happiness" to which as a youth of twenty-four he had ingenuously aspired. He was worth a sum conservatively estimated by a family historian at $150,000. The *chacra* or country estate was valued at another $20,000. He was a financial pillar of his adopted country. When the American consul to Buenos Aires, Thomas Halsey, demurred at asking United States merchants resident in the city to make a large loan

59. Robert M. Harrison to J. Q. Adams, St. Bartholomew, Dec. 1, 1920, cited above, note 51.

60. L. W. Bealer, *Los corsarios de Buenos Aires*, p. 56.

61. John C. Zimmerman, "a young German gentleman of New York," made his advent in Buenos Aires as supercargo of the schooner *Kemp* from Baltimore, which arrived on August 29, 1815, bringing military and naval stores. The firm-name of "Lynch, Zimmerman & Co." first appears in the DeForest papers in October, 1817. J. W. De Forest, *The de Forests of Avesnes*, p. 126.

62. Henry Hill, many years later, told the story of his South American experiences in his inchoate memoirs, *Recollections of an Octogenarian* (Boston, 1884). Eugenio Pereira Salas has described his career in Chile in *Henry Hill, comerciante, vice-consul y misionero* (Santiago, Chile, 1940). Hill's voluminous business correspondence and other papers are now preserved in the Yale University Library.

63. DeForest to William H. Crawford, Secretary of the Treasury, New Haven, Aug. 1, 1820, DeForest Letterbooks, Vol. 7.

to the hard pressed government, DeForest came forward with the money. "Desirous," he proclaimed, "of maintaining the honor and patriotism of the people of my native country to the best of my ability, I·have this day delivered the sum of 6,851 pesos and 6 reals, and assure you as a citizen of these provinces that I will do all I can to assist this government, which I support warmly." [64]

All Buenos Aires knew the North American merchant, Don David of the stocky frame, swarthy features, shrewd dark eyes, and imperious bearing. They told of his prodigious wealth, princely hospitality, and impulsive kindness; of his arbitrary temper and cutting sarcasm. Some remembered the young foreigner who had landed at Buenos Aires at the turn of the century, bringing only his slight baggage of Yankee notions, a ready tongue, and the assurance of youth; and they marveled how far he had come. Now DeForest was on terms of intimacy with the rulers of the state, Pueyrredón, San Martín, Tagle; a secret document of the time listed him among the "individuals who figure in or have some influence on the present affairs of Buenos Aires." [65]

Despite such evidences of prosperity and high social standing, all was not well with this adopted citizen of Buenos Aires. A gnawing anxiety beset him. Now forty-four years old, with a turbulent career behind him, DeForest longed intensely to return to the peace of steady old Connecticut. But what would be the fate of his curiously gotten fortune if he returned to the United States? In more than one case heard in the courts of Baltimore he had ostentatiously figured as owner of privateers that Spain branded as pirates. An American citizen, he had flagrantly violated his country's neutrality law. If the American government were disposed to overlook his offenses, would Spain's agents be equally indulgent? He had a family, hostages to fortune, and dared not risk disaster by one rash, unpremeditated move. Against all contingencies that might arise from his return to the States he must first prepare safeguards. Cares of this sort weighed heavily on DeForest's mind in the closing months of the year 1817.

Two visitors from North America came to know DeForest at this period; but their descriptions of him can hardly be said to

64. DeForest·to José D. Trillo, Buenos Aires, Oct. 18, 1816, Archivo General de la Nación (Buenos Aires), S.1–A.2–A.4, no. 8.

65. H. Zorraquín Becú, *De aventurero yanqui a consul porteño en los Estados Unidos*, pp. 39–40 n.

agree. One was Henry Hill, the supercargo of the *Salvaje* mentioned above, who landed in March, 1817, carrying letters of introduction to DeForest from friends in Baltimore. The merchant was not in his counting-room when Hill called; and the traveler, accompanied by young Manuel Lynch, rode out to the *chacra*. "We found Mr. and Mrs. DeForest writing at separate tables; and she said, with a smile, that she was assisting her husband as clerk, and was copying one of his letters. After I had concluded my business with him, it was in vain that I proposed to return to town before dinner. The writing apparatus was laid aside, and we took a walk among his fruit trees. The figs were delicious, and it was the first time I had ever plucked them from the trees. His house is on a rising ground; the river is in full view, and on the right is the city of Buenos Ayres, with an extensive, verdant plain between. He has a large *hacienda*, or plantation; and the Madeira nuts, peaches and other fruit on the table, were part of its produce. On our way home Don Manuel and I found it pretty warm and dusty, but we had a pleasant ride." [66]

DeForest displayed a kindly interest in his young visitor; at the home of General San Martín's father-in-law he introduced him to the great soldier, just returned from a victorious campaign in Chile; he also gave Hill valuable letters of introduction to correspondents in that country. "Mr. DeForest," wrote Hill many years after this encounter, "was a man of commanding form and fine personal appearance, and naturally was high-spirited, imperious, yet dignified, gentlemanly, affable and very interesting in conversation." [67]

Jeremy Robinson of Massachusetts, who called on DeForest almost one year later, had obtained a commission as special agent of the United States in Lima from President Monroe, only to have his appointment abruptly revoked just before his departure.[68] Robinson nevertheless decided to travel in South America for his health, and also to study the progress of the sciences and letters in that little known part of the world. He sailed for La Plata in November, 1817, in the brig *Columbus*, commanded by

66. H. Hill, *Recollections of an Octogenarian*, pp. 111–112.
67. *Ibid.*, pp. 113–114.
68. On Robinson's travels in South America, see Eugenio Pereira Salas, "Jeremías Robinson, agente norteamericano en Chile (1818–1823)," *Revista chilena de historia y geografía*, LXXXII (1937), 201–236, based on the Jeremy Robinson Papers, Manuscripts Division, Library of Congress. I have made independent use of these papers, particularly of Robinson's Diary.

the future rear-admiral of Chile, Charles W. Wooster. Robinson carried a letter of introduction to DeForest from Darcy and Didier of Baltimore.

The *Columbus* anchored in the port of Buenos Aires on February 4, 1818. Her arrival coincided with the rise of a crisis in the affairs of the American consul to La Plata, Thomas L. Halsey. The Pueyrredón régime, accusing Halsey of furnishing munitions to Artigas and of accepting privateering commissions from the gaucho chieftain, decreed the consul's banishment.[69]

The ruined Halsey met Robinson shortly after his arrival in Buenos Aires, and poured into his sympathetic ear a story of unmerited sufferings. He denied having assisted Artigas or having received privateering commissions from that wandering ruler of the pampas. The author of his downfall, he affirmed, was David C. DeForest, who from motives of commercial jealousy had prevailed upon the Supreme Director Pueyrredón to banish him (Halsey) from the country.

The credulous Robinson listened, believed, and was properly incensed at this insult to the dignity of the United States and at the malignity of DeForest. He did not know that an order from Washington for Halsey's dismissal, based on his well substantiated privateering activities and other charges, was on its way, crossing Pueyrredón's demand for the consul's recall. It was in a hostile mood that Robinson made the acquaintance of the much abused DeForest. In his diary he recorded some impressions of this meeting.

"Dined with Mr. DeForest. He is assuming inflated and impudent in the extreme. A few years ago this gentleman came to this country poor. He acquired some little wealth and applied rather indecorously to the President of the U S for the consular appointment to this place. His rudeness offended the President and he would not listen to Mr. DeForest's application. The consequence has been that he hates and will annoy the Government of the United States by every means in his power. The person who had been appointed to the office was negatived by the intrigues of D[e] F[orest], and his friends in the Senate of the United States, at the same time that D[e] F[orest] professed for him the warmest friendship and esteem. Here we perceive that interest and mercantile habits prostrate every generous principle to their advance-

69. On Halsey and his relations with Artigas, see C. C. Griffin, *The United States and the Disruption of the Spanish Empire*, pp. 151–154.

ment. In fine, this man is a vain, conceited purse proud arrogant arbitrary designing being who has renounced allegiance to his country and disrespects that which gives him subsistence. He has been largely concerned in Privateering as have several other Americans who are citizens of the U S in name [crossed out] in sentiment. Captain M[onso]n has imbibed the same spirit. They live together and like the other Americans here amuse themselves in gossiping and in forming machinations against each other. They all hate Mr. H[alsey] the Consul." [70]

DeForest, Robinson jotted in his journal, had been deeply engaged in the privateering business, and had accumulated so much money that he exacted "homage from every person who approaches him. He at present contemplates returning to the U States but not without fear of being troubled through the cordial but mild embrace of the law. Captain M[onson] is likewise apprehensive of similar danger and inconvenience."

From an undisclosed source Robinson learned that DeForest daily expected to be appointed consul general from the United Provinces to the United States. This intelligence elicited from the peevish tourist the observation: "Very disinterested. Invested with a new nominal allegiance to and a publick function from an unacknowledged Gt. Perhaps it will enable him to avoid the penalties due to a violation of the laws of the U S while a citizen."

One day later DeForest called on Robinson at his lodgings. The merchant confirmed the report that the government of Buenos Aires had appointed a consul general who would shortly depart for the United States. "I am anxious to know," was his tactful query, "whether he will be received or not." Robinson suggested that such an emissary might be received but not formally recognized. "I objected to it the indecent and barbarous banishment of the [U. S.] Consul General Halsey. Mr. DeForest is doubtless the person in question." [71]

DeForest was indeed the person in question. Whether his appointment was suggested by the Supreme Director Pueyrredón or by the merchant himself is not clear. But the arrangement offered obvious advantages to all concerned. For DeForest a diplomatic status signified protection from the meddlesome attentions of American courts. For Pueyrredón and his foreign minister,

70. Jeremy Robinson Diary, Feb. 19, 1818, Manuscripts Division, Library of Congress.

71. *Ibid.*, Feb. 21, 1818.

Gregorio Tagle, it presented an opportunity to send to Washington, where a heated congressional struggle over recognition of the revolted colonies was in progress, an able and resourceful agent to further their cause. Nor would there be any question of remuneration involved. Was not DeForest one of the wealthiest men in Buenos Aires?

Already the amateur diplomat had sent his wife and children to North America in the brig *Aurora*, Captain Searl, which sailed for New Haven in the spring of 1817. Now he prepared to take leave of Buenos Aires, to which he was bound by many strands of experience and recollection. He had first come to this city of azure skies, imposing churches, and white, flat-roofed homes in the remote days of the viceroys, smuggling himself and his little "adventure" across the border from Brazil. He had known here the stormy season of the British invasions, when the *porteños* first gained awareness of their strength and nationality. He had witnessed the uneasy preliminaries of the *Revolución de Mayo;* and from exile he had rejoiced at the downfall of his Spanish enemies. He had contributed to the establishment and consolidation of an independent Argentine state by word and by deed; by the diffusion of republican propaganda, by financial support to the struggling patriot government, and by his leading rôle in the promotion of privateering enterprise against Spanish commerce. In return, his adopted country had afforded him the means of achieving "wealth, honor and happiness."

Preparing to depart for the United States, DeForest gave a notable proof of his gratitude to the people and government of the United Provinces. He presented to the state his *chacra,* to be used for the endowment of the first institution of higher learning in independent Buenos Aires, the Academy of the Union of the South. His communication on this subject, and the letter of acceptance from the government, appear together in a handsomely printed folder evidently published by DeForest. On November 22, 1817, the patron of learning wrote as follows to the *gobernador intendente* of Buenos Aires, Manuel Luis de Oliden:

More than seven years ago I bought an estate [*chacra*] pleasantly situated on the coast of San Isidro, two and a half leagues distant from this Capital, on which I have expended much money, for it served me regularly as a retreat during the summer. For this reason I have a great regard for the said estate, and cannot bring myself to sell it to any private individual, no matter how attractive the offer. But this regard and every other consideration cede to the gratitude which this generous people has always inspired in me by its hospitality and the many other benefits for which I am indebted to it. It is well known that the leaders and public authorities are at present engaged in reestablishing the ancient college [*estudios*] under more liberal and beneficial principles. At the time of the establishment of the Library, which today does so much honor to Buenos Aires, I had the pleasure of collaborating by the donation of some classical works. Since the advantages of reestablishing the college among this great people are even more important, I cannot refrain from taking part in this admirable work as well. Therefore I publicly present this estate to your Lordship, with the accompanying documents of ownership, excepting only two slaves whom I have determined to set free. One only interest moves me—that of making my memory cherished by the sons of this city, and of giving one more proof of my adherence to the cause which it defends. I pray you, therefore, to accept this estate, considering only the motives that inspire this action; and to bring it to the attention of the commissioners for the reestablishment of the college, that they may make use of it in good time.

I hope soon to be reunited with my family in North America, where my concerns have called me for some time. On all occasions it will be highly pleasing for me to perform services for this city, or for its good citizens; and I hope that they will frankly consider me their most sincere friend and fellow-citizen, interested in the glory of this country.

On November 25, 1817, the government of Buenos Aires made the following reply:

This Government has the pleasure of transmitting to you the decree which I affixed yesterday to your representation offering to this country an unequivocal proof of the respect and gratitude that it deserves. The contents of this decree are of the following tenor.

"Acknowledgement is made to Citizen **DAVID CORTES DE-FOREST** of the donation that he freely makes in favor of this city with specific application to the college which it has been ordered to reestablish. The secretary of this Government will go to the home of this worthy Citizen and will thank him for his generous display of gratitude and solicitude for this city, assuring him that this Government will inscribe the names of his esteemed children in the records of the municipality, and will obtain from the most Excellent Supreme Director an order that his portrait be placed in one of the principal halls of the college in order to perpetuate his memory as a benefactor of that establishment. There shall also be established in the new college a scholarship, to be assigned with preference to the children of the donator, and in their absence, to the sons of this country who are descendants of citizens of the United States of North America. For this purpose let there be issued a corresponding order to the Minister of State charged with the reestablishment of the college, transmitting it to the donator for his intelligence and satisfaction." [72]

In these days of his departure from Buenos Aires, DeForest performed another act of sweeping generosity. He freed all his slaves, and gave to each a small sum of money with which to begin life anew. In early March, 1818, he sailed by the *Plattsburg* for the United States, where difficult official duties awaited him. No ordinary test of strength lay before DeForest, but a diplomatic duel with a statesman of great dialectical skill. After meeting and besting all obstacles as smuggler, merchant, and promoter of privateering enterprise, he was about to meet his first serious check at the hands of Secretary of State John Quincy Adams.

72. A copy of this published exchange of letters is preserved in the National Archives (Washington), Department of State, Despatches from Consuls, Buenos Aires, I, Part II.

X

"THE GREAT SOUTH AMERICAN WITCHERY"

A SUCCESSION of emissaries had voyaged from the Río de la Plata to North American shores in quest of aid for their cause since the historic twenty-fifth of May, 1810, birthday of Argentine independence.[1] We have already told of the first mission of this kind, that of Diego de Saavedra and Pedro de Aguirre, sent by the patriot *junta* of Buenos Aires to purchase arms in the United States. It will be recalled that these commissioners at last sailed for home with a sorely needed cargo of munitions, showering blessings upon the friendly neighbor of the North.

The Anglo-American War of 1812 interrupted the flow of envoys from Buenos Aires to Washington. The first visitor with any pretensions to an official character to arrive in the United States after the close of those hostilities was the redoubtable privateering captain, Thomas Taylor, who brought a letter of introduction to President Madison from General Álvarez Thomas, then supreme director of the United Provinces. As we know, Taylor came primarily to foster the progress of his interesting profession, but he also made it his business to inquire into the state of American public opinion on the insurgent cause. His researches led to the conclusion that all classes of the population sympathized with the Spanish American patriots, and that it only required an individual of "brilliance and imagination," invested with an official character by the Buenos Aires government, to set on foot a great movement in support of the revolted colonists. Such a person, Taylor suggested on his return to La Plata, was General William H. Winder of Baltimore, a prominent lawyer whose generous enthusiasm for the cause of freedom knew no bounds. Winder had publicly caned the Spanish consul in

1. For this chapter I have drawn heavily on S. F. Bemis, *Early Diplomatic Missions*, particularly on the excellent account of DeForest's mission, pp. 70–89. Professor Bemis used DeForest's personal papers, and also employed archival materials in the United States, Spain, and the Argentine. There is a brief but appreciative discussion of DeForest's consular activity in A. P. Whitaker, *The United States and Latin America*, pp. 256–259.

Baltimore for outrageous interference with the outfitting of patriot privateers; Winder proposed to leave home, family, and a secure station in life to lead patriot armies in battle against Spanish tyranny.[2] These observations were shortly to bear fruit.

Even before Captain Taylor set foot on North American shores, the Supreme Director Álvarez Thomas had designated Colonel Martín Thompson as agent to the United States (January 16, 1816). His instructions enjoined strict secrecy as to the nature of his mission, which he might divulge only to the President. He should endeavor to secure all possible material assistance, and should urge the government of the United States to use its influence with European powers in favor of the patriot cause. Thompson's mission turned out badly; he entered into unauthorized contracts with army officers for service in Buenos Aires, violated the injunction concerning secrecy, and was finally removed by the new Supreme Director Pueyrredón. Be it from this or other causes, the unlucky agent's mind became completely deranged: his successor reported him in a hospital, "hopelessly crazy." [3]

The next mission from Buenos Aires was directly related to General San Martín's strategy for the winning of continental independence. The Argentine Liberator had already crossed the Andes with his army and gained an important victory over the Spanish royalists at Chacabuco (February 12, 1817); an invasion of Peru from the sea was to follow the complete emancipation of Chile. Accordingly, San Martín, representing the government of Chile, and the Supreme Director Pueyrredón, on behalf of the United Provinces, commissioned Manuel Hermenegildo de Aguirre as chief of mission, and Gregorio Gómez as second, to proceed to the United States and purchase or have constructed there a fleet of armed vessels. By this time the historic congress of Tucumán had formally proclaimed the independence of the United Provinces of South America from Spain (July 9, 1816), but Aguirre's instructions did not direct him to solicit a recognition of independence. A letter from Pueyrredón to President Monroe described its bearer as deputed to the American Chief

2. Thomas Taylor to the Supreme Director Pueyrredón, Buenos Aires, Feb. 19, 1818, Archivo General de la Nación (Buenos Aires), S.1–A.2–A.4, no. 8. Had Taylor known of General Winder's military incompetence, strikingly manifested in the late war with Britain at the battle of Bladensburg and the capture of Washington, he would doubtless have been terrified at this last prospect.

3. S. F. Bemis, *Early Diplomatic Missions,* p. 39.

Executive "in the character of the agent of this Government," and sought for him "all the protection and consideration required by his diplomatic rank and the actual state of our relations." Another missive from San Martín to Monroe stressed the importance of Aguirre's mission to the success of his military projects and compared the struggles of the South American patriots to the trials of the North American revolutionists.[4]

Arrived in Washington, where he found President Monroe absent on a "good feeling" tour of the country, Aguirre was received in a cordial albeit informal manner by Acting Secretary of State Richard Rush. The American official assured his visitor of the sympathy with which the President and people of the United States regarded the independence struggle of the Spanish Americans. He explained that his government, pursuing a policy of strict neutrality, and bound by its treaty of commerce and amity with Spain, must remain aloof from this struggle. At the same time Rush adverted strongly to the advantages which flowed to the patriots from this policy of neutrality. Finally, the secretary advised Aguirre that within the limits of United States law he was free to purchase or have built ships and engage in every other private commercial transaction.

Despite a three day confinement in a New York jail on charges of violating American neutrality legislation—an experience that set the proud creole fairly dancing with rage—Aguirre was moderately successful as concerned the legitimate object of his mission. He had two frigates constructed and dispatched to Chile by way of La Plata. The *Curiacio* later participated in the campaign for the liberation of Peru. Not so the *Horatio*. On arrival at Buenos Aires her suspicious captain refused to hand over the ship until he received payment for a note of 69,541 pesos. Before port officials could seize the vessel he had bolted for Rio de Janeiro, where he sold the frigate to the Portuguese government to satisfy the debt.

An unauthorized adventure in diplomacy turned out less auspiciously for Aguirre. At the opening of Congress in December, 1817, Henry Clay and his partisans launched a spirited attack on the Spanish and South American policies of the administration. They railed against the neutrality act of March 3, 1817, as unfair to the patriots; they protested against the

4. These letters are printed in W. R. Manning, *Diplomatic Correspondence*, I, 352–353.

occupation by United States forces of Amelia Island, a haunt for insurgent privateers, slave-traders, and smugglers off the Florida coast and near the American border; and finally they set up a cry for the immediate recognition of the United Provinces. Aguirre, delighted at this outburst of enthusiasm for his country, hastened to confer with Secretary of State John Quincy Adams, who had taken over the duties of his office from Acting Secretary Rush on September 22, 1817.

In imitation of Clay and his followers, the rebel agent asserted the claim of Buenos Aires to recognition, and complained of the inequalities of the neutrality law and of American occupation of Amelia Island. The imperturbable Adams speedily demolished the groundwork of Aguirre's pretensions. He extracted from the tactless diplomat the confession that he had no new instructions to request recognition;[5] and asked embarrassing questions as to the exact extent of the territory under control of the Buenos Aires government (at this time the Portuguese were in possession of Montevideo and the gaucho chieftain Artigas ruled over the remainder of the Banda Oriental or present-day Uruguay). When Aguirre protested against the occupation of Amelia Island, Adams retorted with the query: Did the government of the United Provinces mean to assume a "superintendency" of all Spanish provinces in both of the continents of America? The United States should be given explicit notice of this fact, that they might regulate their policy toward that government accordingly. Aguirre realized that he had overreached himself, and beat a hasty retreat, assuring the secretary that he spoke for himself only, and without official authority.[6]

In Congress, meantime, Clay was riding hard his "South American great horse."[7] The House, stirred by his persuasive oratory, called on the President to send in all documents relating to Amelia Island and the revolted colonies. Aguirre's representations to the secretary of state, which the agent had carefully

5. Aguirre did tell Adams that he had instructions to urge the recognition of Buenos Aires "as circumstances might occur to favor the demand," but was expressly ordered not to urge it "at the hazard of embroiling the United States with any of the powers of Europe." J. Q. Adams, *Memoirs,* IV, 30, under date of December 24, 1817. But there is nothing of this tenor in the credentials and instructions carried by Aguirre as given in S. F. Bemis, *Early Diplomatic Missions,* pp. 42–45.

6. J. Q. Adams, *Memoirs,* IV, 47, under date of Jan. 22, 1818.

7. The phrase is Adams', *ibid.,* p. 28.

restated in written notes to Adams, would thus find their way into the public prints. The secretary, submitting the required papers to Monroe, appended a statement in which he emphasized that "Aguirre had no diplomatic title, no powers to treat, and that all his demands for recognition had arisen since the assembly of Congress." [8] When, after much debate, the issue of recognition came to the test in the House on March 28, 1818, on a motion by Clay to appropriate $18,000 for a minister and legation in Buenos Aires, it was beaten down by the decisive vote of 45–115. Aguirre's unauthorized and injudicious approaches to Adams had doubtless stiffened administration resistance to the recognition proposal and thereby ensured its defeat.

President Monroe and his secretary of state, it hardly needs to be said, were not unfriendly to the cause of Spanish-American independence. Adams, who on occasion voiced gloomy distrust of the patriots' capacity for self-government and questioned the supposed affinity between the peoples and revolutions of the two continents, was as solicitous as Clay to acknowledge the new states, but only when the fact of their independence and internal stability had been fully established, and when such recognition would not imperil the security of the United States. To satisfy itself completely on the first of these conditions as it concerned the United Provinces, the American government had just despatched a commission of inquiry to Buenos Aires to report on the state of affairs there.[9] Only a few weeks after Clay's crushing defeat, the secretary wrote the United States minister in Spain that if the government of Buenos Aires "should maintain that stability which it appears to have acquired since the Declaration of Independence of July 9, 1816, it cannot be long before they will demand that acknowledgment of right." [10]

The relation of the problem of recognition to the diplomatic interests and security of the United States was more complicated. It was the considered judgment of Adams that from this point of view the time for acknowledgment of the new states had not yet arrived. Delicate negotiations with Spain over Florida and the Western boundary question were in progress; the occupation of

8. S. F. Bemis, *Early Diplomatic Missions*, p. 57.
9. It was composed of Theodorick A. Bland, Caesar A. Rodney, and John Graham. For the mission, see Watt Stewart, "The South American Commission, 1817–1818," *Hisp. Am. Hist. Rev.*, IX (1929), 31–59. The reports of the commissioners are printed in W. R. Manning, *Diplomatic Correspondence*, I, 382–438.
10. Adams to George W. Erving, Washington, April 20, 1818, *ibid.*, p. 61.

Amelia Island had exacerbated the already inflamed peninsular sensibilities; and Adams still feared that if Spain should go to war with the United States over recognition of her revolted provinces, she might find European support. The dangers to which premature recognition might expose the United States became plain from the information which the secretary obtained by circuitous channels in May, 1818, that Great Britain had consented to a general mediation by the European powers to bring about the pacification of Spanish America.[11] To draw England away from collaboration with her reactionary allies on this issue and into a joint acknowledgment with the United States of the independence of the revolted colonies, meantime preserving a posture of strict official neutrality toward the struggle as the best means of averting European armed intervention on the side of Spain, was the prudent course of diplomatic action adopted by the Monroe administration at this juncture. It was a course of policy, as Adams never wearied of reminding importunate South American emissaries, that fully conformed to the true interests of their countries.

The indiscretions of an American special agent to South America were directly responsible for the decision of the Buenos Aires authorities to appoint David C. DeForest as Aguirre's successor at Washington. William G. D. Worthington was sent to Buenos Aires in 1817 to disavow a loan agreement made with the Supreme Director Pueyrredón in the name of the United States government by an earlier agent, Colonel John Devereux, and to promote trade relations between the two countries. Arrived at the Río de la Plata, however, Worthington "swelled upon his agency" until he broke out "into a self-accredited Plenipotentiary," in the words of the angry Adams,[12] and drew up with Pueyrredón a set of articles that amounted to a provisional treaty of amity and commerce.

Encouraged by this seeming portent of recognition by the United States, the supreme director now for the first time addressed a formal request for acknowledgment of independence to President Monroe.[13] At the same time the Buenos Aires government arranged for a more adequate diplomatic representation at

---

11. A. P. Whitaker, *The United States and Latin America*, p. 251.
12. *Memoirs*, IV, 158–159.
13. This letter is printed in W. R. Manning, *Diplomatic Correspondence*, I, 370–371.

Washington. To DeForest, who had his private reasons for wishing to return to North America covered by the immunities of a diplomatic character, Pueyrredón tendered, as we already know, the post of consul general. On the recommendation of Captain Thomas Taylor, the supreme director also appointed General William H. Winder of Baltimore as special deputy of the United Provinces near the government of the United States. A letter from Pueyrredón to the "hero of Canada" besought him to accept the appointment, or, at least, to lend his protection to DeForest, the bearer of Winder's credentials.[14]

DeForest's own instructions (dated February 24, 1818) embodied six articles. The first three placed him under the general obligations of consuls, empowered him to appoint vice-consuls, and declared that until an ambassador or other emissary should be sent to the United States, he was to endeavor to obtain recognition of independence by the United States and all other manner of assistance. Article 4 enjoined DeForest to make every effort to refute the slanders (*especies*) circulated in North America by a group of political exiles from Buenos Aires that included José Agrelo, Manuel Dorrego, and Manuel Moreno, the brother of the famous revolutionary leader.[15] The consul general should not imitate these "detractors," but must seek to win them over to the Pueyrredón régime. The next article authorized DeForest to issue privateering patents in the United States; accordingly, on March 2, 1818, he was given blank commissions for two frigates, six corvettes, twenty brigs, and twenty schooners, with the corresponding officers' commissions, including one made out to our old acquaintance Marcena Monson, now become "colonel and commander-in-chief of the squadron of this state in the North Atlantic." [16] Article 6 suggested a major object of DeForest's mission. "In case our corsairs should occupy some island suitable as a base and to which none of the recognized nations have any right, the said consul is empowered to set up such a municipal government there as may seem best to him, taking possession of the island in the name of this government." [17]

14. Buenos Aires, Feb. 25, 1818, Archivo General de la Nación (Buenos Aires), S.1–A.2–A.4, no. 8.

15. C. C. Griffin, *The United States and the Spanish Empire*, pp. 127–128, describes the activities of this group.

16. A. J. Carranza, *Campañas navales*, III, 242.

17. Confidential instructions for DeForest as consul general in the United States, draft, Buenos Aires, Feb. 24, 1818, Archivo General de la Nación (Buenos Aires), S.1–A.2–A.4, no. 8.

An accompanying letter from Pueyrredón to President Monroe stated that in conformity with the articles agreed upon with the United States agent William G. D. Worthington, he had appointed David C. DeForest as consul general to the United States, with the powers specified in his commission and instructions respectively.[18] "DeForest's credentials," observes Professor Bemis, "were thus based on the unsafe authority of Worthington's unauthorized agreement, and we may presume that the alert John Quincy Adams would not fail to note this, should he find it convenient to do so." [19]

Accompanied by young Manuel Lynch, bound for the United States to learn English and obtain a commercial education, the amateur diplomat sailed from Buenos Aires in the first days of March, 1818, in the United States frigate *Plattsburg*. From this vessel had just disembarked a commission of inquiry despatched by President Monroe to report on the progress of the revolution in the Río de la Plata. DeForest and his companion landed at Baltimore on April 28.

Arrived at that thriving center of privateering enterprise, the envoy placed in the hands of General Winder his appointment as deputy from the United Provinces near the government of the United States. The lawyer, much gratified at the honor thus thrust upon him, asked for time to consider the propriety of acceptance. He immediately notified President Monroe of the designation and sought his opinion on the subject. Monroe unhesitatingly encouraged his old friend to accept the post, and appended a brief but vigorous defense of the administration's South American policy, presumably for the edification of the Buenos Aires authorities.[20] Winder nevertheless finally turned

18. W. R. Manning, *Diplomatic Correspondence*, I, 377–378.
19. S. F. Bemis, *Early Diplomatic Missions*, pp. 73–74.
20. "I have no hesitation to state to you, that the sincere desire of this government, is, that the Spanish Colonies may achieve their independence, and that we shall promote it, by our councils and interest, with other powers, when we have any, and by every honourable and impartial measure, which we can adopt, consistently, with our neutrality, and without compromising, the highest interests of our country. I am satisfied that the true interest of the Colonies, consists, in leaving us perfectly free, to pursue, such course, in regard to them, as we think proper, and that on the ground of interest, there can be no disagreement much less collision between us. It is a miserably shortsighted, and contracted policy, in those who represent the Colonies, or patronize their interest, to pursue a different course, since its tendency is to deprive them of the friendship, of the only power on earth, sincerely friendly to them, and of the immense advantages which they derive, by the supplies, which they receive from us, and from the

down the offer, and in his letter of declination set forth as emanating from himself the substance of Monroe's cogent remarks. He also affirmed that DeForest appeared to have the needful qualifications for his office, and promised to aid the consul general with his advice.[21]

After his visit to Winder, DeForest departed for Washington. At the Department of State, where he left his credentials, he learned that the President had just set out for his home in Virginia and would not return till the following week. This the envoy from Buenos Aires soon found to be a fortunate circumstance, for in the intervening days he could orient himself politically and discover that the campaign launched in Congress for the recognition of the United Provinces by "our own warm friends," meaning Clay and his group, had embarrassed and irritated the President.[22] Shrewdly DeForest concluded that for the present it would be prudent to conceal his intention of soliciting recognition. Meanwhile he lost no time in making the acquaintance of Clay, to whom he presented a letter of introduction from John Graham, one of the commissioners sent by the President to Buenos Aires.

Responding to a note from Secretary of State Adams, DeForest appeared for an audience at the department on the afternoon of May 7, 1818. Adams must have eyed his visitor with a peculiar interest. He knew more of the privateering past of this adventurer from Connecticut than DeForest suspected. Thomas L. Halsey, ex-consul of the United States in Buenos Aires, had lately furnished the secretary with some gratuitous information on that subject.[23]

After the customary exchange of civilities, Adams turned to the business at hand. He explained to DeForest that the treaty which Worthington had presumed to make with the Supreme

countenance which we give them and for what purpose encounter this danger? Equally satisfied I am, that were we ever to engage in the war, in their favour, they would be losers by it." Monroe to Winder, Washington, May 11, 1818. This correspondence between Monroe and Winder has been printed in the *Hisp. Am. Hist. Rev.*, XII (1932), 457–461.

21. Winder to Gregorio Tagle, Baltimore, June 5, 1818, Archivo General de la Nación (Buenos Aires), S.1–A.2–A.4, no. 8.

22. DeForest to Tagle, Baltimore, May 17, 1818, Archivo General de la Nación (Buenos Aires), S.1–A.2–A.4, no. 8.

23. See Halsey to Adams, Buenos Aires, Jan. 25, 1818, National Archives (Washington), Department of State, Despatches from Consuls, Buenos Aires, I, Part 2.

Director Pueyrredón at Buenos Aires, and on which DeForest's appointment was based, had been made without authority and was therefore wholly null and void. Under existing circumstances, he went on, it was not deemed prudent to acknowledge the independence of the United Provinces, and consequently De-Forest could not be formally received in the capacity of consul general, since that would be tantamount to a recognition of his government. He was free, however, to reside anywhere in the United States and to act in his official character as if he were received in due form. He might hold correspondence with the Department of State and would receive all proper attentions and respect from the American government.

DeForest mildly rejoined that his agency was only commercial in nature, and should not be regarded as bearing a political character. The United States had sent a similar agent to Buenos Aires, where he was duly accredited; and the government of the United Provinces had not thought there would be any objection to granting a like status to DeForest. It was an appointment of very little consequence, to be sure; he, DeForest, had not solicited it; it had been given to him on the eve of his return to the United States, where he intended to remain, in order to prevent the irregularities committed by privateers flying the flag of Buenos Aires, irregularities of which the Supreme Director Pueyrredón entirely disapproved. After these cautious and self-deprecatory remarks, DeForest asked whether he should show his commission to Adams, and whether he would receive an answer to his written application for an *exequatur*.

The secretary readily perceived the purport of DeForest's clever and plausible suggestion that an exchange of commercial agents could be made by the two countries without a formal recognition of the independence of Buenos Aires by the United States. He immediately rebuffed this ingenious effort to smuggle recognition in by the back door. The United States, Adams pointed out, had appointed many consuls to reside at colonial establishments. They were seldom received with their regular titles, but were generally allowed to act as commercial agents. At Buenos Aires, it was true, Consul Halsey had been formally received. But this was a wholly voluntary act on the part of the Buenos Aires government, which might have declined to do so without any offense to the United States. DeForest's appointment as consul general, on the other hand, was expressly based on the Worthington agreement, which was entirely disavowed. As to writing, the cautious Adams thought it unnecessary; it would be more consistent with delicacy if they understood each other verbally. If DeForest should apply in writing for an *exequatur*, however, he would receive an answer in the same manner.

DeForest hastened to assure the secretary that his government was not disposed to urge any point which might be disagreeable to the United States; he would be careful not to take any step which might embarrass the administration. In reply to a question from Adams, he observed that his commission did not interfere with that of Aguirre, which was merely to procure arms, naval stores, and an armed vessel. In this connection, he confirmed that Aguirre had no authority to ask for recognition, had flouted the supreme director's wishes not to press the United States government on that subject, and had been instigated to his actions by other parties.[24]

The consul general from Buenos Aires had not ventured to broach in this initial conference a major object of his mission: the occupation of an island in the Gulf of Mexico as a base of privateering operations, similar to the lately extinguished establishment at Amelia Island. The next day, in the course of a second conversation with Adams, he skirted rather undiplomatically about the subject. If the government of the United Provinces should send an expedition to take Florida, he asked, would the American government take any measure to prevent it?

The secretary stiffly replied that the same law by virtue of which the United States had lately taken possession of Amelia Island[25] would apply in such a contingency to the remainder of Florida. The United States had a claim upon that province for indemnities long due from Spain, and could not suffer its occupation by a third party.

DeForest assured the secretary that the government of Buenos Aires had no part in the dubious proceedings of the adventurers who had established themselves at Amelia Island, and was entirely content with the recent occupation of the place by the United

24. The sources for this conference are the entry in J. Q. Adams, *Memoirs*, IV, 88–89, under date of May 7, 1818; and DeForest to Tagle, May 17, 1818, cited above, note 22.

25. The reference is to the act of Congress of January 15, 1811, voicing the famous "non-transfer" principle. In his interview with DeForest, Adams inadvertently stated that the law had been in existence "ever since 1815,"

States. But the possession of a port in the Gulf of Mexico would greatly aid the United Provinces in privateering operations against Spain, and if they could not take Florida there was no port in the Gulf to which their corsairs could resort.

Adams drily replied that the law of 1811 had been made without any intention to injure the interests of Buenos Aires, but while it remained in force the President was bound to execute it. He added that the commissioners sent to South America had been instructed to give suitable explanations on this subject to the supreme director at Buenos Aires.

DeForest wisely decided not to press the matter further. He informed the secretary that he would let his reception as consul general rest on these conversations without any exchange of notes.[26] Then, by prior arrangement with Adams, he went to call on the President.

The disciple of Jefferson did not scruple to show his ardent sympathy with the patriots of Buenos Aires. He lamented the cause which prevented a formal recognition of DeForest, and hoped for a speedy removal of these obstacles. "He observed that the world was in such a state that much caution was required; and that, having our commercial relations placed on an equal footing with those of Spain, was as much as could be done for us at this moment." [27]

After these unpromising exchanges with Adams and Monroe, DeForest returned to Baltimore. There Manuel Moreno, brother of the revolutionary apostle, and an exiled opponent of Pueyrredón, sought him out. The refugee, evidently in straitened circumstances, was eager to be permitted to return to Buenos Aires. As directed by his instructions, DeForest received the repentant Moreno in friendly fashion, and accepted his professions of renewed allegiance to the supreme director at their face value. He introduced the exile to General Winder as one who might be usefully employed "in any business relating to our country," meaning of course privateering business; and wrote home a favorable report on Moreno's attitude and actions.[28]

26. The source for DeForest's second interview with Adams is the entry in Adams' *Memoirs*, IV, 89–90, under date of May 8, 1818. DeForest does not mention it in his letter to Tagle of May 17, cited above, note 22.

27. DeForest reported on this interview in his letter to Tagle of May 17, 1818, cited above. He mentions the conference as held on May 9; Adams, in his *Memoirs*, gives the date as May 8.

28. DeForest to Tagle, May 17, 1818, cited above.

At Buenos Aires, where the authorities had built great hopes on the weak foundations of the Worthington agreement, DeForest's report on his seemingly barren conferences with Adams and the President caused disappointment. The supreme director informed the congress of the United Provinces in secret session that the planned dispatch of a commissioner to the United States should be deferred, for he would probably suffer the same slights as had the consul general sent there.[29] Gregorio Tagle, Pueyrredón's secretary of foreign affairs, was also vexed by what he considered the unreasonable refusal of the government of the United States to receive DeForest.[30]

In reality, DeForest's mission had not been altogether futile up to this point. His discreet approaches to Adams and Monroe had been in refreshing contrast to the importunities of his predecessor, Aguirre, and had contributed to a more favorable opinion of the Buenos Aires government on the part of the administration. To this kindlier disposition can probably be ascribed the moves toward acknowledgment of the United Provinces made by Adams in the summer of 1818. Thus, in mid-August, the secretary instructed the ministers of the United States at the courts of England, France, and Russia to inquire of these governments how they would regard a recognition of the independence of Buenos Aires by the United States, and what position they would take if Spain declared war on the United States in consequence of such recognition. Later that month, he wrote to Monroe that if the Buenos Aires government would moderate its territorial claims and agree to place the United States on the most-favored-nation footing (as Pueyrredón had declined to do in the disavowed agreement with Worthington), he would think the time had come when such acknowledgment could be made without breach of neutrality.[31]

Unaware of these hopeful developments, with the advent of summer the unrecognized consul general had set out on a tour through the "Northern and Eastern States of this great and

29. Emilio Ravignani, ed., *Asambleas constituyentes argentinas* . . . (7 vols., Buenos Aires, 1937–1939), I, 536. Pueyrredón also advanced as reasons for delaying the appointment the lack of a person with suitable qualifications and the difficult situation of the treasury.

30. Tagle to Bernardino Rivadavia, Buenos Aires, Sept. 10, 1818, in Universidad de Buenos Aires, *Comisión de Bernardino Rivadavia ante España y otras potencias de Europa* (2 vols., Buenos Aires, 1933–1936), I, 303–304.

31. In this appreciation of DeForest's mission, I have followed A. P. Whitaker, *The United States and Latin America,* pp. 258–259.

growing Republic." [32] At New Haven he rejoined his family, and arranged for the construction of a large and stately home on the Green by David Hoadley, the "self-taught architect" of Connecticut.[33] After a festive reunion with his parents at Watertown, DeForest journeyed across the land of steady habits to the town of Boston. There the arrival of an envoy from distant Buenos Aires attracted some attention. By official invitation, DeForest attended a "visitation of schools," and afterwards dined in the company of the selectmen of Boston.[34] William L. Shaw, secretary of the Boston Athenaeum, who proposed to visit Buenos Aires in search of "Coins, Medals and other curiosities peculiar to South America," called to ask for letters of introduction; and Captain John Downes of the United States frigate *Macedonian*, bound for the Pacific "with a view to protecting the trade of the U. S. from marauding Spaniards on the coast of Chile," made the same request.[35]

When Congress opened, in November, 1818, DeForest was in Washington, now joined by his handsome young wife. By this time the commissioners sent to Buenos Aires had returned with reports that agreed that Spain could never reconquer the former viceroyalty, though they were divided on the virtue and stability of Pueyrredón's government. On the plains of Maipú, San Martín had won a great victory over the royalists of Chile. General Andrew Jackson had made his famous incursion into Florida in the summer of 1818, provoking a fresh crisis in the relations between the United States and Spain. From the congress of Aix-la-Chapelle, meeting that autumn, came the report that the European allies had agreed not to use force in the mediation under way between Spain and her revolted colonies.[36] Contemplating these diverse events, DeForest gathered renewed hope for his formal reception by the Washington authorities.

32. DeForest to Gregorio Tagle, Boston, Aug. 20, 1818, Archivo General de la Nación (Buenos Aires), S.1–A.2–A.4, no. 8.

33. On Hoadley, see George Dudley Seymour, *New Haven* (New Haven, 1942), pp. 239–243. The DeForest house stood on the northwest corner of Church and Elm streets, facing the Green. It was remodeled in 1878–1879 for Mayor Joseph B. Sargent. In 1910 it was demolished to provide a site for the new county court house. For views of the house, see *ibid.*, pp. 711–713.

34. DeForest to the selectmen of the town of Boston, Exchange Coffee House, Aug. 17, 1818, DeForest Letterbooks, Vol. 6.

35. DeForest to Lynch, Zimmerman and Co., Boston, Aug. 24, 1818; DeForest to General José de San Martín, Boston, Aug. 24, 1818, *ibid.*

36. DeForest to Tagle, Dec. 12, 1818, Archivo General de la Nación (Buenos Aires), S.1–A.2–A.4, no. 8.

Having already learned, perhaps from Aguirre with whom he had several conferences during the summer, that the question of Spanish-American independence was much mixed up with the party politics of the country,[37] DeForest now rashly undertook to follow Aguirre's mischievous example of collaborating with the opposition in Congress. He conferred with Henry Clay, leader of the anti-administration group, and with that skillful politician contrived a plan of action. They agreed that DeForest should renew his solicitations for a formal reception as consul general from the United Provinces, but in writing, so that Congress could call for the record and DeForest's notes be printed for their effect on public opinion.

In conformity with this plan, in early December, 1818, the Buenos Aires agent addressed to Secretary Adams a note requesting that he be accredited as consul general from the United Provinces of South America. DeForest submitted that his unofficial standing prevented him from protecting the commercial interests of his countrymen in American courts, thus placing him on an unequal footing with the consuls of Spain. Though he made no direct claim to a recognition of the independence of Buenos Aires, he affirmed that the reports of the commissioners lately returned thence established beyond a doubt that the United Provinces were truly independent; that their inhabitants possessed capacity for self-government; and that "they look up to this great republic as a model, and as to their elder sister, from whose sympathies and friendship they hope and expect ordinary protection at least." [38]

This communication led to a long conference with Adams on December 14. The secretary again set forth the view that to accredit DeForest as consul general would constitute a formal recognition of the government of the United Provinces. The United States, earnestly asserted Adams, was using its influence to produce a simultaneous acknowledgment of that government by other powers as well as the United States. There was reason, he continued, to believe that this influence had produced favorable effects; when the proper time came, "recognition would not be withheld." The patriots of Buenos Aires, he avowed, would one

37. DeForest to Tagle, Boston, Aug. 20, 1818, cited above, note 32.
38. DeForest to Adams, Washington, Dec. 9, 1818, in W. R. Manning, *Diplomatic Correspondence*, I, 515.

day be more distinctly aware of the exertions made by the American government in their behalf.

DeForest grew impatient with these diplomatic subtleties. "I am not a negotiator," he brusquely reminded Adams, "but a merchant, and my commission is only that of a Consul; should I recommend to the Supreme Director to send out here a Minister with full powers?"

"Not at present," replied the secretary, "because the objections to his reception would probably still exist." Adams then informed DeForest that the act of recognition, when made, would not involve the United States in controversy over the Banda Oriental, Santa Fé, Paraguay, or any other provinces contesting the authority of the Buenos Aires government. Further, the reported refusal of the Supreme Director Pueyrredón to accord the United States most-favored-nation treatment, on the ground that certain privileges must be reserved for Spain as a possible reward for renunciation of her claims to rule over the Río de la Plata, cast serious doubt on the integrity of the independence which the United Provinces professed to enjoy. The United States, declared Adams, would not ask any commercial favors as the price of recognition, and would regard the concession of such exclusive privileges to any other nation as "evidence rather of dependence transferred than of independence."

At DeForest's request, the secretary agreed to embody these ideas in a written answer to his caller's notes.[39] This Adams did,[40] and in a second note sharply protested against the excesses of Buenos Aires privateers and the outfitting of such vessels in North American ports in violation of the neutrality laws.[41] Even as he administered this rebuke to the Buenos Aires government, however, the secretary was drafting instructions to the United States minister in England to inform the British government that the United States would probably recognize the independence of the United Provinces "at no remote period." Only the objections of the President and other members of the cabinet ultimately caused

39. The sources for this interview are the account in Adams, *Memoirs*, IV, 190–192, under date of December 14; and DeForest to Tagle, Georgetown, Dec. 18, 1818, Archivo General de la Nación (Buenos Aires), S.1–A.2–A.4, no. 8. At one point I have altered the indirect discourse of Adams' entry to direct discourse, making no other change in the text.

40. Adams to DeForest, Washington, Dec. 31, 1818, W. R. Manning, *Diplomatic Correspondence*, I, 82–85.

41. Jan. 1, 1819, *ibid.*, pp. 88–89.

this statement of intention to be qualified by the phrase, "should no event occur which will justify a further postponement." [42]

On Christmas Day, 1818, with Monroe's previous consent, De-Forest and his wife appeared at the President's drawing room. Monroe's republican court unstintingly admired the Connecticut beauty. DeForest did not resent the attentions lavished on his Julia. He wrote little Pastora that all the world admired her mother so much that he was afraid of losing her. "May you excel your mother in everything, my little Darling," wrote the loving parent. [43]

But the Spanish minister Onís was sorely vexed by the presence at this official reception of the unrecognized agent of a revolted province. "Last Wednesday," wrote Don Luis to his government, "finding myself at what is called here the Drawing Room, where the President and his wife hold court together, I saw a rather handsome woman in the *salon* standing beside one of my daughters next to the fireplace, which is the spot of most distinction at this time of the winter. I observed that she seemed to feel at home, and that a great many people were paying homage to her. When I asked who she was, I was told that she was Mrs. Forest, the wife of the Consul General from Buenos Ayres, and they pointed out to me, near her, an uncouth, coarse-looking man, six feet six in height, [44] saying that he was her husband, a millionaire, who a few years ago was a stableboy in this country. Without saying anything, I immediately picked up my daughters and went home, with the British Minister and his wife following me, although this might have been by chance and not for the same reason. This is the second time that I have found such gentry in this court. The first was in the time of the previous President, Mr. Madison, when I met up with the famous Gual, who then called himself Minister of Cartagena and Caracas, but having indicated my displeasure to those who could suggest to the President that he should not return, I did not see him any more. I do not think this will be the case now, because DeForest enjoys a high degree of protection, above all from Clay's party, and the Government

42. A. P. Whitaker, *The United States and Latin America*, p. 264; Adams to Richard Rush, Washington, Jan. 1, 1819, W. R. Manning, *Diplomatic Correspondence*, I, 87.

43. Washington, Dec. 30, 1818, G. B. Griffin Notes. This excerpt was first printed in S. F. Bemis, *Early Diplomatic Missions*, p. 81.

44. DeForest was actually 5 feet 11½ inches in height, as shown by his military record, contained in a Memorandum Book among his papers.

does not care to collide with him. Nevertheless . . . I shall continue to leave any social gathering where I find myself together with gentry of this kind, for it does not seem proper that the King's Minister should sanction with his presence the tacit recognition of these revolutionaries." [45]

A few days after this episode, the French minister Hyde de Neuville, happening to be at Adams' office, complained to the secretary of the inconvenient social aspirations of the agent from Buenos Aires and his lady. He said that DeForest had called on him, and that Mrs. DeForest had paid a visit to Madame de Neuville. "He did not know why. They must be sensible that neither he nor Madame de Neuville could return their visits." Adams assured the perplexed Frenchman that his concern was unfounded. "De Forrest was a citizen of the United States, and as such had been received at the President's. But he was not recognized as Consul from Buenos Ayres, and I myself had not returned his visit." [46]

In following the story of DeForest's efforts to secure formal recognition of his diplomatic character, and thus of his government, we must not lose sight of his interest in wresting from Spain an island in the Gulf of Mexico that should serve as a base for privateering operations, as authorized by his instructions. Although the project by which he hoped to achieve this purpose proved abortive, it illustrates in a most suggestive manner the close and complex interplay between the movement for Spanish-American independence and the steady pressure of the United States to gain strategic security and round out its borders at the expense of the dissolving Spanish empire.

In the letter from which I have just quoted, the Spanish minister Onís had more to relate concerning the activities of the troublesome agent from Buenos Aires. He informed his government that DeForest, Manuel Moreno ("a man of the greatest talents"), the Venezuelan agent Lino Clemente, and the adventurer Pierre Laffite were planning to hold one or more secret meetings with Clay and other persons "in this government." In these conferences the conspirators would discuss what must be done to secure recognition of the independence of Buenos Aires

---

45. Onís to Casa Irujo, Washington, Dec. 29, 1818, Archivo Histórico Nacional (Madrid), Estado, legajo 5643, apartado 1. This extract from Onís' despatch was first printed in S. F. Bemis, *Early Diplomatic Missions,* pp. 81–82.

46. Adams, *Memoirs,* IV, 210.

by the United States, and would also prepare a plan of attack against the possessions of his Catholic Majesty on the North American continent. This last project had the approval of the American government, because it knew that Great Britain was meditating the seizure of a port on the coast of Venezuela, or perhaps the islands of Puerto Rico and Santo Domingo, with the aid of Spanish-American corsairs; and it wished to use the rebel forces for its own ends (*trata de sacar partido del mismo plan*). The administration had therefore proposed to the filibusters that immediately after the return of Pensacola and St. Marks to Spain,[47] they should fall upon and occupy these posts and St. Augustine as well, and then turn them over to the United States! At the head of this enterprise American officials wished to install Pierre Laffite, in whom they placed great confidence, remembering his notable services at the defense of New Orleans. Yet it was Laffite, repenting his past misdeeds against Spain and avowing his sincere love for *la Patria*, who had revealed this intrigue to Onís, offering at the same time to assist in trapping and destroying the filibusters.[48]

The alarm which this cloudy report of the dubious adventurer Laffite inspired in the Spanish minister is more understandable than may appear at first view. At the close of the year 1818 the painfully protracted negotiations between Adams and Onís were at a standstill, with the two diplomatists deadlocked over the question of the international western boundary.[49] Under the circumstances, it was not unreasonable for Onís to believe that Monroe's government, despairing of a satisfactory adjustment of the dispute with Spain, might resort to measures roughly analogous to those by which President Madison, having stirred up revolt in West Florida, had been enabled to proclaim the occupation of that province in 1810, and which Monroe, then secre-

47. General Andrew Jackson had captured these places during his campaign against the Florida Indians in the spring of 1818.

48. Onís to Casa Irujo, Dec. 29, 1818, cited above, note 45. On the Laffites and their secret connections with Spain, see Harris Gaylord Warren, *The Sword Was Their Passport: A History of American Filibustering in the Mexican Revolution* (Baton Rouge, La., 1942), especially Chapters 5, 6, 9, and 10. My account of the filibustering project in which DeForest figured is largely taken from this work, pp. 214–232, and from H. G. Warren, ed., "Documents Relating to George Graham's Proposals to Jean Laffite for the Occupation of the Texas Coast," *Louisiana Historical Quarterly*, XXI (1938), 212–219.

49. Philip C. Brooks, *Diplomacy and the Borderlands: the Adams-Onís Treaty of 1819* (Berkeley, Cal., 1939), covers these negotiations authoritatively.

tary of state, had employed less successfully through the agency of General George Mathews in East Florida in 1811.[50] As a matter of fact, Laffite's allegations and Onís' fears were not entirely unfounded. The indiscretions of a presidential agent, about to be related, gave color to the belief that the United States government was conniving in rebel schemes to seize Spain's possessions in North America. In these schemes DeForest was designed to play a certain part.

A group of Napoleonic officers, ostensibly seeking a refuge for the exiled officers of the fallen emperor, made a settlement early in 1818 on the Trinity River above Galveston, thus within territory in dispute between Spain and the United States. To this colony they gave the hopeful name of Le Champ d'Asile. The French lodgment gave concern to both claimants of the debatable ground between the Sabine and the Rio Grande. It was feared that the exiles aspired to place Joseph Bonaparte on a Mexican throne. The viceroy of New Spain organized a military expedition against the French settlement. About the same time Monroe's government resolved to send an agent, George Graham, who should protest to the colonists against their occupation of American territory and ascertain the real ends of their venture. Adams suspected that the Frenchmen might actually be instruments of Spanish policy in Texas. The Graham mission also offered an opportunity to warn off the celebrated brothers Laffite. These adventurers of shifting allegiance, ousted from their smuggling and privateering establishment at Barataria by American troops in 1814, had lately installed a new seat of lawless enterprise on Galveston Island. But Adams' written instructions to Graham were silent on this subject.

The agent, arrived at Galveston on August 24, 1818, discovered that the French exiles had already fled thither from Le Champ d'Asile before the threat of a Spanish attack. Graham nevertheless made known to General Charles Lallemand, leader of the hapless settlers, his government's views as to their alleged encroachment on American territory. Lallemand proved properly submissive, and Graham, relenting, assured the Napoleonic veteran that in the event of an occupation of Galveston by the

---

50. On the West Florida question, see Isaac J. Cox, *The West Florida Controversy; 1798–1813, a Study in American Diplomacy* (Baltimore, 1918); on East Florida, see R. K. Wyllys, "The East Florida Revolution of 1812–1814," *Hisp. Am. Hist. Rev.*, IX (1929), 414–445, and the careful study of the Mathews affair in Julius W. Pratt, *The Expansionists of 1812* (N. Y., 1925), pp. 76–115.

United States, the members of his expedition and their property would not be harmed. Monroe's emissary then decided to seek explanations from Jean Laffite. The master of Galveston ruled over his island domain from a large, mastless brig grounded in the bay, his "dwelling, storehouse and arsenal," reported Graham to Secretary Adams.[51] In the ensuing exchange of views, Laffite avowed most disinterested motives for having come to Galveston: "that of offering asylum to the armed vessels of the revolution and that of being able . . . to fly to the aid of the United States if circumstances should demand."[52] He had not known that the United States laid claim to the entire coast from the Sabine to the Rio Grande, asserted the affable corsair, but was ready to quit Galveston as soon as he could assemble his forces.

Beguiled by these fair words, Graham now made to Jean Laffite and General Charles Lallemand a series of proposals for which his instructions gave not the least warrant. He allegedly suggested that the Laffites, the noted privateersman Louis Aury, and Lallemand should unite their forces to defend Galveston against Spanish attack. The United States would assist these filibusters in occupying successively all the points on the coast from Galveston to the Rio Grande. American forces would then go through the motions of attacking these places, which the corsairs should surrender to the United States for a suitable compensation. When Laffite observed that his privateering commissions were from the shadowy patriot government of Mexico, Graham advised him to take out patents from the more stable régime at Buenos Aires, and helpfully supplied him with a letter to Consul General DeForest at New York. All these proposals Laffite pretended to embrace, but took good care to relay them to his Spanish employers.

On his return to Washington, Graham reported to the secretary of state on his mission. He apparently failed to reveal the full scope of his negotiations with the adventurers at Galveston. Adams nevertheless registered his serious concern over the agent's proceedings in his diary.

"He had a sort of negotiation, it seems, with Lallemand and Lafitte, from which it appears that Lallemand's case is desperate. Graham's transactions with Lafitte, as related by himself, did not exactly tally with my ideas of right, and they were altogether

51. H. G. Warren, *The Sword Was Their Passport*, p. 218.
52. *Ibid.*, p. 219.

unauthorized. He says Lafitte told him that he had commissions
from the Mexican Congress, but they were like Aury's commissions, and he [Graham] advised him to take a commission of
Buenos Ayres, and gave him a letter to De Forrest, at New York,
to assist him in obtaining one, and that Lafitte took his advice,
and immediately dispatched a man to New York for that purpose. Now, I should not be surprised if we should hear more of
this hereafter, and not in a very pleasant manner. But it was all
of Graham's own head, and, in my opinion, not much to the credit
of its wisdom. He is for taking immediate possession of Galveston,
and so am I." [53]

Jean Laffite had indeed taken Graham at his word and sent an
emissary, one V. Garrot, to negotiate with DeForest. Their conference took place on November 16, 1818, in Philadelphia. Since
DeForest did not speak French, an interpreter was present. After
reading the letter from Graham, which asked him to give Pierre
Laffite "the flag with the dispatches from Buenos Aires," and to
name the authorities who should head the government to be established by the corsairs in the Gulf of Mexico, the rebel agent
displayed a lively interest in the filibustering project. He asked
Garrot on what point of the Spanish dominions Laffite planned to
make his establishment.

The messenger replied that no decision had been reached on
that subject. Operations of such importance required mature
deliberation. He presumed that Laffite had fixed his attention
more particularly on the Gulf of Mexico, but about the rest
nothing could be said with certainty. If DeForest could obtain
from President Monroe a promise that the United States would
postpone the occupation of Galveston for one year, suggested
Garrot, during that time the corsairs could be engaged in select-
ing another convenient port.

DeForest agreed to make this request of the President. Learning from Garrot that Laffite had six ships at his command, the
Buenos Aires agent seemed impressed, and observed that if these
forces were joined with Aury's it would be possible to take possession of Puerto Rico or Santo Domingo. After giving assurances
of his full support to Laffite's enterprise, DeForest informed
Garrot that he would leave for Baltimore in a few days to arrange
with the merchant Thomas Tenant for the necessary arms and
supplies. Then he would go to Washington, where he hoped to

53. Adams, *Memoirs*, IV, 175–176.

meet with Pierre Laffite.[54] Pierre was then in the capital, conferring with Onís.

The affair made progress, and by the end of December, 1818, DeForest could send the following note to Manuel Moreno, now his trusted lieutenant:

"The time has now arrived when I shall probably be able to come to a determination to relate the plan I spoke to you about when I last saw you. The Gentlemen who have the power to carry the plan into Execution, arrived here last evening; and if you will come up here on Monday I have no doubt something will be done very much to your advantage, for, my object will be to chasten the enemies of Buenos Ayres in a honorable way; and to place you where you can make a fortune rapidly." [55]

Gathered in secret conclave at Washington, as foretold by Pierre Laffite to Onís, Pierre, DeForest, Moreno, and possibly others, concerted their plans. They agreed that Moreno should take command of the projected expedition against "some port or place in or near the Gulf of Mexico." The precise point of attack was apparently left for later determination, but DeForest seems to have contemplated a descent on Florida. The size of the armada to be employed is suggested by a letter from DeForest to Manuel Lynch in New York, directing him to deliver to Moreno twenty privateering patents for craft of the following description: one ship, seven brigs, and twelve schooners.[56] Moreno, acting as representative of the Supreme Director Pueyrredón of Buenos Aires, would hold the occupied territory as a colony of the United Provinces, "under whose laws it should be governed as a rendezvous for the privateers of that country." [57] The promoters even settled the mode of division of the anticipated spoils. "Moreno and No. 19 [Pierre Laffite] will have a part of all the cargoes taken by them, all the payments incurred for anchorage, condemnation, and other charges which they will divide between them; one per cent will be given to Consul Forestt, who will issue corsair commissions, and one per cent will be for the Minister of Buenos Ayres who has signed said commissions." [58]

54. Garrot to Pierre Laffite, Philadelphia, Nov. 17, 1818, in H. G. Warren, ed., "Documents Relating to George Graham's Proposals to Pierre Laffite."

55. DeForest to Manuel Moreno, Georgetown, Dec. 26, 1818, DeForest Letterbooks, Vol. 6.

56. DeForest to Manuel Lynch, Washington, Jan. 6, 1819, ibid.

57. DeForest to Henry Didier, Washington, Jan. 4, 1819, ibid.

58. H. G. Warren, The Sword Was Their Passport, p. 228.

As late as the middle of January, 1819, DeForest buoyantly envisaged the rise of a new and more successful Amelia Island, a privateering paradise whither the corsairs of Buenos Aires could conveniently bring Spanish prizes for summary condemnation by Laffite's henchman Garrot, designated in the plan as prize-court judge. He brushed aside certain objections advanced by the more cautious Henry Didier of Baltimore. "The negotiations between this Country and Spain," argued DeForest, "appear to be pretty much at an end: and the U. S. cannot consider it any interference with her affairs, if any enemy of Spain should take possession of Florida. The thing is practicable; and I am confident the U. S. would not complain in the least. If effected, and the War with Spain ended, a cession of it might be profitably made to the U. States . . ." [59]

These rash assertions of course overlooked Secretary Adams' emphatic warning to DeForest, given in his second interview with the Buenos Aires agent, that the United States would not tolerate a rebel occupation of Florida. Nor were the negotiations between Adams and Onís as moribund as DeForest believed. On January 11, 1819, after receiving authority from his government to reopen the suspended treaty negotiations, Onís wrote to the secretary proposing to renew their conversations with a view to further compromise. [60] Thereafter negotiations proceeded at an accelerated pace, and on February 22, 1819, Adams scored his greatest diplomatic triumph with the signing of the treaty by which Florida became American territory and the boundary of the United States was drawn clear across the continent to the Pacific Ocean.

This happy and unexpected consummation immediately destroyed DeForest's filibustering hopes. He forthwith severed his connections with the Laffites, whose integrity he had evidently begun to doubt, and fixed his attention again on the central struggle for his official reception by the government of the United States as consul general from the United Provinces.

Early in January, 1819, DeForest sent a carefully prepared reply to Adams' two notes of December 31, 1818, and January 1, 1819. He reiterated his contention that the reception of a

59. DeForest to Henry Didier, Georgetown, Jan. 13, 1819, DeForest Letterbooks, Vol. 6.
60. P. C. Brooks, *Diplomacy and the Borderlands*, p. 155.

consular agent from Buenos Aires was a distinct and separate question from an acknowledgment of independence. "I do not profess to be skilled in the laws of nations, nor of diplomacy . . .; yet I must say, that I cannot understand the difference between the sending of a consular agent duly authorized to Buenos Ayres, where one was accredited from this country, four or five years ago, and has continued ever since, in the exercise of the duties of his office, and the reception of a similar agent here." He only sought to be received as a consular agent, "having never agitated the question of an acknowledgment of our independence as a nation, which most certainly is anxiously desired by the Government and people of South America, but which, being a political question, I have never asked." [61]

This note was clearly timed to accord with an appropriate move by anti-administration forces in Congress. On January 14, 1819, Clay's group pushed through a resolution requesting information as to whether any independent government in South America had asked for recognition of a minister or consul general, and what reply had been made.

This latest attempt to embarrass the administration with the "great South American witchery" moved the harassed Adams to bitter reflection. "In this affair," he confided to his diary, "everything is invidious and factious. The call is made for the purpose of baiting the administration, and especially in fastening upon the Secretary of State the odium of refusing to receive South American Ministers and Consul-Generals. I am walking on a rope, with a precipice on each side of me, and without human aid beyond myself upon which to rely. . . . DeForrest's notes are cunning and deceptive. To the last and longest of them I have not replied. It must be sent in under the call, and if unaccompanied by a refutation of its contents, advantage will be taken of it to censure the course of the Executive, and perhaps even to force the recognition of the Southern independents. I must, therefore, demolish the arguments in De Forrest's last note, which is indeed not a difficult task, but which must take time and many words." [62]

Thereupon the sturdy little secretary set himself to the task of replying to DeForest's "cunning and deceptive" note. This state-

61. DeForest to Adams, Georgetown, Jan. 8, 1819, W. R. Manning, *Diplomatic Correspondence*, IV, 516–519.
62. Adams, *Memoirs*, IV, 223–224, under date of Jan. 20, 1819.

ment, together with the correspondence he had exchanged with DeForest and Lino de Clemente of Venezuela, Adams sent in to the President for transmission to Congress.

The secretary of state explained that the government had declined to have further communication with Clemente because he had been one of those who signed the commission of the adventurer Gregor MacGregor to take possession of Amelia Island. DeForest was charged with no offense, but his credentials were void because they were founded on Worthington's unauthorized treaty. "Mr. De Forest's credential letter asks that he may be received by virtue of a stipulation in supposed articles concluded by Mr. Worthington, but which he was not authorized to make; so that the reception of Mr. De Forest, upon the credential on which he founds his claim, would imply a recognition, not only of the Government of the Supreme Director, Pueyrredón, but a compact as binding upon the United States, which is a mere nullity." Adams also noted that in the previous May the agent had declared himself entirely content with his informal reception, but that "shortly after the commencement of the present session of Congress" he had renewed his solicitations.[63] The secretary thus indicated his suspicion that DeForest was collaborating with Clay's opposition group.

Adams was now resolved to rid himself forever of the troublesome envoy from Buenos Aires. When DeForest called at his office again, on January 22, 1819, Adams found occasion to remind his visitor that he was still a citizen of the United States and hence liable to prosecution for violation of the neutrality laws.

Disquiet was suddenly written on DeForest's face. "When I informed you that I had no intention of returning to Buenos Aires, but had come finally to settle here," he said, "I did not expect the information would ever be used against me. Would I be considered by law to have been a citizen of the United States while at Buenos Aires?"

"It is unnecessary for me to give you an opinion on that point," replied Adams. "You had better consult a lawyer upon it. It is not my intention to make any use to your disadvantage of anything you have said to me. Although the information you gave me was voluntary, under no injunction of secrecy or intimation of confidence, I have never mentioned it to any other person than the

63. Adams to President James Monroe, Washington, Jan. 28, 1819, W. R. Manning, *Diplomatic Correspondence*, I, 89–94.

President, and shall never notice it publicly unless it should be necessary in the discharge of my public duties. But it is in candor due to you to let you know that the recognition of yourself as Consul General of Buenos Aires, should it hereafter be granted, will in no wise divest you of your character as a citizen of the United States."

Somewhat reassured by Adams' words, DeForest unburdened himself to the secretary. "For the last seventeen years," he said, "I have resided principally at Buenos Aires, and have become a citizen of that country. In their revolutionary struggle with Spain I have taken a very decided and active part, particularly in the business of privateering. I have now returned to this country with the view of remaining here, and am building a house at New Haven. But if Spanish subjects can molest me here for what I did while an inhabitant of Buenos Aires my situation will be very perilous."

DeForest also confirmed what Adams had suspected—that he had conferred with Clay on the question of recognition. He assured the secretary, however, that he was now convinced that Clay's proceedings had injured rather than aided the patriot cause; he, DeForest, was entirely satisfied with the Spanish-American policy of the administration.[64]

Adams' veiled threat had served its purpose. DeForest beat a precipitate retreat from Washington, settled down in New Haven, and never again crossed the path of the formidable secretary of state. The shadows of his privateering past already hung darkly about him. "You do not appear to know," he was soon writing to former associates in Buenos Aires, "how much anxiety I have had on account of my fears of suits brought by Spanish claimants, although I have openly pretended to the contrary. Captain M[arcena] Monson, however, has always shown his fears, and even to this day keeps very retired, and has no property except what is covered by some friend." [65]

In its own good time Monroe's government accorded to the new Spanish-American states that recognition for which De-Forest had unsuccessfully labored. When the President sent his

64. This account of DeForest's last interview with Adams is based on the entry in the latter's *Memoirs*, IV, 225. I have altered indirect to direct discourse, but have made no change in the original sense of this material.

65. DeForest to Lynch and Zimmerman, New Haven, July 2, 1820, DeForest Letterbooks, Vol. 7.

celebrated message to Congress of March 8, 1822, recommending an appropriation for the dispatch of diplomatic missions to five of these states—the United Provinces of Río de La Plata, Chile, Peru, Colombia, and Mexico—he did so not in consequence of partisan political pressure but from a variety of considerations in which the decisive victories of patriot armies, the final ratification of the Adams-Onís Treaty by Spain, the passing of the danger of European intervention, the desire to strengthen the influence of the United States in Spanish America, and Adams' belief that the legal conditions for recognition had at last been satisfied, all played a certain part. Congress, almost without a dissenting voice, voted the required appropriation on May 4, 1822.

Monroe's message encouraged DeForest to write to Secretary Adams, claiming for Buenos Aires the honor of being the first state to be recognized, with himself as *chargé d'affaires* and consul general. Adams replied that as an American citizen he could not serve as *chargé d'affaires;* that his invalid credentials did not entitle him to be received as consul general; and that the department had been notified of the intention of the new government of Buenos Aires to revoke DeForest's commission.[66] Manuel Torres, the aged and infirm representative of Colombia, had the distinction of being first to be received. Formal diplomatic relations with the United Provinces of La Plata were established by the appointment of Caesar A. Rodney as first United States minister to that country (January 27, 1823).

In June, 1823, DeForest received official notification from the new Rivadavia government of the recall of his commission as consul general. He was to send to Buenos Aires his archives, together with any remaining privateering patents and an explanation of the status of those he had used.[67] In a belated reply to Rivadavia, DeForest pleaded the want of a "convenient opportunity" for not having written earlier. Perhaps he feared to send the incriminating privateering material in his possession by ordinary channels. There is evidence that Spanish agents intercepted at least one letter directed to him.[68] DeForest complained

66. W. R. Manning, *Diplomatic Correspondence,* I, 159–160.

67. Bernardino Rivadavia to DeForest, March 13, 1823, in *Documentos para la historia argentina,* XIV, 202–203.

68. In the Archivo Histórico Nacional (Madrid), Estado, legajo 5567, expediente 13, there is an intercepted letter from the noted Argentine patriot Tomás Guido to DeForest, sent from Guayaquil, Jan. 3, 1821. Guido wrote that he would continue to keep DeForest informed concerning developments in "this important

that Rivadavia's communication was the first he had received from the government of Buenos Aires since the establishment of the new régime in 1821; and that this note did not even acknowledge receipt of any dispatches from him, "of which I have made many, most of them in triplicate. Nor does it intimate to me how and when, I am to be rewarded for my services, during the time I have been in their employ." He bore his adopted country no ill will, however, on that account. "With my best wishes for the happiness of Buenos Aires, I have the honor to remain . . . David C. DeForest." [69]

It was not until September 23, 1824, one year later, that a messenger turned over DeForest's official archives to the first recognized minister to the United States from Buenos Aires, Carlos de Alvear.[70] They included, in addition to the exchanges of notes with Secretary Adams, 432 unused privateering patents and officers' commissions that had been issued to DeForest in connection with his mission to North America, and two used and surrendered patents.[71] With this action DeForest wrote *finis* to the diplomatic chapter of his career. His qualities of a pertinacious, bold, and resourceful fighter had not availed to change the set course of the Spanish-American policy of the United States, guided by the firm and skillful hand of John Quincy Adams.

section of the globe, in whose fate you have always displayed such a lively interest."

69. DeForest to Bernardino Rivadavia, New Haven, Sept. 7, 1823, Archivo General de la Nación (Buenos Aires), S.1–A.2–A.4, no. 8.

70. Dr. Thomas B. Davis, Jr., is preparing for publication a study of Alvear's mission to the United States. For an important aspect of this mission, see T. B. Davis, Jr., "Carlos de Alvear and James Monroe: New Light on the Monroe Doctrine," *Hisp. Am. Hist. Rev.*, XXIII (1943), 632–649.

71. Memorandum of Carlos de Alvear, acknowledging receipt of DeForest's official archives, New York, Sept. 24, 1824 (copy), Archivo General de la Nación (Buenos Aires), S.1–A.2–A.4, no. 10.

XI

EPILOGUE

SINCE the early months of 1819, conforming with the broad hint of Secretary Adams not to annoy the administration any more with his diplomatic attentions, DeForest had quietly resided in the town of New Haven. With commerce he had no further concern. Until the middle of 1823 he continued to style himself consul general of the United Provinces of South America, a title flattering to his vanity, but this shadowy office imposed no serious duties. For the rest, he had only to enjoy the leisure that his ample means made possible. One of his first actions on returning to New Haven was to search out and reimburse with interest the creditors of his youthful venture in Maine. In his prosperity he was mindful of his brothers and other kinsmen; among his relatives DeForest divided $15,000, no inconsiderable fortune for those days.[1]

The stately house on the Green that David Hoadley had built was ready for occupation on July 1, 1820. Contemporaries of DeForest regarded his house as "the handsomest residence in the state."[2] In the basement of his home the envoy from Buenos Aires placed a marble tablet engraved on both sides. On one side was an inscription recording the names, with dates and places of birth, of himself, his wife, and his five children. On the other side was a whimsical injunction to future owners of the house ever to honor the anniversary of the Revolution of Buenos Aires.

"To the owner of this House.
David C. DeForest,
A native citizen of Huntington in
this state; and at present Consul
General of the United Provinces of
South America, of which Buenos
Ayres is the Capital, where he

1. J. W. De Forest, *The de Forests of Avesnes,* p. 156.
2. Henry Howe, "New Haven's Elms and Green," Chap. 20, *Daily Morning Journal and Courier* (New Haven), Jan. 1, 1884.

resided for many years; and
assisted in establishing its
Independence. greeting.
I have caused this
beautiful building to be erected
for your use, as well as mine; &
have taken much pains to accom
odate you, for which you will
never pay; & being no relative of
mine, I demand: that you assemble
your friends together on every
25th day of May in honor of
the Independence of South
America; it being on that day
in the year 1810, that the
Inhabitants of
Buenos Ayres
established a free Government
New Haven, 1820

David Hoadley, Arch't.
Horace Butler, Mason

D. Ritter, Sculp." [3]

The coming of the Don, as New Haveners were quick to call
the swarthy man from Buenos Aires, was a memorable event in
the life of the little town. The mystery of DeForest's reputedly
vast fortune excited speculation; and about him gossip weaved
tales that grew in the telling. In this wise the Don acquired the
fame of having been a pirate. A genial story-teller of the last century who spent some youthful years in "getting learning" at Yale
College attests to the persuasive power of this legend. Recalling
DeForest as a stern man with black-eyed lovely daughters and a
son called Carlos who was handsome but effeminate, he comments:
"I never saw him that I did not dream of bloody decks, fierce sea
fights, a pirate's doom, and I had a general idea that his cellar,
instead of containing barrels of cider, metheglin, and bins of
apples, was filled with kegs of Spanish gold coin, diamond neck-
laces, finger rings, and breast-pins, in barrels. To me the Don was
a mystery never solved." [4]

3. This tablet is now in the possession of the New Haven Colony Historical
Society of New Haven.
4. [Joseph A. Scoville], *The Old Merchants of New York City,* by Walter
Barrett, clerk (5 ser., N. Y., 1863–1870), IV, 204–205.

In recital to the youngest and most credulous sort, this fable was appropriately embellished. Imaginative parents told their offspring that in the cellar of DeForest's mansion was a deep sink or well containing hogsheads of doubloons. Monstrous serpents, kept there for the purpose, guarded the treasure. "So great was the terror inspired by this statement that often small children on their way to school avoided passing by the house for fear those snakes would be out after them." [5] Yet the Don was kind to children, and his friendliness sometimes conquered the dread that his fame inspired. "He was a pompous, arbitrary man," recalled one contemporary, "but I loved as well as feared him, as he always had a playful word or a ready joke for children who he knew." [6]

In New Haven, as in Buenos Aires, DeForest practiced a hospitality that also became legendary. His great house, says one account, was open to "the wise, the witty, the struggling scholar, and the grace and fashion of town." [7] To his receptions at seven o'clock in the evening came many distinguished folk, among them James Gates Percival, the shy poet-geologist and New Haven's literary lion; DeForest's counsel and particular friend Judge David Daggett; and the learned lexicographer Noah Webster. When General Lafayette came to New Haven in August, 1824, it was at the home of "David C. DeForest, esquire, late consul general from Buenos Ayres and the provinces of the Rio de la Plata," that he paused to take refreshment and rest from his triumphal procession through the town. DeForest was then away, placing one of his daughters in a Montreal school, and it was his wife who received the comrade of Washington at the door, no doubt with three profound curtsies, an importation from Spanish America not wholly approved by the sober people of New Haven. The editor of the *Columbian Register* duly noted the impressions of the revolutionary hero. "No such splendid mansion, with its brilliant furniture, was here in 1778. From the portico in front he surveyed the beautiful Green, full of people, with the long line of troops, the buildings around, and the fine foliage of the trees. A lively sensibility at once appeared. He was struck with the beauty of the scene. Such another prospect can

5. Henry Howe, "New Haven's Elms and Green," Chap. 20, *Daily Morning Journal and Courier* (New Haven), Jan. 1, 1884.

6. "New Haven in Old Times," *Daily Palladium* (New Haven), Feb. 24, 1869.

7. "A Former Townsman," *Daily Morning Journal and Courier* (New Haven), Feb. 21, 1873.

hardly be presented in America." [8] Later, standing under the
portrait of DeForest by Samuel F. B. Morse, Lafayette drank a
toast to the absent master of the house.

Morse painted two portraits of DeForest in 1823. At that
period the "American Leonardo" [9] was living with his father
Jedidiah, the celebrated geographer, on Hillhouse Avenue in New
Haven. Morse's attention was already divided between art and in-
ventions, with neither pursuit proving very profitable, and he undoubtedly rejoiced to receive this message from the local magnate:
"Mr. D. C. DeForest's compliments to Mr. Morse. Mr. De-
Forest desires to have his portrait taken such as it would have
been six or eight years ago, making the necessary calculations for
it, and at the same time making it a good likeness in all other
respects. The reason is not to make himself younger, but to appear to children and grandchildren more suitably matched as to
age with their mother and grandmother." [10]

For this portrait DeForest sat in a riding dress of blue coat
and red vest that heightened the desired youthful appearance.
Morse painted a spruce and vigorous gentleman whose features
express energy, shrewdness, and good humor. About this time
Morse also painted a companion portrait of Mrs. DeForest in the
yellow satin dress she wore at President Monroe's drawing-room
in 1818. This canvas brilliantly communicates the classic beauty
that Monroe's republican court so greatly admired. These portraits now hang in the Yale University Art Gallery.

For presentation to the Academy of La Unión del Sud in Buenos Aires, which his donation had helped to found, DeForest commissioned Morse to paint a second and more authentic likeness
of himself. In this picture DeForest is dressed in a formal suit of
black. From the lapel of his coat hangs what appears to be a
badge decorated with the blue-and-white Argentine colors. The
head, observes a student of this canvas, is a superb pictorial and
psychological synthesis, in which the prematurely gray hair con-
trasts with the face, still smooth and ruddy "in that intensive
second youth which Providence is wont to bestow on generous
natures as they near the fifty year mark." The heavy eyebrows,

8. J. W. De Forest, *The de Forests of Avesnes*, p. 155.
9. Carleton Mabee, *The American Leonardo, A Life of Samuel F. B. Morse*
(N. Y., 1943).
10. Letter dated New Haven, March 30, 1823. Edward Lind Morse, *Samuel
F. B. Morse: His Letters and Journals* (2 vols., Boston, 1914), I, 243.

the compressed lips, the solid and obstinate chin, bespeak energy and daring. But this effect is softened by a cordial, almost benign expression: "Neither gravity nor ostentation; a frank, affectionate, and absolute simplicity." [11]

This portrait DeForest sent to Buenos Aires together with a number of other artistic pieces: an engraving of a symbolic representation of the independence of the United States, with the coats of arms of the thirteen original states and a copy of the Declaration of Independence of July 4, 1776, with "facsimiles of the signatures of the great and good men who constituted the Congress that made it"; an engraving by Asher B. Durand of John Trumbull's painting of the signing of the Declaration, "containing the portraits of the members of the North American Congress of 1776"; and a landscape by Henry C. Pratt, a pupil of Morse, depicting the DeForest mansion in New Haven and some adjacent buildings. "Of these paintings," wrote DeForest with patriotic pride, "permit me to assure you, Sir, that all, and every part thereof, is the work of Americans. The landscape is sent to show the style of Architecture in this part of the New World, and a Mansion on which waves the Flag of South America on every twenty-fifth of May, surrounded and cheered by the inhabitants of the little city in which it stands." [12]

These tokens of his friendship DeForest sent to Buenos Aires in charge of the first United States minister to the provinces of the Río de la Plata, Caesar A. Rodney, who duly delivered them to President Achega of the Academy of La Union del Sud. The portrait of DeForest by Morse, unsigned by the artist, hung in the halls of the University of Buenos Aires until the close of the nineteenth century, when it was placed in the newly founded Museo Nacional de Bellas Artes. About 1910 the then director of the Museo officially ascribed the unknown masterpiece to the Spanish painter Goya; and this attribution was accepted until 1921, when a letter of inquiry from Dr. Louis S. de Forest, a relative of DeForest, reopened the question. Subsequently evidence sent from the United States conclusively established that Morse had painted the anonymous canvas. The whereabouts of the other art objects sent by DeForest is unknown.

11. Atilio Chiáppori, *Maestros y temperamentos* (Buenos Aires, 1943), "Un Goya yanqui y un yanqui porteño," pp. 105–106.
12. DeForest to Domingo Vicente de Achega, President of the University of La Unión del Sud, New Haven, April 10, 1823, DeForest Letterbooks, Vol. 8.

As mentioned in his letter to President Achega, DeForest had already begun annual celebrations in New Haven of the Argentine Independence Day, the twenty-fifth of May. The first such commemoration was held in 1821. "On Friday the 25th inst.," reported the *Columbian Register*, "the anniversary of the independence of Buenos Ayres was celebrated in this city in handsome style. The day was ushered in by the discharge of a national salute. At about 11 o'clock, a. m., a large company of gentlemen assembled at Butler's County Hotel, agreeably to a general invitation which had been publicly given in the newspapers; but the concourse was so great that it was found necessary to adjourn to the State House, where a neat and appropriate address was delivered by Robert Lockwood, Esq. After which the company returned to Butler's Hotel, and drank a number of patriotic toasts, and partook of some refreshments which had been prepared for the occasion. At noon and sunset the national salute was repeated. Soon after 8 o'clock, p. m., a very numerous company of ladies and gentlemen convened at the elegant mansion of Don David C. DeForest, and passed the evening in great hilarity."

The friends of South American liberty drank to "the city of Buenos Ayres," to "General San Martín and the Army of Peru," to "the gallant little navy of Chile," and finally a fervent toast went up to "the Holy Alliance and the Devil—may the friends of liberty check their career, and compel them to dissolve partnership." [13]

DeForest held a similar observance in 1822. Before the next twenty-fifth of May he had been divested of his consular office, but during the brief years of life that remained to him he continued to commemorate, more simply and privately, the day that had marked a turning point in the history of the Río de la Plata and in his personal fortunes.

The Don gave one more proof of loyalty and attachment to his adopted country. At his suggestion, six young Argentines came to the United States, intrusted to his care, in order to study English and otherwise prepare themselves for mercantile careers. First to come was Manuel Lynch, a brother of DeForest's former partner in Buenos Aires. Manuel went to school at an academy in Hudson, New York, served an apprenticeship in the counting-

13. *Columbian Register* (New Haven), May 26, 1821; see also *Connecticut Herald* (New Haven), May 28, 1821.

house of Lockwood De Forest in New York City, and having completed his training sailed for home at the end of 1819.[14] Other youthful *porteños* followed him to North America: Pedro Martínez y García, José María and Francisco Rodríguez de Vida, Patricio Basabilbaso, and Pedro J. Trellechea. Some DeForest placed in the academy at Hudson; others he sent to a nearby school in Huntington.[15] After gaining a competent knowledge of English, these lads were expected to acquire practical commercial experience in a counting-house. Although their relations were generally harmonious, some sharp clashes of wills occurred between DeForest and his charges. Of Pedro Martínez y García, "a very gentlemanly and well behaved young man," he wrote that "we have never differed except on the amount of money he ought to spend. He feels much hurt at my foolish ideas." [16] It is worthy of note that young Patricio Basabilbaso took advantage of his sojourn in the United States to court and marry a North American bride before returning to Buenos Aires where he became a prosperous merchant.[17] Many years were to pass before DeForest's pioneering conception would be taken up by governments, universities, and private foundations to become an accepted and integral feature of inter-American cultural relations.

Having assisted in the foundation of the first seat of higher learning in the land of his adoption, DeForest fittingly enough became a benefactor of Yale College in the town of New Haven where he had made his home. In 1821 he offered to the college a donation of $5,000, to be held at 6 per cent interest until January 1, 1850, when the principal, amounting to $25,941, should yield an annual interest of $1,556, to be expended as follows: $1,000 for the support and education of DeForest's assigns at the college; $500 for the purchase of books, maps, and charts to be placed in an alcove of the college library, with the name of DeForest written thereon and on each volume or other item thus purchased; and $56 to purchase a gold medal to be awarded to the best orator of the senior class, and to be called the DeForest medal.[18]

14. DeForest to Patricio Lynch, New Haven, Oct. 14, 1819, DeForest Letterbooks, Vol. 7.

15. DeForest to José Rodríguez de Vida, New Haven, Oct. 13, 1819, *ibid.*

16. DeForest to Manuel Martínez y García, New Haven, Oct. 2, 1819, *ibid.*

17. E. Udaondo, *Diccionario biográfico argentino,* p. 129.

18. DeForest to his Excellency Ethan A. Brown, Governor of the State of Ohio, New Haven, Nov. 5, 1821, DeForest Letterbooks, Vol. 8.

When this proposal was laid before the corporation of Yale College, in meeting assembled, it appears to have raised a storm of controversy. According to DeForest himself, several of the trustees opposed acceptance of the gift, "principally on the ground of its having a tendency to the establishment of an aristocracy; and although a majority was in favor of it they did not press a vote then, but adjourned its further consideration till the next commencement." [19] J. W. De Forest, in his family history, affirms that the opposition was led by a certain unnamed trustee, "a locally illustrious gentleman," who had just donated $1,000 to the college library and whose feelings were hurt by the magnitude of DeForest's offering.[20] The records of Yale College, silent on this point, disclose only that on September 11, 1821, the president and fellows of the college "voted that the Proposal of David C. DeForest to deposit $5,000 in the Treasury of this Corporation on certain terms and conditions be [laid over to] the next meeting of the Board, and that James Hillhouse and Elizur Goodrich, Esq.[s] be a committee to confer with Mr. DeForest on the subject of said Proposal." [21] According to DeForest's biographer-nephew, this committee requested the would-be benefactor to withhold his donation until the dissenting minority of the board could be reconciled to it.[22]

DeForest, never one to bear slights with equanimity, was understandably resentful of this rebuff. In his anger he considered offering his $5,000 on the same terms to the projected State University of Ohio, and actually began negotiations toward that end.[23] But he may have thought better of it, or perhaps the legislature of Ohio was equally suspicious of aristocratic influences, for when Secretary Goodrich and Treasurer Hillhouse called on DeForest again in 1823 he was ready to renew his tender to Yale College with somewhat altered conditions. Now he proposed that $1,000 of the anticipated annual income of the fund, amounting to $1,556 in 1852, should be devoted for the education and support at Yale College of four direct male descendants of his mother, Mrs. Mehitable Lockwood, and "in default of such descendants the same sum to be applied to the education of others

19. *Ibid.*
20. J. W. De Forest, *The de Forests of Avesnes,* p. 157.
21. DeForest Fund Records, Yale College 1823 to ——, in Yale Memorabilia Room, Yale University Library.
22. J. W. De Forest, *The de Forests of Avesnes,* p. 157.
23. DeForest to his Excellency Ethan A. Brown, New Haven, Nov. 5, 1821, cited above, note 18.

of the name of DeForest, giving preference to the next of kin of the donor," or, in default of candidates of that name, to indigent young men of good talents who would assume the name of De-Forest. The donor assumed that $1,000 would support and educate four scholars each year, but "as this may depend on the value of money and other articles, nothing definite can be determined." He further stipulated that "in the selection of candidates for the bounty herein provided, the Religious or Political opinions of themselves or their families should not operate against or for them, in any case; but a preference shall always be given to those who are of moral and virtuous conduct; and it is left wholly at the discretion of the Corporation of Yale College to make the selection." In addition, there should be presented an annual gold medal worth $100, for superiority in English composition and declamation, the president and professors being judges, and every member of the senior class a candidate for the prize.[24]

The lone trustee mentioned above, supported by one member of the faculty, again opposed accepting DeForest's gift. He is reported to have denounced it as un-American: "It is contrary to the spirit of our American institutions. It is an attack upon republican equality. Here is a family which is to have special privileges; its young men are to be made literary aristocrats. As an American, I protest against it." [25] But on September 9, 1823, the corporation overrode his protests and voted to accept DeForest's offer. The fund finally accumulated and became available in 1852. In 1864 the DeForest heirs agreed to an alteration in the terms of the scholarships fund, so that—in default of DeForests —other qualified candidates need not change their names. To this day the David C. DeForest Scholarships and gold medal for oratory are coveted prizes at Yale University.

The Don continued to give generously of his time and money to liberal causes and to charitable works. When the citizens of New Haven assembled at the county house on December 17, 1823, "for the purpose of concerting measures to aid the Greeks in their glorious struggle for independence," David C. DeForest was elected along with his friends David Daggett and Noah Webster to the committee on resolutions.[26] Two months later the

---

24. *A Copy of the Acts and Doings Respecting the DeForest Fund at Yale College in New Haven (Conn.), Established in the Month of September, 1823.* New Haven, S. M. Dutton, printer, 1823.

25. J. W. De Forest, *The de Forests of Avesnes*, p. 157.

26. *Columbian Register*, Dec. 20, 1823.

Register carried an account of a feast "given at the Alms-House in this town, to the poor, in commemoration of Washington's birth day, by David C. DeForest, Esq. which is the third and not the least dinner served up in style at 4 o'clock, and abundant." [27] Hospitable as ever, DeForest's "feasts of grapes" attracted particular mention. The discriminating editor of the *Register* reported of one of these affairs that "the grapes were all excellent of their kind, but those denominated the La Fayette, were very superior in flavor and richness." [28]

New Haveners did not suspect that this worthy citizen and pleasant host was beset by tormenting fears that very likely contributed to his prematurely gray hair and hastened his death. The lawsuits that he had sought to avoid, threatening disgrace and the forced restitution of his privateering profits, became painful reality by 1821. One suit concerned the Spanish merchantman *Sereno*, taken by the patriot corsair *Congreso* in 1816, and illegally condemned by the Buenos Aires prize court.[29] The Royal Philippine Company commenced another action for the value of their ship *Triton* and its cargo, taken by Captain Marcena Monson of the *Tupac-Amarú*.[30] Against these attempts on his fortune and honor, for so he regarded them, DeForest conducted a vigorous legal defense. He was immersed in these affairs when, on a wintry evening in February, 1825, he fell ill. The next day he was waging a losing struggle with pneumonia; and on February 22 he died, aged fifty-one. He was buried in the Grove Street Cemetery of New Haven, in the presence of a great number of mourners. "There were so many country wagons hitched along the fences of the Green," wrote an eye-witness, "that one was reminded of the fourth of July." [31] From the poor of the town came a laboriously worded message of sympathy for DeForest's wife and children.

Of the eight children born to DeForest in Buenos Aires and

27. *Ibid.*, Feb. 28, 1824.
28. *Ibid.*, Oct. 9, 1824.
29. There is a docket on the case of the *Sereno*, containing proceedings from 1816 to 1818, in the archives of the United States district court at Baltimore. In the Spanish archives is a memorandum or note on the case which indicates that in 1827 it was settled in favor of the Spanish claimants, who collected $25,000 from DeForest's heirs. Archivo Histórico Nacional (Madrid), Estado, legajo 5561, expediente 13.
30. J. H. DeForest to John Wells, New Haven, May 29, 1821, DeForest Letterbooks, Vol. 8.
31. J. W. De Forest, *The de Forests of Avesnes*, p. 160 n.

New Haven, only three daughters and two sons lived to maturity. The three girls, all acclaimed for their beauty, made excellent marriages.[32] David Curtis, bold and adventurous like his father, took to the sea; in January, 1838, aged only eighteen, he fell to his death from the masthead of a sealing vessel in the south Pacific. Carlos María, less vigorous in body and temper, left New Haven at an early age and settled in Bradford County in Western Pennsylvania, where he lived and died obscurely. Julia DeForest did not marry again. A visitor to Saratoga Springs in the summer of 1833 often saw "the accomplished widow" on the arm of the courtly Vice-President of the United States, Martin Van Buren.[33] She died in New Haven at the dawn of New Year's Day, 1873, aged seventy-seven, having survived her husband almost forty-eight years.

The career of David C. DeForest spans and embodies a quarter-century of relations between the United States and Buenos Aires in the great epoch of Spanish-American emancipation. That quarter-century witnessed, to use the happy phrase of Professor Arthur P. Whitaker, the discovery of Latin America by the people of the United States. The progressive disintegration of the Spanish Empire in America opened the way for a notable increase of commercial, ideological, and political contacts between the republic of the North and the former Spanish colonies. The consciousness of a common opportunity and a common peril in the face of a hostile monarchical Europe inspired sentiments of hemispheric solidarity and yearnings for inter-American collaboration in the struggle against Spanish tyranny. A multitude of North Americans actually foreswore neutrality and rendered effective military assistance to the rebels. The friendly government of the United States opened its ports to rebel cruisers, permitted the free flow of munitions to the patriots, and conducted a vigorous diplomatic defense of the new states against the menace of an armed European intervention. An outpouring of books, pamphlets, and newspaper articles in the United States informed interested readers concerning the progress of the revolutionary struggle in Spanish America. Cultural relations multiplied as

32. Francisca Tomasa Isabel, the eldest daughter, married a son of Judge Van Ness of Columbia County, New York; Julia Nicanora married a son of Hiland Hill, a banker of Catskill, New York; and the youngest daughter, Pastora Jacoba, married a son of the prominent New York City lawyer, George Griffin.

33. Henry Wikoff, *The Reminiscences of an Idler* (N. Y., 1880), p. 59.

learned societies in the United States entered into correspondence with Spanish-American savants and the first students from Chile and Buenos Aires arrived in North America.

DeForest's life provides a remarkably complete record of this process of inter-American acquaintance and coöperation in the first great international crisis of the Americas. It mirrors the course of the early relations between the United States and Buenos Aires from the first furtive contacts in the days of the viceroys to the formal exchange of diplomatic representatives a quarter-century later.

DeForest himself shaped those relations in a large measure. At the dawn of the nineteenth century he helped to blaze a trail for United States commerce to the Plate ports; as early as 1805 he urged President Thomas Jefferson to establish a consulate in Buenos Aires. As a resident merchant in the provincial capital he drew on an arsenal of ruses to evade Spain's restrictive laws, and diligently taught the use of these devices to other North American traders. He also became a carrier and interpreter of North American republican doctrine to discontented creoles: mingling with such fathers of the *Revolución de Mayo* as Juan Larrea and Juan José Castelli he spoke to them of the rights of man, the governments of the world, and the independence of Buenos Aires. Expelled from La Plata by Viceroy Cisneros, allegedly for his liberal sentiments, DeForest returned after the *veinte-cinco de mayo* to become a promoter of privateering enterprise against Spanish commerce. The exploits of the *Congreso*, the *Tupac-Amarú*, the *Mangoré*, and other corsairs outfitted in Baltimore through DeForest's initiative attest to the important military contribution of the United States to the winning of Argentine independence. His mission as consul general of the United Provinces of La Plata at Washington was a milestone in the establishment of diplomatic relations between the United States and his adopted country. Finally, by his generous donation for the support of the first institution of higher learning in independent Buenos Aires; by his presentation of North American art objects to that institution; and by his encouragement to young *porteños* to study in the United States, DeForest broke new ground in the field of cultural relations between the two countries.

BIBLIOGRAPHICAL NOTE

Bibliographies and Guides

Cecil K. Jones, *A Bibliography of Latin American Bibliographies* (2nd ed., Washington, 1942), is of broader scope than the title indicates; the section on Argentina yielded many useful historical titles and clues for research. Samuel F. Bemis and Grace G. Griffin, *Guide to the Diplomatic History of the United States, 1775–1921* (Washington, 1935), was indispensable for the diplomatic relations between the United States and revolutionary Buenos Aires. An informing discussion of authorities and sources introduces the section on "La revolución en el Río de la Plata" in the monumental work of Antonio Ballesteros y Berreta, *La historia de España y su influencia en la historia universal* (8 vols., Barcelona, 1919–1936), VII, 318–321; there is a supplementary list of titles on pp. 467–468. The "principal bibliographies" appended to the chapters of the *Historia de la nación argentina,* discussed below, have also been useful. Two publications largely devoted to historical bibliography, the *Boletín* of the Instituto de Investigaciones Históricas of the University of Buenos Aires (Buenos Aires, 1922–   ), and the *Anuario de historia argentina* (Buenos Aires, 1940–   ), published by the Sociedad de Historia Argentina, were of value for the annual increment of writings on the colonial and revolutionary periods in La Plata. The best guide to the minor figures of the Argentine revolution is Enrique Udaondo, *Diccionario biográfico argentino* (Buenos Aires, 1938). I have consulted numerous published guides to the manuscript collections of the Library of Congress, the National Archives (Washington), and other depositories in the United States; similarly full analyses do not yet exist for the archives of the Argentine Republic.

Manuscripts

The manuscript material on which this work is based has been obtained from the manuscript collections of the Yale University Library, the Library of Congress, and the National Archives in Washington, and the United States District Court in Baltimore.

The richest and by far the most useful source for this study has been the David C. DeForest Collection in the Yale University Library. The eight letterbooks, seven journals or diaries, and five account books which form the bulk of this collection allow a comprehensive reconstruction of DeForest's life from 1798 to his death in 1825. These papers also constitute a rich and hitherto untapped source for the commercial and political history of the Río de la Plata in the late colonial and revolutionary periods. They appear to be fairly complete; the most important missing item is a letterbook for the years 1815–1817, containing much correspondence on privateering affairs. It should be noted that while we have almost all of DeForest's outgoing letters, copies of which he entered in his letterbooks, we do not have any of the letters sent to him. This is a pity, for among DeForest's friends and correspondents were such *próceres* of the Argentine revolution as Juan Larrea, Juan José Castelli, Manuel Belgrano, and Bernardo Monteagudo.

In the John W. De Forest Collection, also in the Yale Library, I found among the papers of this distinguished novelist, a nephew and biographer of DeForest, a folder of notes and transcripts drawn off for him from family papers by Colonel George Butler Griffin, the son of one of DeForest's daughters. Particularly useful here were transcripts from the now missing letterbook containing DeForest's privateering correspondence. In the Hiram Bingham Collection in the Yale Library, I consulted profitably a set of abstracts and transcripts made by Professor Bingham from British Foreign Office material in the Public Record Office (London), relating to the Spanish-American Wars of Independence. They were valuable for evidence of early Anglo-American commercial rivalry in La Plata and the reports of British merchants on conditions in Buenos Aires on the eve of the *veinte-cinco de mayo*.

Two collections of personal papers in the Division of Manuscripts in the Library of Congress were especially helpful. The Jonathan Meredith Papers yielded documentary material (a privateering contract between DeForest and the government of Buenos Aires, instructions to privateering captains, and the like) that usefully supplemented information obtained from other sources. In this collection there is also much evidence of the privateering interests of DeForest's arch-foe, Thomas L. Halsey, sometime United States consul in Buenos Aires. The Jeremy Robinson Papers contributed the interesting diary of the traveler in South America of that name, with its acid characterization of DeForest and his motives for desiring a consular appointment in the United States.

For DeForest's diplomatic career, the most valuable source in the Manuscripts Division of the Library of Congress was photocopies of material from the Archivo General de la Nación (Buenos Aires), sección Gobierno, Estados Unidos, S[ala] 1, A[rmario] 2, A[naquél] 4, Núm[eros] 8, 9, and 10. This material comprises correspondence between United States consuls and the government of Buenos Aires; the file of instructions and reports of DeForest and other early missions from Buenos Aires to the United States; and correspondence between DeForest and the first recognized minister from Buenos Aires, Carlos de Alvear. Comparison with DeForest's letterbooks, in which he entered copies of all his official despatches, shows that the reports from him in the Buenos Aires archives are fairly complete. In the Library of Con-

gress I have also made use of photocopies of material in the Archivo
Histórico Nacional (Madrid), Estado, legajos 5552–5576, 5636–5648
inclusive; scattered information obtained here is cited in my footnote
references.

In the Department of State Division of the National Archives (Washington), the following series were of limited assistance: Consular Letters, Buenos Aires, Vol. 1, parts 1 and 2, for occasional references to
DeForest in consular despatches from Buenos Aires; Consular Letters,
St. Bartholomew, for the excesses of patriot privateers in West Indian
waters; and Domestic Letters, for a remonstrance from Secretary of
State Adams to Spanish-American governments concerning these excesses.

The Admiralty Records of the United States District Court in Baltimore contain much material on privateering under the flag of Buenos
Aires. The most important material consulted here was the docket of the
case of the *Sereno,* which DeForest finally lost to Spanish claimants, to
the great financial loss of his heirs. There are scattered references to
DeForest in other privateering cases recorded here.

Newspapers

La Gaceta de Buenos Aires (facsimile edition, 6 vols., Buenos Aires,
1910–1915), published by the Junta de Historia y Numismática Ameri-
cana of Buenos Aires, was useful for some details of DeForest's commercial activity in Buenos Aires, 1812–1818. For his New Haven years
(1818–1825), I have relied chiefly on the *Columbian Register* and the
Connecticut Journal, both published in New Haven. I am indebted to
many other newspapers for scattered information cited in footnote references.

Printed Sources

In the notable continuing series, *Documentos para la historia argentina*
(Buenos Aires, 1913–   ), published by the Facultad de Filosofía y
Letras of the University of Buenos Aires, the following volumes were of
particular value: Vol. 7, *Comercio de Indias; consulado, comercio de
negros y de extranjeros, 1791–1809,* for contraband trade between the
United States and the viceroyalty of the Río de la Plata, and commercial
matters generally; Vol. 12, *Territorio y población; padrón de la ciudad
de Buenos Aires,* for the dates and places of DeForest's residence in
Buenos Aires; and Vol. 14, *Correspondencias generales de la provincia
de Buenos Aires,* for DeForest's diplomatic mission to the United States.
*Documentos relativos a los antecedentes de la independencia de la Re-
pública Argentina* (Buenos Aires, 1912), a publication of the Facultad
de Filosofía y Letras, was helpful for political conditions in Buenos
Aires after the British invasions.

William R. Manning, ed., *Diplomatic Correspondence of the United States Concerning the Independence of the Latin American Nations* . . . (3 vols., N. Y., 1925), was indispensable for the early missions from Buenos Aires to the United States; Vol. 1 contains the exchange of notes between DeForest and Secretary of State Adams. In his *Memoirs,* edited by Charles F. Adams (12 vols., Philadelphia, 1874–1877), the secretary made fairly detailed entries of his interviews with DeForest; these accounts usefully supplement DeForest's own reports in the Buenos Aires archives. The *Writings of John Quincy Adams* (7 vols., N. Y., 1913–1917), edited by Worthington C. Ford, supplement the *Memoirs* as a helpful source for Adams' Spanish-American policy. C. K. Webster has illustrated British policy, a constant factor in Adams' diplomatic calculations, with selected documents from Foreign Office archives bearing on *Britain and the Independence of Latin America* (2 vols., N. Y., 1938).

Louis Effingham de Forest printed two early letters of DeForest in "A Trip Through Brazil in 1802," *Brazil* (N. Y.), Year IX, no. 101, March, 1937. These are the only DeForest papers that have appeared in print.

Secondary Works

For the ancestry of David C. DeForest I have drawn on two family histories: John W. De Forest, *The de Forests of Avesnes (and of New Netherland)* (New Haven, 1900); and Mrs. Robert W. de Forest, *A Walloon Family in America* (2 vols., N. Y., 1914). Jane DeForest Shelton, *The Salt-Box House* (N. Y., 1929), is a charming evocation of eighteenth-century life in DeForest's birthplace, the town of Stratford. W. A. Robinson, *Jeffersonian Democracy in New England* (New Haven, 1916); and Richard J. Purcell, *Connecticut in Transition* (New Haven, 1918), depict the economic changes and shifting climate of opinion that moulded the thoughts and aspirations of the young DeForest.

Samuel E. Morison, *Maritime History of Massachusetts, 1783–1860* (N. Y., 1921), is a vigorous account of the great outward thrust of American commerce of which DeForest's early ventures formed an incident. Harry Bernstein, *Origins of Inter-American Interest, 1700–1812* (Philadelphia, 1945), illustrates with the aid of numerous printed sources and some manuscript material an unsuspected wealth of early contacts between North and Spanish America; trade with La Plata is discussed on pp. 33–51. A pioneering little work, rich in information but lacking the apparatus of scholarship, is Charles L. Chandler, *Inter-American Acquaintances* (Sewannee, Tenn., 1915); there are a number of references to DeForest. Three articles by the same author are useful for the proportions and character of early United States trade to La Plata: "The River Plate Voyages," *American Historical Review,* XXIII (1918), 816–826; "United States Merchant Ships in the Río de la Plata (1801–1809) as

Shown by Early Newspapers," *Hispanic-American Historical Review,* II (1919), 26–54; and "The United States Shipping in the La Plata Region, 1809–1810," *ibid.,* II (1920), 159–176. Roy F. Nichols, "Trade Relations and the Establishment of the United States Consulates in Spanish America, 1779–1809," *ibid.,* XIII (1933), 289–313, shows how Spain's maritime distresses during periodic wars compelled the opening of her colonial ports to United States trade; commerce with La Plata is only briefly discussed. Dorothy B. Goebel, "British Trade to the Spanish Colonies, 1796–1823," *American Historical Review,* XLIII (1938), 276–318, reveals with the aid of British archival material how financial exigencies and the rise of revolutionary crises in the Spanish colonies furthered English trade penetration unsanctioned by the Spanish government; the discussion of trade to La Plata, while helpful, suggests only slight familiarity with Argentine printed material. Roberto C. Simonsen, *Historia economica do Brasil* (2 vols., São Paulo, 1937), provided background information for DeForest's smuggling activity in Brazil.

Two standard works, Ricardo Levene, *A History of Argentina* (Chapel Hill, N. C., 1937), translated and edited by William S. Robertson; and F. A. Kirkpatrick, *A History of the Argentine Republic* (Cambridge, Eng., 1931), were useful for general reference as concerned the Argentine struggle for independence. For particular episodes, however, I have relied in the main on the pertinent contributions to the coöperative *Historia de la nación argentina* (Buenos Aires, 1936–   ), under the general editorship of the erudite Professor Ricardo Levene. This vast and continuing enterprise is planned to cover in ten volumes the course of Argentine history from its beginnings to the definitive organization of the nation in 1862. Two supplementary volumes will bring the history down to the 1912 electoral reform. Vol. IV, *El momento histórico del virreynato del Río de la Plata;* and Vol. V, *La revolución de mayo hasta la asamblea general constituyente,* have been most useful in the writing of this study.

The British invasions of 1806–1807, of which DeForest became an unwilling observer, gave a powerful stimulus to the movement for independence in Buenos Aires. The best account in English, based on the then available printed material, is by Bernard Moses, "The British in Buenos Aires," in *Spain's Declining Power in the New World* (Berkeley, Cal., 1919), pp. 337–371. Juan Beverina, "Las invasiones inglesas," in *Historia de la nación argentina,* IV, section 2, is a convenient summary of the military operations. Paul Groussac, *Santiago de Liniers, conde de Buenos Aires* (Buenos Aires, 1907), is a wise, witty, and learned biography of the French-born hero of the *reconquista.*

Napoleon's seizure of the Spanish throne in 1808 precipitated a crisis of the old régime in the Spanish-American colonies. Bartolomé Mitre, *Historia de Belgrano y de la independencia argentina* (4th ed., 3 vols.,

Buenos Aires, 1887–1888), is a broad study of the process of Argentine independence, based on extensive archival research, and framed about the life of the patriot leader Manuel Belgrano. For particular trends and events leading to the *veinte-cinco de mayo,* the following contributions to the *Historia de la nación argentina,* V, section 1, have been most helpful: Ricardo R. Caillet-Bois, "Las corrientes ideológicas europeas del siglo XVIII, y el virreinato del Río de la Plata"; Ricardo Levene, "Intentos de independencia en el virreinato del Plata (1781–1809)"; and by the same author, "La asonada del 1º de enero de 1809." Argentine historians are not in accord as to the influence exerted on the course of revolutionary events by Mariano Moreno and his famous memorial on the advantages of free trade. Diego Luis Molinari, *La representación de los hacendados de Mariano Moreno, su ninguna influencia en la vida económica del país y en los sucesos de mayo* (2d ed., Buenos Aires, 1939), subjects the original documents to searching analysis and vigorously rejects any suggestion of such influence; an affirmative and probably more widely accepted position, embodying conclusions based on many years' research in the subject, is taken by Ricardo Levene, "Significación histórica de la obra económica de Manuel Belgrano y Mariano Moreno," in *Historia de la nación argentina,* V, section 1. The same author contributes two masterly surveys of the *Revolución de Mayo* to Vol. V, section 2 of the *Historia:* "Los sucesos de mayo," an authoritative statement of the train of events; and "El 25 de mayo," a thoughtful essay on the nature and ends of the revolution. Other contributions to this volume, narrating the rise and fall of successive patriot governments down to the *asamblea general constituyente* of 1813, have been useful for general reference. Volume VI of the *Historia,* which continues the story of the revolution, had not appeared at the time of this writing.

With the aid of ships and crews supplied by merchants in the United States, the Buenos Aires government launched an effective privateering campaign against Spanish commerce. North American investigators have delved deeply into this picturesque theme. Theodore S. Currier, *Los corsarios del Río de la Plata* (Buenos Aires, 1929), is a useful preliminary account based exclusively on printed material in the United States. Lewis W. Bealer, *Los corsarios de Buenos Aires* (Buenos Aires, 1937), exhausts published sources in Argentina and the United States, but does not exploit archival sources in either country. Charles C. Griffin, "Privateering from Baltimore during the Spanish American Wars of Independence," *Maryland Historical Magazine,* XXXV (1940), 1–25, illuminates the organization and practice of privateering industry with the aid of admiralty records in the federal court archives of Baltimore and other seaboard cities. Theodore S. Currier, *Los cruceros del "General San Martín"* (Buenos Aires, 1944), a case study in privateering also based on United States court records, appeared after most of the work on this book had been completed. Angel Justiniano Carranza, *Campañas navales de la República Argentina, cuadros históricos* (4 vols., Buenos Aires, 1911–1914), a eulogistic history based largely on archival sources, was helpful for scattered information on DeForest's privateers.

To the United States the patriots of Buenos Aires early turned for support and encouragement. Samuel Flagg Bemis, *Early Diplomatic Missions from Buenos Aires to the United States, 1811–1824* (Worcester, Mass., 1940) (reprinted from the *Proceedings* of the American Antiquarian Society for April, 1939), a definitive study founded on exhaustive research in United States, Argentine, and Spanish archival material, as well as the DeForest papers, was invaluable for DeForest's consular mission to the United States. Of the voluminous literature on the relations between the United States and the new Spanish-American states, only three works need be mentioned here. Frederic L. Paxson, *The Independence of the South-American Republics; A Study in Recognition and Foreign Policy* (Philadelphia, 1903), a pioneer monograph that exploits United States and British archives, contains the first scholarly though brief account of DeForest's diplomacy. Charles C. Griffin, *The United States and the Disruption of the Spanish Empire* (N. Y., 1937), a multi-archival study, places in useful focus the intimate interplay between United States boundary disputes with Spain and the Spanish-American struggle for independence; there is only brief mention of DeForest's mission. Arthur P. Whitaker, *The United States and the Independence of Latin America, 1808–1830* (Baltimore, 1941), a broad survey founded on prodigious research in United States, European, and South American archives, has for its main theme the retreat from Jefferson's "large policy of 1808" to the more cautious policies of Madison and Monroe; it contains a judicious appraisal of DeForest's efforts to gain recognition for Buenos Aires. Harris G. Warren, *The Sword Was Their Passport: A History of American Filibustering in the Mexican Revolution* (Baton Rouge, La., 1942), a monograph based on Spanish and United States archival material, was invaluable for DeForest's projects to establish a base in Florida for the privateers of Buenos Aires.

There are a few slender writings that seek to encompass the life of DeForest as a whole. J. W. De Forest devoted two chapters to his uncle in a family history, *The de Forests of Avesnes (and of New Netherland)* (New Haven, 1900). Within its limitations (source material was apparently confined to a few early letters of DeForest, a number of extracts from DeForest's letterbooks and account books, and the *Memoirs* of John Quincy Adams), this is a useful preliminary sketch, but the historical observations are practically worthless. Atilio Chiáppori, "Un Goya yanqui y un yanqui porteño," *La Nación* (Buenos Aires), May 20, 1934, 2ª sección, p. 2 (reprinted in a collection of essays by the same author, *Maestros y temperamentos*, Buenos Aires, 1943, pp. 105–135), weaves a highly impressionistic account of DeForest's life about the Morse portrait of DeForest in Buenos Aires; aside from information on this painting it was of no value. Horacio Zorraquín Becú, *De aventurero yanqui a consul porteño en los Estados Unidos: David C. DeForest, 1774–1825* (Buenos Aires, 1943) (reprint from the *Anuario de historia argentina, IV*, 1942), has diligently combed printed material in the United States and Argentina, but did not avail himself of archival sources close at hand; this pleasantly written little study was helpful for some sections of my narrative. Señor Zorraquín Becú promises a closer analysis of DeForest's mission to the United States in a work as yet unpublished, "Inglaterra, la diplomacia norteamericana y el reconocimiento de la independencia argentina." Madame Courtney Letts de Espil has published a series of four popular articles on DeForest in *La Nación* (Buenos Aires), Nov. 12, 26; Dec. 10, 24, 1944, with the aid of some Argentine printed sources and a few extracts from the DeForest papers. Mention should also be made of the brief but accurate biographical sketch of DeForest in the *Dictionary of American Biography*.

INDEX